Effective Negotiation

From research to results

Essential reading for students and professionals in the fields of business, law and management, *Effective Negotiation* offers a realistic and practical understanding of negotiation and the skills required in order to reach an agreement.

In this book Ray Fells draws on his practical background and extensive experience as a teacher and researcher to examine key issues such as trust, power and information exchange, ethics and strategy. Recognising the complexity of the negotiation process, he gives advice on how to improve as a negotiator by turning the research on negotiation into practical recommendations. It includes:

- how to negotiate strategically
- negotiating on behalf of others
- cultural differences in negotiation.

The principles and skills outlined here focus on the business context but also apply to interpersonal and sales-based negotiations, and when resolving legal, environmental and social issues.

Effective Negotiation also features a companion website with lecturer resources.

Ray Fells is Associate Dean in the Faculty of Business, University of Western Australia.

Effective Negotiation

From research to results

RAY FELLS

CAMBRIDGE UNIVERSITY PRESS
Cambridge, New York, Melbourne, Madrid, Cape Town, Singapore, São Paulo, Delhi

Cambridge University Press
477 Williamstown Road, Port Melbourne, VIC 3207, Australia

www.cambridge.org
Information on this title: www.cambridge.org/9780521735216

First published 2010

Cover design by Sardine Design
Typeset by Aptara Corp.
Printed in China by Printplus

National Library of Australia Cataloguing in Publication data

Fells, Railton Edward.
Effective negotiation : from research to results / Ray Fells.
9780521735216 (pbk.)
Includes index.
Bibliography.
Negotiation.
Contracts.
Covenants.
302.3

ISBN 978-0-521-73521-6 paperback

Contents

Acknowledgements

To Joan Keogh and other former colleagues at the Advisory Conciliation and Arbitrary Service in the UK, who taught me the need to be practical when fixing disputes and to Zoe Hamilton and the staff at the Press for their advice and patience.

1 An introduction to negotiation

We negotiate a great deal – more than we realise. Sometimes it goes smoothly, sometimes it seems difficult. While there is much advice about how to negotiate and be a 'winning negotiator', the actual experience does not seem as straightforward as books suggest. Why? Because negotiation is a complex process. This book grapples with these complexities while recognising the idiosyncrasies of both the negotiation process and the negotiator.

This opening chapter explores some core complexities of negotiation, providing a foundation for later chapters. Although this book will focus on the business context, the principles and skills can be applied in other contexts such as interpersonal negotiation, sales or when resolving legal, environmental and social issues. Very few people are employed solely as professional negotiators; for most of us it is just an integral, perhaps unrecognised, part of our job. Figure 1.1 is a 'map' developed from an exercise within a company to identify who has to negotiate with whom and over what. It shows that throughout an organisation, negotiation is deeply embedded as a way of getting things done. Even this map does not show the full complexity of the internal negotiations particularly in the production stage where managers and supervisors are constantly negotiating with each other over scheduling and the use of resources.

The advice offered in this book is based on good research yet is pragmatic, recognising the difficult contexts within which negotiations take place. Box 1.1 lists five recommendations that seem to be at the heart of the many suggestions that emerge throughout the ensuing chapters. These are not five keys to success but are offered, along with the rest of the book, with the aim of guiding the reader's progress towards being a better negotiator.

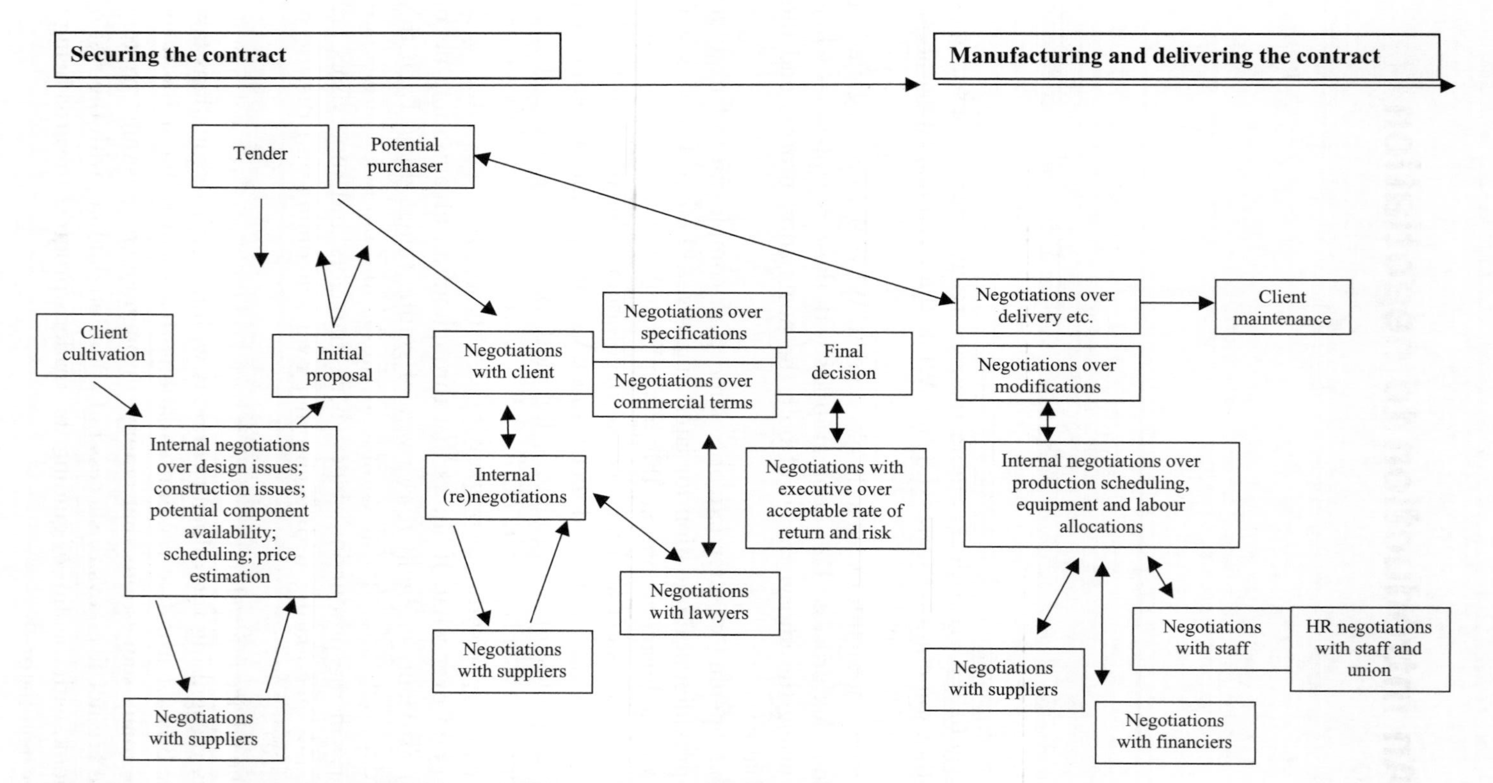

Figure 1.1: A map of negotiations within and around an engineering fabrication company

Box 1.1: Advice to negotiators – an 'up-front' summary

Be pragmatic – negotiation is messy

Negotiation – like politics – is the art of the possible.

Remember – at ALL times – that negotiation is two-sided

Others can make choices too!

Be inquisitive and acquisitive

Always ask 'why?' and 'what if?' and 'can we get a better outcome than this?'

Create a new script

Be confident managing the process but be prepared to improvise.

Treat others with respect

This is the only golden rule.

What is negotiation?

Starting with a definition may seem 'academic' but it highlights some key points about negotiation that provide some preliminary but important practical insights.

> Negotiation is a process where two parties with differences which they need to resolve are trying to reach agreement through exploring for options and exchanging offers – and an agreement.

Firstly, negotiation is a **process** – a sequence of activities, perhaps with an underlying pattern. It is not a single event – choices are made along the way. It is not mechanical or deterministic – the choices negotiators make affect how agreement is achieved and what the agreement will be. The process of negotiation and how to manage it effectively will be explored in Chapters 4 and 5.

Secondly, we need **two parties** for a negotiation. Having more than two parties does not alter the fundamental duality of the process. Chapter 9 examines how a negotiation becomes more complex when constituencies or other parties have an interest in the outcome of the negotiation and Chapter 10 considers the impact of cultural differences.

Thirdly there must be **differences**. If there are no differences there is no need to negotiate and because there are differences, we can expect some conflict and competition. The task of unravelling differences is examined in Chapter 6.

The parties must **need to resolve** their differences. It is this need that generates cooperation between the parties. The need to settle their differences also helps negotiators understand their power; this important aspect of negotiation is explored in the next chapter.

That negotiation involves **trying to reach agreement** suggests that negotiators might not always succeed and also that reaching a good agreement takes some effort. If an agreement is reached easily then it is probably not a good negotiation; it is likely that some value has been left on the negotiating table.

There are two broad ways agreements can be found. The negotiators can **explore** possibilities and develop **options** that might possibly resolve the issue. This is the creative aspect of negotiation and is how negotiators add value. Ways of doing this are explored in Chapter 7. Secondly, and more commonly, negotiators can **exchange offers** around and between their stated positions which involves compromise and can be competitive. Competitive negotiation and offer strategies are discussed in Chapter 8.

Finally, negotiations result in an **agreement**, which might be an agreement to walk away. The notion of 'agreement' sounds positive but nothing about negotiation guarantees that an agreement is a positive outcome; the parties might agree but only reluctantly. While the focus of a negotiation is on reaching agreement the most important aspect of any negotiation is not the agreement itself, but how it is implemented. The agreement is only a part of the outcome to any negotiation.

Some initial practical implications

The above definition shows some of the complexities inherent in any negotiation and why it is not straightforward. Firstly, negotiation is a mix of **competitiveness** *and* **cooperation**. Some aspects of the process will generate competitive interactions while others will require cooperation if agreement is to be reached. This is why negotiation is regarded as a 'mixed motive' interaction (Schelling, 1960, p. 89); there is competitiveness because each negotiator is standing in the way of the other achieving their goal but at the same time, cooperation is needed because without the other's help neither will achieve anything at all. Managing this mix of competitiveness and cooperativeness can be a challenge.

Secondly, negotiation is about an issue – *what* the differences are between the parties – but it is also a process – *how* the parties will try to resolve their differences. Therefore negotiators have to manage both the **issue** and the **process** to achieve a good outcome.

Thirdly, negotiation involves **choice**. Negotiators are constantly faced with choices throughout the negotiation. They have to manage the balance of cooperation and competitiveness; they face choices over how to deal with the issue and how to manage the process. These choices flow through into actions and reactions. This issue–process–action distinction will recur throughout this book.

Although negotiators constantly make choices about how the negotiation should proceed, they do not have control. This is because of the fourth important point about negotiation: that it is **two-sided**. This fundamental and obvious point is often ignored by negotiators when they plan and implement their strategies. Ignoring the other party is a mistake that even effective negotiators make (Sebenius, 2001).

Fifthly, although the definition of negotiation offered earlier is neat, succinct and has an inherent logic, the process it seeks to define is **messy**. The parties' differences may not become clear until well into a negotiation. The pressures to resolve their differences will probably change during the negotiation. Negotiators might try to exchange offers before exploring for options; it may be not until they start to trade offers that they finally clarify their real differences. Entering into a negotiation with a good understanding of the process will help reduce the messiness, but negotiation will never be entirely straightforward.

There are two further practical implications to consider, one relevant before a negotiation, the other once it is over. Firstly, identify the key elements of negotiation based on the definition given above by preparing a **preparation checklist** (see Appendix 1). This will provide the negotiator with a framework to use during the negotiation process. (Other aspects of preparation are explored throughout the book.) Secondly, since any negotiation is less than straightforward it always gives a negotiator the opportunity to learn and improve. Rackman and Carlisle (1978) found that once a negotiation was concluded it was the skilled negotiators who took time out to reflect upon what had happened, why it happened, and what could have been done differently and better. This action–reflection model is where real learning can take place. Similarly comparing negotiations provides good insights into ways to improve one's negotiating (Gentner, Loewenstein and Thompson, 2003). A **negotiation review checklist** is provided in Appendix 2.

The DNA of negotiation

What makes a negotiation 'work'? There are several elements that might be regarded as the 'DNA of negotiation', elements that are 'hard-wired' into the process of reaching an agreement. They are integral to the strategies negotiators can employ and so need to be understood to manage the process more effectively. They can be used, or abused.

Describing negotiation in terms of DNA creates an image that helps our understanding of the process. The DNA helix represents two parties who seem to be jostling for position yet are inextricably linked, an indication of the competitiveness and yet cooperation inherent in any negotiation. The twists reflect that negotiation is not straightforward. The links between the two strands of the DNA can be viewed as the key elements or 'links' which give life and structure to a negotiation – reciprocity, trust, power, information exchange, ethics and outcome.

Reciprocity is a feature of many social interactions including negotiation. What one party does tends to be matched or reciprocated by the other. This does not happen all the time but often enough to influence the pattern and progress of the negotiation. It is an aspect of the process that can be managed.

Trust is an expectation that the other party will act in a beneficial rather than exploitative way. A lot of emphasis is placed on building trust, particularly when trying to create a cooperative negotiation, but trust is fragile and is easily overestimated. Thinking about trust leads to thinking about the behavioural **ethics** in negotiation.

Another important feature of a negotiation is **power**. Paradoxically this has a great deal to do with the consequence if the parties were *not* negotiating. The power that negotiators have relates to the alternatives open to them – ways other than negotiation to achieve their desired objectives. Negotiation can be viewed as a process whereby the alternatives that negotiators think they have are changed.

The lack of power, reflected in concern about having only a poor alternative, brings negotiators to the negotiating table and keeps them there. The level of trust between the parties determines the quality of the agreement they will then achieve. To a large extent this trust is built through reciprocity.

Information, or more often the *lack* of it, is central in reaching an agreement and so forms another link in the negotiation DNA. No matter how much negotiators prepare, there are always things that they do not know (but wish they did). Many of the strategies and tactics are designed to improve the negotiators' understanding of what is and is not possible as an outcome. Because of this, negotiation can be viewed as a process of **information exchange**, particularly information about possible solutions on the one hand and walk-away alternatives on the other.

Finally, as suggested in the definition of negotiation, the reason for entering into a negotiation is to reach an agreement and so the **outcome** is another part of negotiation's DNA. The better the negotiation, the better the outcome. Negotiators are often encouraged to achieve a 'win-win' agreement but the notion of a 'win-win' agreement is not as clear (or as achievable) as we would like to think.

None of these elements – reciprocity, trust, ethics, power, information and outcome – are clear-cut, they are not mechanistic or precise. This is why negotiation is complex, relatively difficult and unpredictable. To be a good negotiator means having a practical understanding of a negotiation's DNA which helps a negotiator manage the process while recognising that he can never eliminate all the uncertainty and difficulties.

The DNA imagery has its limitations – the two strands never meet, perhaps signifying that the parties never reach agreement! However, having an image or script that resonates with the key aspects of negotiation creates a mental framework to help a negotiator guide the process to an agreement. A visual image sometimes has more 'life' than a carefully formulated definition, such as that presented at the start of this chapter. The DNA image is just one of several images that appear throughout this book to help the reader's practical understanding of negotiation.

2 The essence of negotiation

The previous chapter suggested that negotiation is like DNA with some critical elements 'hard wired' into the process. This chapter examines the two strands of our negotiation DNA: the parties and the key elements that hold them together, namely reciprocity, trust, power, information exchange, ethics and outcome.

Parties to the negotiation

The two strands of our negotiation DNA represent the two parties, each with its objectives and priorities. Most business negotiations are conducted by individuals acting on behalf of organisations so even when these negotiations are one-on-one, the 'shadow' of the organisation is often in the background. When thinking about the 'party' to a negotiation, it is important to consider the interactions between the other party's negotiators and those who they represent. These 'intra-party dynamics' are explored in Chapter 9.

But what of the individual negotiator? One characteristic of negotiation is that it is 'messy', one reason being because people are different. We each try to do things in different ways and we react differently to what is happening around us or to us. Our personality impacts on how we negotiate, but how much?

Do I make a difference?

As we get older our personalities become more set, so it would be of little help to learn that a personality different from ours is necessary for effective negotiation. Fortunately, attempts to identify the impact of personality on negotiation effectiveness have not found any significant, practical effects (Bazerman et al., 2000). While we may develop a particular way of defining problems or reacting to conflict, more research is needed (Sandy, Boardman and Deutsch, 2000). It seems that some of the structural and dynamic aspects of negotiation tend to moderate the effects our personality might have.

Nevertheless, we cannot excuse our personality and behave as we wish and we cannot rely on our personality as a substitute for becoming more competent. Negotiators need to be 'smart' (Fulmer and Barry, 2004). There is evidence that cognitive ability – the ability to analyse and plan – and perspective-taking ability – being able to discern and understand a point of view other than your own – help a negotiator manage a negotiation more constructively (Barry and Friedman, 1998; Kemp and Smith 1994; Kurtzberg, 1998). The ability to perceive and manage emotions in oneself and in others – emotional intelligence – also contributes to a negotiator's effectiveness (Barry, Fulmer and Van Kleef, 2004; Foo et al., 2004). The advice of the Greek philosopher Plato to 'know thyself' is useful for negotiators (Deutsch, 1990; Raiffa, 1982). It helps us understand how we might approach the task of negotiation, how we might react and what effect we have on other negotiators. This self-awareness can be instructive and while it may not change who we are, it might help us change what we do. For example, being aware of those events in a negotiation which might cause us to be anxious or angry, gives us an opportunity to plan what to do – perhaps to summarise, repeat our main points or openly reflect on our feelings.

Our personality may not have a determining impact on negotiations but how we approach a negotiation certainly does. Unfortunately the way that we think sometimes hampers effective negotiation. The first is a tendency to regard issues as win-lose situations even when they are not (Bazerman and Neale, 1983; Pinkley, Griffith and Northcraft, 1995). This can lead to an understanding of negotiation as a game or contest in which there are winners (us) and losers (you). This shapes our whole approach to the task of negotiating. It means that we tend to view negotiation as having a completely competitive script and so we act accordingly. For example, when negotiators know the walk-away point of the other party they tend to open competitively, placing a high offer that seeks to claim the bulk of the available value (Buelens and Van Poucke, 2004). Negotiators tend to make high demands when the other negotiator has made a low one (Pruitt and Syna, 1985).

Given the power of reciprocity – which is particularly strong if we have come to the negotiation with a reputation for competitiveness (Tinsley,

O'Connor and Sullivan, 2002) – our competitiveness is often matched by the other party. This then reinforces our (mistaken) belief that negotiations are necessarily competitive and that the only way to get a good outcome is to be more competitive than the opponent. The result is that negotiators who fail to see what opportunities there might be for joint gain often *both* end up losing (Thomspon and Hastie, 1990; Thompson and Hrebrec, 1996). In fact, research suggests that self-oriented competitive bargainers do not fare well (Beersma and De Dreu, 1999; Schneider, 2002; De Dreu, Weingart and Kwon 2000). Even if negotiators who are only interested in their own outcome try to engage in cooperative strategies they cannot do so consistently enough to reap the benefits from true cooperation (Kern, Brett and Weingart, 2005).

Related to this is a tendency to attribute greater differences to situations than actually exist (Robinson et al., 1995). This can be reinforced by a tendency to stereotype others and expect them to behave in a particular way. It is not surprising that if we think negotiation is a win-lose affair and we believe that the other party is extreme in their demands, then we will draw on a competitive rather than a cooperative stereotype. These biases can also prejudice cross-cultural negotiations. When negotiating with someone from China we might instinctively assume that we are negotiating with a Sun Tzu strategist rather than a Confucian gentleman (Fang, 1999).

A bias towards a win-lose view of negotiation frames our preparation and our interpretation of the other party's words and actions. The author and a colleague in the United States asked their students to undertake a negotiation over the internet. One of the virtues of online negotiating is that it provides a full transcript. As part of their reflection, the Australian students commented on how competitive the Americans were, giving quotes from the text to support their view. Closer examination of the transcript revealed that the Australian students had used the same language. (Incidentally, the American students made the same critical comments of the Australian negotiators, while again doing the same things themselves.)

Researchers have discovered a long list of cognitive, emotional and motivational effects on the way negotiators approach their task (Thompson, Neale and Sinaceur, 2004), some of which are listed in Box 2.1. They don't make for good reading! They are examples of what Sebenius (2001) calls 'skewed vision' but the difficulty for people with skewed vision is that they don't know they've got it because to them everything seems straight!

Box 2.1: Some biases of negotiators (developed from Thompson, Neale and Sinaceur, 2004)

Overconfidence

We think others (e.g. an arbitrator) are going to judge in our favour.

We think that our coercive tactics will work on the other party but theirs will have no effect on us.

Which is why we don't give much attention to information exchange and why we make fewer concessions because we think our best alternative to a negotiated agreement (BATNA) is better than it probably is.

Fixed-pie perception

We tend to view our positions and interests as being diametrically opposed.

Which is why we enter a negotiation competitively and also devalue any concessions the other party might make. (We also do this because we don't really understand their situation.)

Anchoring

We tend to give greater weight to early information or positions, particularly if it is clear.

Which is why we get stuck defending a position that is untenable.

And why it is easier to negotiate around positions than interests.

Extremism

We tend to think that the other party's positions are more extreme than they are.

Which is why we expect the other party to make more concessions and to devalue any concessions they make – they should not have been holding their position in the first place!

Illusion of transparency

We tend to think that others can understand us and discern our motives more than they actually can.

Which is why we stay stuck in our positions and don't do much to create a bridge of understanding between both parties (because that understanding is presumed).

Knowledge of other

We tend to ignore how the other party might be thinking, or why, and attribute their behaviour to themselves rather than their situation.

Which is why we are not very good at predicting the effect our strategy and tactics will have on the other party.

How can we counter innate bias? Firstly, biased thinking can emerge from a lack of critical thinking. Ensure that those within your negotiating team who suggest a contrary perspective are always given scope to express themselves. (If negotiating alone, talk through your preparation with someone you trust and who is prepared to challenge your thinking.) Secondly, biases and prejudices can stem from our ignorance of the other party. Ensure full attention is given to the perspectives of the other party, taking time to understand, as best one can, their situation and their motivations. Thirdly, as some of these biases are going to lead to negotiation difficulties and poor outcomes, we might usefully learn from our mistakes by reflecting on our own negotiation performance. However, when doing this we do need to be aware that the very biases that caused the weaknesses in the negotiation will affect the reflection process and will encourage us to explain away our faults. It helps to get a second opinion.

Finally, as suggested earlier in the chapter: 'know thyself'. We can be more alert to our biases and prejudices if we understand how we act and react – particularly when under pressure. This can be done by seeking wise counsel and by reflecting on one's own negotiation performance. Some self-reflection tools are provided in Appendix 3.

Dealing with others' differences

Can 'personality' be used as a tactic? Can the other party's perceived personality weaknesses be used to our advantage? Even the phrasing of the question conveys a competitive orientation that is probably not helpful to the negotiation. A typical personality tactic would be to get the other negotiators annoyed, lose their tempers and so then reveal some critical information or make an unwarranted concession. However, negotiation is both two-sided and messy. The hoped-for results of any tactic are not guaranteed. If the other negotiators control their annoyance and reciprocate the personality tactic with one of their own, are you sure you can then hold your temper and not do the very things you were hoping to entice from across the negotiating table?

Similarly, what if the other negotiators are 'emotional' – speaking a lot, interrupting, speaking loudly, quickly and in an unstructured and exaggerated manner? Negotiators use emotional outbursts as a tactic because they feel deeply about an issue and so get 'carried away', because someone pushed a 'trigger' or simply because it works for them. Some ways to deal with this are listed in Box 2.2. (Remember we all show emotion of some sort when we negotiate.) Female negotiators seem to react less to statements which might trigger an emotional response (typically anger or frustration) because they view negotiation in relationship terms, emotion being part of a relationship (Schroth, Bain-Chekal and Caldwell, 2005). For male negotiators, emotion gets in the way of fixing the dispute and so they react to it more.

Box 2.2: Dealing with emotion in negotiation

Treat people with respect

Do listen, show you are trying to understand.

Do allow for exaggeration.

Don't use put-downs yourself.

Don't challenge people's statements.

Treat yourself with respect

Don't get angry or frustrated.

Do retain your belief that you *can* find a good solution.

Restate what you want to achieve (but don't press others to agree).

State your own feelings too, but briefly.

Reflect on what others are saying

Recognise the emotional component.

Build on their statements about the substantive issues.

Seek to manage the process

Talk about where the present dynamic is leading.

Suggest alternative ways of interaction.

When considering the effect of gender on negotiation, we face the same problem as with personality – that there are no definitive links between gender and negotiation behaviour. It is more the case that the situation influences how negotiators approach their task, particularly in shaping one's expectations and goals (Kray and Babcock, 2006). As a simple but important example, if society conditions us to believe that women earn less than men, then a woman going for a job probably does not expect to earn as much and so just accepts what is offered at the job interview.

There is no reason for a male superiority complex or for women to feel they have to negotiate like men to be successful (which incorrectly presumes that men, however they negotiate, are successful). The socialisation of roles into gender should not be allowed to hide the fact that sexes are equally competent at negotiating. Female negotiators are seen as being more 'cooperative' by which is meant that they show more concern for others and make lower demands (Walters, Stuhlmacher and Meyer, 1998). When this is the case (as we will see from our strategy analysis in the next chapter), it is not surprising that they don't get such good outcomes but when they have set the same goals as men, they do just as well (Calhoun and Smith, 1999).

However, women might challenge the definition of negotiation in Chapter 1 because of its task orientation. Halpern and Parks (1996) found that female negotiators defined a situation more broadly than their male counterparts, such as considering who might be affected in the future, reflecting a more relationship-driven motivation. Following from this, the ensuing discussion might be viewed more as an opportunity to talk through a problem than a negotiation to fix it. This leads to a more collaborative perspective and less use of confrontational tactics. 'Negotiation' is less clearly separated from other conversations (Kolb and Coolidge, 1991), a consequence being that women can find themselves in situations where men are negotiating but they are not.

We might presume to give some gender-specific negotiation advice for when negotiating with someone of the opposite sex. Male negotiators should look at the broader perspective and include other people's concerns while backing off from making threats or using sarcastic humour while female negotiators should raise their expectations through good research and not let their goals become diluted for the sake of others achieving theirs. However, this is not specifically gender-related advice; it is useful advice for all negotiators whoever they are negotiating with. Again, self-reflection (Appendix 3) is important.

Reciprocity

If you try to 'wind up' the other negotiators, they are likely to do the same to you! A common feature of any social interaction is reciprocity – the tendency of one person to match what the other is doing. This is embedded in the way we relate to each other whether in informal gatherings or sitting across a negotiation table.

Reciprocity is a central dynamic of negotiation (Putman and Jones, 1982). Morton Deutsch, one of the father figures in social conflict research (that is, research into how to *avoid* conflict), realised that while we might look to the context, personality traits and other sources of conflict, the cause of any conflict behaviour being displayed by the person across the negotiating table is likely to be one's own behaviour. The reverse is also true, that if a negotiator acts cooperatively this too is likely to be matched by the person opposite. Deutsch (1990) called this his 'crude law of social relations'. It is a 'crude' law, a general trend to reciprocate, not precise matching ('negotiation is messy'). Nevertheless it is a powerful dynamic. Brett, Shapiro and Lytle (1998) found this matching behaviour strong enough to be called the 'bonds' of reciprocity.

The phenomenon has important implications for how negotiations unfold. The raison d'être of any negotiation is 'two parties with *differences . . .*' and the typical bias is to expect negotiations to be zero-sum. It follows that if negotiators give little prior thought to their negotiations then before too long they will be emphasising their differences, overlaying this with a bit of competitiveness, which then is reciprocated, and this contentiousness is in turn reciprocated . . . (Eyuboglu and Buja, 1993). A conflict spiral develops to no one's advantage. This is the positional bargaining described by Fisher, Ury and Patton (1991) where potentially beneficial solutions are not considered and where, even if the parties find a reasonable agreement, the process of achieving it has been so poor that neither is happy with the outcome.

The reverse reciprocation is also true. If one party is cooperative then the other is also likely to develop a cooperative approach. For example if one negotiator refrains from interrupting, it is likely that the other negotiator will cease to interrupt, allowing the negotiations to proceed more smoothly. So while the strength of reciprocity is a danger as it can easily lock negotiators into a conflict spiral, it is also an opportunity to establish and maintain cooperative interaction.

Converting conflict into cooperation: the power of 'tit for tat'

A lot of research into conflict and cooperation has involved the Prisoner's Dilemma game, which focuses on a key feature of negotiation. This feature (which negotiators tend to forget) is that the outcome of a strategic or tactical choice depends on what the *other* party does ('negotiation is two-sided'). The important practical implication is that negotiators should 'second guess' the other negotiators' options and motivations as well as their own.

The Prisoner's Dilemma situation is described in terms of cooperation (the choice which would maximise joint benefit; implying trust) and defection (the choice which would maximise own benefit; implying no trust). To cooperate is to make whatever move that may lead to joint benefit; to defect means to make a move that will disadvantage the other party for your own gain. An alternative view is to regard cooperation as a move towards the other party whereas the 'defection' move is not really a defection (implying mistrust, deceit etc.) but simply standing firm on one's present offer. These choices, which are brought into sharp focus in the Prisoner's Dilemma, apply most clearly in the negotiation end-game when parties make a series of offers to achieve an agreement. It is also relevant when negotiators consider whether to exchange information.

The reciprocity or matching behaviour we find occurring in negotiations has been incorporated into a formal strategy known as 'tit for tat'. It emerged undefeated from an experiment by Axelrod (1990) to see which strategy fared best when played against all other strategies in a repeated Prisoner's Dilemma game.

The essence of the 'tit for tat' strategy is that a negotiator matches what the other party has just done. If the behaviour is positive, such as providing information, then a potentially virtuous circle is established and the negotiations can make progress. Figure 2.1 reflects a process of information exchange in negotiations between an equipment manufacturer in the oil and gas industry and one of its raw material suppliers. They could not agree on a supply price. The manufacturer's negotiator, Michael, stated that a key concern for him was the funding arrangement over the life cycle of the project. Susan responded with information about her company's financial requirements leading to Michael going into more detail of his company's position. As a result, they were then able to work out a payment schedule that benefited the manufacturer at no cost to the supplier. This then enabled Michael to meet Susan's expectation on price.

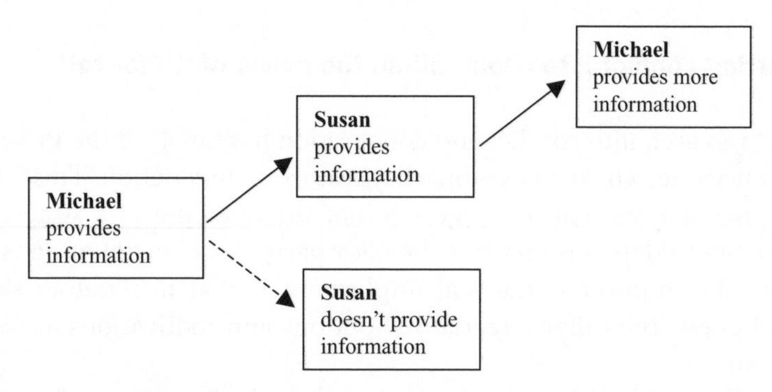

Figure 2.1: Negotiator choice and positive reciprocity in information exchange

If, however, Susan had not responded positively (Figure 2.2) Michael would have found himself in a difficult position having shared some information to move the negotiations forward but not getting a cooperative response. He would have had to try again to encourage cooperation by providing yet more information. While this seems a conciliatory move, giving something when nothing has been received can also look like weakness. Susan is now in an even more advantageous position. If this pattern continued the outcome would probably have been in her favour at the expense of Michael and his company.

According to the 'tit for tat' strategy the correct response to a refusal to provide information is not to give any more information oneself. This

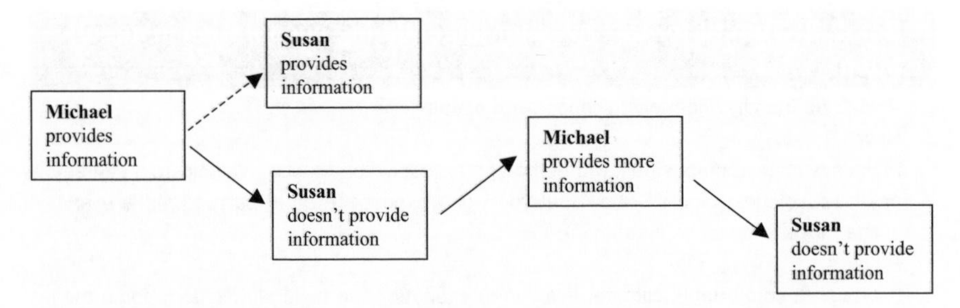

Figure 2.2: Negotiator choice and non-reciprocity in information exchange

looks like a recipe for a deadlock and conflict spiral so how does this 'tit for tat' behaviour lead to cooperation?

At the very least the parties must continue to interact in some way rather then end their negotiations. If they keep the process going and continue to match each other's behaviour then it is easy to recognise what is occurring and to appreciate that the situation cannot be exploited (Axlerod, 1990). As a rule to guide behaviour, matching the other's moves benefits from its clarity. 'What accounts for tit for tat's robust success is its combination of being nice, retaliatory, forgiving and clear. Its niceness prevents it from getting into unnecessary trouble. Its retaliation discourages the other side from persisting whenever defection is tried. Its forgiveness helps restore mutual cooperation. And its clarity makes it intelligible to the other player, thereby eliciting long term cooperation' (Axlerod, 1990, p. 54). Negotiators realise that they will not make any progress if they continue doing what they are doing and that they must adopt more cooperative strategies to achieve a good outcome.

The basic principle of 'tit for tat' can be developed into some 'rules' to help manage a negotiation. As noted earlier, negotiations are about the issue and the process. The 'tit for tat' strategy can help both aspects, such as encouraging information exchange or building trust, or when making concession. The rules all begin (conveniently) with the letter F (Box 2.3).

Rule 1: be nice or **friendly** and make a cooperative opening move. This does not mean a negotiator has to be soft on the issue and be 'cooperative' by making some initial concessions 'to get things going'. Using the distinction between the issue and the process, a negotiator can state her opening position (anticipating the other party to disagree) and at the same time through language and demeanour indicate a willingness to find a solution that meets both parties' needs.

Box 2.3: The 'tit for tat' rules for engendering cooperation in negotiation

Rule 1: be friendly and make a cooperative opening move

Issue

Make a 'yes-able' proposition, rather than an excessive one which will indicate a degree of reasonableness and so show that you won't expect the other party to make every single move to reach an agreement.

Process

Establish a comfortable climate, allow the negotiations to build slowly, don't force the pace; send general messages of the need to work together to see what might be achieved.

Rule 2: be firm and match the other's behaviour

Issue

Be clear from the outset on any genuine non-negotiables; state and restate underlying interests; match the other party's statements of interest/position with your own; make concessions to match the other party (concession size will be contingent upon the expected outcome).

Process

Don't over-argue the other's points, just match them with your own; match (perhaps slightly understate) the other party's threats.

Rule 3: be forgiving

Issue

Do not try to recoup any 'losses' from a previous negotiation; do not focus on retrieving setbacks in the current negotiation – look at the overall package being negotiated.

Process

Do not refer to earlier negotiations unless necessary (and then not in terms of win or loss); keep a future/solution orientation.

Rule 4: be facilitating

Issue

Hold positions on the issue and don't press for change from the other party.

Process

Make suggestions about a likely sequence of moves against the backdrop of a probable stalemate but ensure that the message includes a restatement of position.

Rule 2: be **firm** and match the other's behaviour. If the other negotiators simply reiterate their previous position, then you should repeat yours and not feel obligated to reduce your position in an attempt to overcome the impasse.

Rule 3: be **forgiving** if having tried to be cooperative (friendly, Rule 1) and it was not matched, be firm (Rule 2) but do not seek to 'punish' the other party for their uncooperativeness.

Because of Rule 2 be 'firm', the other negotiators will, in time, realise the only way to get you to cooperate is to cooperate themselves if they want an agreement. Further, because of what you have demonstrated through

Rules 1 and 3 ('friendly' and 'forgiving') the other negotiators will know that if they cooperate you will not exploit their cooperativeness and so they have some confidence that a genuine pattern of cooperation will be established.

Brett, Shapiro and Lytle (1998), in testing the strength of reciprocity and exploring how a conflict spiral can be broken, found that non-reciprocity *can* work. If the other negotiator is using arguments based on power, then to respond with interest-based arguments can break the cycle. While it *can* work it might not and so it is a strategy with risk. They suggest that a safer strategy would be to make a mixed message that involves making a power statement to match the other party (firmness) and an interest-based statement to provide an alternative. Drawing on the work of Rackman and Carlisle (1978), Brett et al. (1998) found that labelling the behaviour of the other party and suggesting a way forward also looked positive (though in their research experiment there were few examples of these behaviour strategies). These findings can be made into a further 'tit for tat' rule.

Rule 4: be **facilitating** – Talk about the process and provide other ways of proceeding. As an example, negotiations between two production managers are becoming increasingly positional; each worried about being left with additional costs through having to meet the other's deadline. A constructive contribution might be:

> [Scott] 'I know your deadline is three months and I've said my department cannot supply that many components in less than four (*Rule 2: be firm)* but as I said at the outset *(referring back to your friendly opening under Rule 1*), fulfilling this contract is important to both our departments so what if we talk about what the key drivers are behind your time frame and mine? That might offer us a way forward' *(Rule 4: be facilitating)*.

However, negotiation is messy. Just because one negotiator makes a facilitating move does not mean that the other will respond. If Ian's reply is:

> I've told you what has to happen. We need your components in three months to meet our deadline.

Then by Rule 2 Scott's appropriate response would be:

> I've made it equally clear we cannot do the work you require in less than four.

Rule 4 means a negotiator *talks* about the process and other ways of proceeding but does not embark on them until the other negotiator shows signs of reciprocating. In time, perhaps following another facilitating move by Scott, Ian might also respond with a mixed message:

> We are tied to our deadline. Three months. Though I can see what we are asking is difficult; the components are complex.

This gives Scott the option of responding to the firm part of Ian's statement ('We are tied to our deadline') or to the facilitating part ('I can see what we are asking is difficult') which has opened another avenue for discussion. This is where Rules 1 and 3 ('friendliness' and 'forgiveness') come into play again, shown by what the negotiator does *not* do. It is not an opportunity for Scott to take the facilitating comment as a sign of Ian backing down and haranguing him about how unreasonable he has been for even thinking that three months was possible. 'Tit for tat' tells us that this will only lead to Ian responding in kind. Instead Ian's facilitative response should be reinforced by a similar comment from Scott about the pressures deadlines (plural, recognising Ian's deadline too) and then shifting the dialogue slowly but surely into a new discussion, perhaps about rescheduling some of the processes.

The GRIT strategy

Osgood (1962) suggests the graduated and reciprocated initiatives in tension reduction (GRIT) strategy as another way to break a competitive 'tit-for-tat' conflict spiral. In the GRIT strategy, a party seeking to break the deadlock outlines its intentions which involve two elements. Firstly, it foreshadows plans to take firm action against the other party. However, this action will be delayed. Secondly, it makes a number of conciliatory gestures – small, non-costly concessions, which may include *not* doing something it had previously threatened to do. The GRIT strategy relies on the other party responding positively to one of these conciliatory gestures (to forestall the eventual unwelcome firm action). This means there will have been two successive cooperative moves and the reciprocity of competitive moves has been converted to reciprocity of cooperation.

The GRIT strategy is predicated upon the parties having a long-term relationship and the issues they have to negotiate can be fractionalised or dealt with incrementally (not being 'either/or' issues or issues of principle). Cold war diplomacy – the context in which this strategy was developed – is far removed from business negotiations but the essential principles of GRIT can still be used. Consider a situation where the parties in a supply contract are disputing every point – deliveries are late or wrong; schedules are always changing – and then 'resolving' them by referring to the small print in the contract. The GRIT strategy would involve, firstly, making it clear that to continue at present would mean that both parties would lose. Secondly it would involve making a series of small concessions as situations arise but against the backdrop of potential credible action to address the future of the relationship. The party trying to bring about change might accept the other's error, or bear some variation costs rather than contest them. They would make it clear that they are doing this, not 'for the good of the relationship' (which looks very much like appeasement) but rather because 'we are trying to make this contract work and we plan to accommodate the variations for the next six months but we have also asked our lawyers to pursue the compliance issues under the contract'. If the other party reciprocates by giving ground on another of the issues in dispute (as they ought, according to the 'tit for tat' strategy) then progress can be made (such as suggesting a mid-term operational review of the whole contract) and the legal proceedings can be halted. If the other party does not reciprocate, then no more concessions should be given (other than those announced) and the legal budget increased.

The GRIT strategy is a complex one to manage. However, a key point in the strategy, the idea of doing things gradually, has broader application as will be seen in strategies to build trust and develop a willingness to exchange information.

Trust

Another link in the DNA of negotiation is trust, 'one of the cardinal underlying characteristics of fruitful negotiation' (Zartman and Berman, 1982, p. 27). Trust is one of the great imponderables in negotiation. It seems to be important (and it is) but it is hard to know what trust is, and it is even harder in the middle of a negotiation to know whether one should trust the negotiator sitting across the table. Trust is related to personal qualities such as credibility, integrity and honesty but in the context of a negotiation it is more focused. Trust is an understanding that the other negotiator is willing to cooperate in some way to achieve an outcome – to engage in problem-solving or to match a concession in a trading situation (Pruitt, 1981).

Some people are inherently more trusting than others. In the absence of any evidence to the contrary, they are more likely to take statements and actions by others at face value rather than doubt them. More generally, trust expects the other person to 'do the right thing'. Examples would be giving money to someone to post off to a charity, trusting that they will post it all and not keep a dollar or three for themselves, or believing that when the real estate agent says, 'there are three other clients looking at this property' that there *are* three clients, and that they are separate, not three from the same family.

Trust can be made more secure by finding out more about the people and their trustworthiness, perhaps through any previous dealings with them. We would probably expect a friend to pay in all the money to the charity but be less sure about an unfamiliar work colleague. We might trust the veracity of the real estate agent if that agent had been recommended by neighbours as someone who really looked after them when they were buying their house.

We might also put some checks on the others' behaviour to make them more reliable. For example, when donating to a charity through another person we could ask for a receipt (which, of course, changes an act from being a trusting one to a distrusting one as far as the other person is concerned) or ask the real estate agent some follow up questions about the other clients. It is easier to keep check on other people's actions than their words. Unfortunately, negotiation is typically first about what people say rather than what they do.

Types of trust

Lewicki and Wiethoff (2000) identify two broad types of trust. The first is calculus-based trust. As its name suggests, this is trust based on weighing up the consequences of trusting compared with not trusting. The trust involved in giving the money to a work colleague might be an example. You are prepared to trust him because you estimate that he will realise that if he short-changes you you will find out and he will be embarrassed. You have calculated that he will know that not doing what he has been asked is not worth the risk. Added to this may be your knowledge of his past behaviour, particularly his reliability in keeping promises.

Identification-based trust is more relationship oriented and is built on an understanding of the other party and their expectations. Your friend can be trusted to forward the money to the charity more than a work colleague because she understands how important you think the work of the charity is and so will want to do what you've asked. She will probably give you the receipt without you asking as a natural way to reinforce the trust between you.

In both examples, the orientation is positive, and the trust has to do with cooperation and beneficial results. On the other hand, distrust is the expectation that the other people will take advantage of you for their own ends (Lewicki, McAllister and Bies, 1998). However, the lack of trust does not necessarily mean the presence of distrust. When starting to buy a car we may be wary of car salesmen because of their generally poor reputation but we don't have any reason to distrust the particular salesperson that we are dealing with; we will typically let him earn our trust as negotiations proceed.

Situation-specific trust

We cannot do much about our inherent predisposition to trust other people or about the other negotiator's innate trustworthiness. Of more immediate interest is what trust means in the negotiation itself. Lewicki and Stevenson (1997) make an important point that the type of trust we need to build depends on what we are trying to achieve. If the negotiation is a single transaction it is only necessary to build calculus-based trust. This would involve behaving consistently, undertaking commitments made and being clear to the other negotiator about the adverse consequences of not behaving in a similar fashion. Johnson and Cullen (2002, p. 343) found that there are a number of actions that managers could take which the other party would regard as indications of trust (Box 2.4).

Box 2.4: Ways that managers can demonstrate trust (Johnson and Cullen, 2002, p. 343)

Deliver on promises.
Deliver more than expected.
Make a concession.
Hold back rather than exercise power.
Resolve a conflict in a way that demonstrates procedural and outcome fairness.
Share information.
Be accommodating and flexible in a crisis.
Give opportunities to participate in discussion/decision making.

If the intention is to build a relationship for the future then the parties must work to build identification-based trust through frequent interactions to get to know and understand the other party and their long-term interests. This is particularly so for negotiators who are perceived to be in a strong position. Those in the low-power position take a calculative approach and will expect the stronger party will use their power to exploit (Rubin and Zartman, 1995). It is necessary to build identification-based trust by promoting shared values to overcome this (Olekalns, Lau and Smith, 2007). One difficulty, of course, is in trying to understand the other negotiator's intent. Many negotiators have participated in a social dinner followed by an enjoyable karaoke session (with resultant hangover) only to be faced with a very competitive bargaining session the following morning.

We can be more specific in trying to identify what trust is needed in a negotiation. What negotiators are really interested in is whether – at the present point in the negotiation – they can trust the other party. This question arises when there is a risk because without risk there is no need to trust.

There are three main points in a negotiation process where the need to trust is salient. The first is when information is provided by the other negotiator – is it true? The risk is that the information is false (or more often, is incomplete) and so decisions we make turn out to be unwise. Secondly, there are critical times when to make progress a negotiator needs the other party to reciprocate her actions – can they be trusted to do so? The risk is that she might offer some information in the expectation that the other will do likewise only to find that they do not. (As an example of the complexity of trust and distrust in negotiation, the fact that they have not reciprocated does not make them untrustworthy; it just indicates that they were not ready to establish a pattern of information exchange at that point in the negotiation. If they used the information so gained against the first negotiator, then this *would* indicate that they are not trustworthy.) The third situation calling for trust in a negotiation is whether the other negotiators can be relied upon to do what they have said they will do, such as honour their promise to come to the next meeting with a new proposal.

The presence of risk means these situations can be portrayed in terms of the Prisoner's Dilemma and so the strategies to build reciprocity that were outlined earlier in this chapter can also help build trust. In particular, the distinction between the issue and the process that is inherent in all negotiations enables a negotiator to talk about the need for trust (Rule 4: be facilitating) while standing firm (Rule 2) on the issue being negotiated. Only when there is an indication from the other party that they are also willing to trust, is the next move – providing information or making a concession – actually made (Fells, 1993).

This very pragmatic, situation-specific trust will strengthen as the negotiations progress. While dealing with the specifics of the issues a negotiator can encourage the development of calculus-based trust by referring, from time to time, to the adverse consequences of not reaching agreement. Identification-based trust is built on common interests and values as they become evident over time and should be reinforced at every opportunity. It is important that negotiators – both personally and on behalf of any organization they may be representing – demonstrate integrity by following through on any commitments they have made, large or small.

The important implication for negotiators is that the trust required in these specific situations is separate from whether the other negotiators are inherently trustworthy. It helps if they are but if they are not, this does not mean agreement cannot be reached. If a negotiator so shapes the situation that it is in the other party's interests to do what they have promised (calculus-based trust over the agreement's implementation) then this may be all that is needed. In these cases negotiators may trust simply because they feel they have no alternative. This leads to the next of the essential elements of negotiation – power.

Power

Power has been wonderfully defined as getting other people to do what you want them to do and having them like it (attributed to President Roosevelt). Power is at the heart of any negotiation because having to negotiate is an acknowledgement that you don't have enough power to achieve your objectives without the involvement of others. Negotiators do well to remember Magenau and Pruitt's observation that power is a slippery concept (Magenau and Pruitt, 1979, p. 197) – it can be exercised in many ways and while we know that we need to have power it is difficult to know how much of it we have. One of the dangers for negotiators is that people whose position is getting stronger tend to overestimate their power and so make even larger demands; however people whose power position is falling do not reduce their demands (Sivanathan, Pillutla and Murninghan, 2008). The practical implication of this is that convincing the other negotiators that they are in a weaker position than they thought will not automatically lead to them making concessions. As Magenau and Pruitt (1979, p. 198) crucially observed: just because I think I have more power than you does not mean you think you have less power than me. Power is not a zero-sum commodity.

Making sense of power in negotiation

Power can take many forms and so is difficult to categorise or measure. An early representation by French and Raven (1959) identified power by its sources: expert knowledge; an ability to reward or punish another; one's position of authority; or respect that others confer. While it is intuitively appealing to look to one's power base it might not be very helpful. Expert knowledge may be valuable (and negotiators cannot hope to secure a good outcome if they have not found out the facts surrounding the issue under negotiation) but two knowledgeable people, one on either side of the table, should each be able to make a good case as to why the other is wrong. (On the other hand, they might come up with an entirely new solution, which is a different sort of power altogether.) Further, trying to evaluate where the power lies is difficult – for example how can I balance my referent power against your coercive power?

We can 'translate' most of the sources of power into the notion of alternatives. Why, for example, is an expert's opinion listened to and accepted? Using specialised knowledge, the experts are able to demonstrate that their suggestion is better than any other option on the table (including the option of walking away) so everyone is drawn to agree to it.

Similarly, the view that 'information is power' (Dawson, 1999, p. 222; Lewicki, Minton and Saunders, 2006, pp. 188–9; Winkler, 1981, p. 141) can lead negotiators to withhold information in the belief that to do so makes them more powerful whereas to release information makes them more vulnerable. The critical issue here is 'information about what?' A negotiator who is cagey about revealing what he really wants to achieve should not be surprised if the other negotiator seems unwilling to cooperate. On the other hand, if he can get the other negotiator to understand *why* he is holding to a particular position then a cooperative approach is more likely to emerge. (This distinction between the 'what' and the 'why', positions and interests, is explored more fully in Chapter 6.) The judicial provision of information about the background to the issue, one's goals and preferences and the real reasons for not agreeing to the other party's proposals adds power in the sense of providing the opportunity for creative solutions to emerge.

The one piece of information that all negotiators want to know is 'at what point is the other party going to settle?' This becomes particularly important when the parties are trying to finalise an agreement and when the same question is asked in another way, 'at what point will they walk away?', which again shows the importance of alternatives.

Not surprisingly power is often associated with competitiveness and getting your own way. A classic definition of power is that of Dahl (1957, pp. 202–3) who stated, 'my intuitive idea of power, then, is something like this: A has power over B to the extent that he can get B to do something that B would otherwise not do.' Similarly Chamberlain and Kuhn (1965, p. 170) define bargaining power as 'the ability to secure another's agreement on one's own terms'.

Bargaining power has been described as the power to fool and bluff, 'the ability to set the best price for yourself and fool the other man into thinking it was your maximum offer' (Morgan 1949). Bacharach and Lawler (1981) bring the notions of subjectivity and perceptions into their understanding of bargaining power. The uncertainty and ambiguity of negotiation together with bargainers processing information imperfectly provides opportunities for tactical action to alter the perceptions of the other party. Reshaping the other party's understanding of their interdependence – who needs whom the most to get the outcome they are seeking – can increase one's bargaining power irrespective of the actual situation. In a similar manner, Lewicki and Litterer (1985, p. 241) offer a straightforward definition of power as, 'the ability to get another party to do something they ordinarily would not do by controlling the options they perceive open to them'.

If power is the ability to get someone to agree to something then emerging solutions can become a source of power. Fisher (1983) talks about the power of an elegant solution. Consider two countries in dispute over territory. A river going through the territory would be an obvious place to put the boundary and is an example of what Schelling (1960) showed when he identified a rather disconcerting phenomenon for negotiators, namely that we can reach solutions without actively problem solving. (He called it 'tacit bargaining'.) If we 'stand back' from a situation, it often speaks to us and an outcome becomes obvious, a 'mutually prominent alternative' (Schelling, 1960; Pruitt, 1981). This is essentially what Fisher, Ury and Patton (1991) suggest when they advocate using objective standards. In these cases the 'power' lays not so much with either party as with the proposed solution and that power is derived from it being manifestly better than anything else either party might come up with.

The power of knowing when not to negotiate

We feel we are in a strong negotiating position when we believe that we don't have to negotiate at all. Rubin and Brown (1975, p. 7) state that the parties to a negotiation are 'at least temporarily joined together in a special kind of *voluntary* relationship' (emphasis added) and Lax and Sebenius (1986, p. 11) regard negotiation as 'a process of potentially opportunistic interaction'. These observations reflect the key point that negotiators should continue negotiating only for as long as they expect the outcome will be better than what they might achieve in other ways. Fisher Ury and Patton (1991) portrayed this fundamental point with their notion of the best alternative to a negotiated agreement (BATNA).

The word 'alternative' is often taken to mean a different outcome as, for example, when a supplier offers a flat-rate price increase across the range of its products as an alternative to the previously proposed percentage increase. However, the word 'alternative' in the acronym BATNA refers to an alternative way of securing one's objective. So the supplier might decide to post its prices, which have all increased by a similar percentage, on the company website leaving it up to the buyer to place purchase orders at the new prices. This unilateral action to secure the desired price rise is an alternative to negotiating the price increases with customers. This, in essence, is how many commodities are traded internationally. Buyers and sellers – such as an iron ore miner and a steel mill – may negotiate a supply contract for the coming year that locks them together for the duration of the contract. Alternatively, there is a 'spot' market for iron ore – some miners are prepared to sell their ore once they've dug it out of the ground; some steel mills are prepared to look to the spot market for their supplies. So the key point for our miner and steel mill when they enter into negotiations for their next supply contract is that they each have an alternative way of pursuing their objective. They don't necessarily have to negotiate but they will stay and negotiate for as long as the expected outcome seems better than what they might achieve through spot market trading.

An example: the power of alternatives

A prominent architect had a 'falling out' with a company supplying air conditioners. He was so annoyed with the company that he never included any of its products in his design specifications unless it was the only one that could possibly do the job. The company felt the adverse sales effect of this, missing out on opportunities to supply its products to major construction and renovation projects. A new manager took over the company and resolved to get the architect's business back by giving him first-class treatment whenever he placed an order. Despite this the architect refused any overtures to use more of the company's products in his design specifications.

The new manager's strategy was not working. He realised what needed to be done only when he considered the architect's situation when he *did* place an order. The fact that the architect had placed an order meant he could not get the necessary equipment anywhere else. The architect's alternatives were nil. Consequently, the manager told his staff that when the architect next placed an order it should be given a low level of priority.

A few days after the next order from the architect came in, the manager phoned him to say 'you may be wondering why we have not given your order priority and processed it straightaway for you'. The architect was indeed wondering! The manager continued that since the architect was only an occasional customer his orders were – quite naturally – given lower priority than those who placed more regular orders and bought larger volumes. He was just phoning to tell the architect the situation in case he might be worried about any delay and so want to place his order elsewhere.

The architect was worried about a delay (which he had not anticipated) but he knew he could not go anywhere else. Before long, he placed some large orders and since everyone understood how they were now placed, the relationship prospered. The lesson of this story is clear. Consider *their* alternatives as well as your own to work out where the power lies.

Information exchange

Getting a realistic appreciation of the walk-away alternatives is just one, albeit crucial, aspect of negotiation. Equally important is gaining an understanding of interests and priorities as this lays a foundation for improved outcomes (Thompson, 1991; Olekalns, Smith and Walsh, 1996; Butler, 1999). However, even when negotiators prepare very well, there will still be some things they do not know, or are not sure of when they enter the negotiation. (Even when an agreement has been reached, the negotiators will probably still have unanswered questions, even if it is only 'would they have settled for less?') So it follows that encouraging effective information exchange is critical. From this perspective, negotiation is a learning process by which the negotiators, through the exchange of information, begin to understand their true situation.

When information is exchanged, there is then the question of how that information will be used – whether to create individual or joint gain. Murninghan et al., (1999) found that negotiators who stood to gain from doing well use information effectively to get good outcomes for themselves. Using information in this way reinforces the notion that information is power and so negotiators should be reluctant to share it. Even so, it is important to gain – and because of reciprocity, this also means exchange – information as the negotiations unfold.

Exchanging information about what?

The facts surrounding the issue are important in any negotiation. For example, if a mining company is negotiating a contract for the supply of tyres then issues of delivery logistics – journey times, routes, truck availability, the lifting gear needed to get the tyres off the truck (those tyres are big!) – will influence, perhaps even determine what can be agreed. A solution might emerge simply because the two parties bring different information to the table. In our tyre-supply negotiation, both parties probably have a good understanding of what it takes to deliver tyres and the only information the parties hold back is their respective financials. However the potential supplier might provide information about deliveries to other sites in the region and the mine operator might say something about their tyre store which, if deliveries are as frequent as the supplier is proposing, will now be empty most of the time. The supplier might then realise that he could perhaps rent the 'vacant' store as a regional depot for his own operation. In this way the additional information provided the basis for a previously unrealised outcome.

This information exchange is 'enabling' power in the sense of enabling the parties to agree to something they otherwise would not have by making a better outcome available. Thus the negotiators can create value through information exchange. Had they not exchanged this information they would probably have had an essentially competitive price/cost negotiation.

It is even easier to find opportunities to create value if each party clearly understands the goals, priorities and limits of the other party. Priorities might dovetail allowing one party to gain but not at the expense of the other. At the very least, learning more about the goals and priorities of the other party gives you an insight into how to put forward your proposal persuasively.

Cautious information exchange

Negotiators can learn about the other party's priorities by listening carefully to their presentations and statements and by asking open-ended questions. We read earlier that reciprocity is strong in negotiation so (and in accordance with the rules of 'tit for tat') being friendly and providing information is the first step to generating information exchange. However, we should not expect the information exchange to be complete. Much of the information provided (and withheld) early in the negotiation is usually shaped to present the party's situation in a favourable light. This can continue for only so long and it usually becomes apparent that further disclosure is needed for any more progress to be made. How should this be done?

When negotiators feel that to give information might convey weakness rather generate cooperation they will be reluctant to answer questions openly. In this situation, the power of reciprocity might be harnessed, 'What you are asking me is quite difficult to disclose, but there are some costings of yours that would help me understand the situation better, so if we both had more information . . . ' may get the process started.

Another approach is to 'drip feed' information, a practice that draws on the gradualism of the GRIT strategy as well as the rules of 'tit for tat'. If the negotiations are stalled through an information deadlock, initiate the process of drip feeding by providing some limited information (Rule 1: be friendly) but do not provide any more (Rule 2: be firm) until the other party reciprocates. If necessary, talk about the deadlocked situation and the need for more openness (Rule 4: be facilitating). Only when the provision of information is reciprocated should some more information be provided, again waiting for it to be reciprocated. In this way, the trust between negotiators can slowly build and information can then be exchanged rather more confidently.

Negotiators can also learn about the goals and priorities of the other party through their rejection of their offers. Getting to understand why a party says 'no' to an offer can yield valuable insight into what they really want. Rather than respond to a rejection with more reasons why it should be accepted, a good negotiator will seek to clarify the reasons for the rejection (Rackman and Carlisle, 1978). Insights can also be gained by repackaging a rejected offer into something of similar value. If the tyre suppliers' offer was rejected, then rather than lower his price to make it more acceptable the supplier might repackage it by, for example, increasing the frequency of tyre deliveries while reducing the penalties on late deliveries. By keeping the financial value of his offer much the same, his repackaged offer may tease out the relative importance of the two issues to the mine operator.

Some negotiators are high context communicators, able to 'read' a situation not only from what is being said but also from information about the inferred meanings from the context. (See Chapter 10 for more on cultural differences.) Low context negotiators who like the facts and a straight 'yes or no' answer often have more difficulty discerning the other party's underlying motivations, priorities and limits. Negotiators who are more individualistic in their orientation (that is, not too concerned about the other party) are less likely to be willing to offer information about their own priorities and so have to rely more on the offer-packaging approach to gain an understanding of the other party's priorities (Olekalns and Smith 2003).

Ethics

Ethical behaviour is another link in the DNA of negotiation, or perhaps more correctly, unethical behaviour is a mutation that distorts the process and outcome. It is very difficult to 'repair' a negotiation once there has been unethical behaviour.

Ethics is not a stand-alone phenomenon. We are ethical – or not – over how we handle the other DNA links of reciprocity, trust, power, information and outcome. The problem is in defining what is 'unethical behaviour'. This relates particularly to information exchange and the use of power (which are examined more closely below) but surveys of ethically ambiguous tactics (such as by Anton, 1990; Robinson, Lewicki and Donahue, 2000) have found that some tactics are regarded as more acceptable and are used more than others. For example, participants did not have much difficulty with tactics associated with competitive bargaining such as asking for more than they wanted and concealing their bottom line. They were less accepting of actions to manipulate others and had doubts about how one might obtain information on the other party (buying information is not okay). Misrepresentation and bluffing are generally seen as unethical with providing false information being the worst.

Even so, negotiators use deception frequently (Murninghan et al., 1999; Schweitzer and Croson, 1999). It seems as if deception is part of many negotiators' tool kit. This gives rise to a very practical difficulty. Honest disclosure increases the likelihood of an improved outcome (Paese, Schreiber and Taylor, 2003) but the honest disclosure is only effective in helping move the negotiations forward if it is *seen* to be honest or at least is readily verifiable. In a private hospital one of the key factors that determine the hospital's profitability is the extent to which the operating theatres are fully used. During wage negotiations, if the hospital management resists a wage claim on the grounds that 'the theatre utilisation rate is down' the credibility of this statement will not be helped if the management then refuses to provide the utilisation figures on the grounds of 'commercial in confidence'.

Ethics, information exchange and the bottom line

As discussed earlier, one of the main times in a negotiation where there is a need to trust relates to whether the information being provided is true. To provide false information is unethical (and unlawful) and this includes providing information in a way designed to create a false impression. If asked a question they do not wish to answer, negotiators have a number of

Table 2.1 Handling 'inaccurate' information in negotiation

Prevention	Diversion	Detection
Being honest with oneself Being obviously prepared Asking questions Not rushing the negotiation Taking notes	Asking questions Restating the main points Summarising	Not making automatic assumptions, deliberate deceptions or responding competitively Seeking repetition or clarification Presenting your understandings Seeking time to confirm

options rather than to give a misleading answer. They can ask a question in return, restate their main points or summarise (Table 2.1). Such responses will divert the discussion giving the negotiator time to consider what response to give if the question is asked again. A good negotiator will have thought ahead about difficult questions that might be asked and will have prepared answers to them.

Showing that you have done your research prior to the negotiation and that you would prefer to take your time rather than press on quickly to the deal-making closure would deter the other negotiator from attempting any tactical misinformation as it is likely to be exposed. Asking direct questions cuts down the risk of the other party deceiving through omission but all answers need to be tested for their veracity (Schweitzer and Croson, 1999). If misinformation is suspected then rather than direct confrontation, asking for a restatement or clarification will cause the other negotiator to reconsider – even if they repeat the inaccuracy they will know it has not been believed. Responding by outlining one's own understanding of the situation would have the same effect. If, on reflection, it is believed that the deception was deliberate, consider whether to continue negotiating. If agreement is necessary then one option is to include a contingency provision in the agreement. If the other party is insisting they can deliver the raw materials by a certain date (which you seriously doubt) then an additional clause about penalties for late delivery would be important.

Negotiators regard misrepresentation as unethical but why do they tend to conceal or misrepresent their bottom line position? Rather than see the question of 'reveal or not' as an ethical one, we can consider it and make a judgement in the context of the process of negotiation. A premier league soccer club is prepared to pay £30 million for a striker it wants on its team. Its recruiting manager makes an offer of £25 million to the player's club in London. The manager of the London club, who is seeking to maximise the transfer fee, challenges the worth of the offer by asking 'is that your best price for my leading goal scorer?' To respond openly and reveal that the club's board had authorised an additional £5 million would put the recruiting manager at a disadvantage because few negotiators expect the other party's early positions to be their final one. (An early final position distorts the negotiation dynamic because the other negotiator expects yet more concessions to be made later but there are none to be given.) As a transfer deadline nears, the two clubs reopen their stalled negotiations. The offer of £25 million is tabled again and draws the same response, 'is that your best price for my leading goal scorer?' It is a question of judgement, not ethics, whether to reiterate that the £25 million offer is all that is available.

Ethics and the exercise of power

Negotiators who believe they are in a strong position often use overly competitive tactics (Crott, Kayser and Lamm, 1980) but to do so can easily backfire. An oil company embarked upon a round of negotiations with the leaseholders of its service stations. The company was facing competitive pressure from food retailers who were expanding into motor retail and service stations. As a result, it needed to renegotiate the leases on terms more favourable to itself and so it developed what was known the FUD strategy. The company negotiators would set out to instill fear, uncertainty and doubt in the station leasees' minds prior to negotiating new terms for the leases. At the same time the company's website declared that it worked in a cooperative partnership with its station owners, customers and clients. Clearly the negotiating team did not read this or perhaps they were given such a tough negotiating target by their board that they felt the only way they could achieve their targets was through a drastic competitive strategy. When the FUD strategy became public, the company issued an apology on its website.

Ethics and the agreement

The question of ethics may arise in how the negotiators implement the agreement. Commitments made as part of an agreement must be honoured but an agreement cannot cover all possible changes in circumstances that may occur during its life. Negotiators from some cultures place more emphasis on the relationship than on the precise terms of the agreement and so would not see it as unethical to seek changes to those terms when their circumstances change. As world prices of resources showed signs of falling rather than continuing to rise, an Asian steel company was reported to have renegotiated the price of a contracted iron ore shipment even after it had already reached the Asian port (*Australian*, 9 October 2008, p. 4).

Being ethical

Few negotiators set out to be unethical but often the pressure of achieving an outcome leads to unethical actions. In negotiations over television rights one very senior company lawyer admitted he had lied in the negotiations (*West Australian*, 13 December 2005, p. 12). The court asked 'is it your view that in pursuit of an important business objective it may be legitimate to tell lies?' The lawyer's response was 'I don't think that's the right thing to do. I was desperate to try to get funds from them to facilitate the acquisition of the ... rights, and things were moving very fast.' Approximately $10 million was at stake at this point in the negotiation.

Similarly with the oil company negotiators – a succession of strategic and tactical decisions in pursuit of an objective resulted in an unethical approach to the negotiation. (Just so readers don't think it is only corporate negotiators who act unethically, in one union negotiation in the Pilbara some union members put a jack under a section of rail and so prevented all movement of trains – hardly a case of 'good faith bargaining'.) In the intensity of a negotiation and the pressure of the moment the need to achieve a particular objective can justify many decisions, particularly when no single step in the strategy is illegal. However, a good negotiator applies some tests.

As we have noted earlier, negotiation is two-sided and a critical element in preparation is to do one's preparation from the perspective of the other party. Taking this two-sided approach, a negotiator should always ask, 'how would I feel and react if the other party did to me what we are proposing to do to them?' This is a good test to apply but even here we might – as we often do – apply a different standard to ourselves. A stronger test – the one that came to be applied in the oil company case – was the publicity test, 'would I be comfortable with everyone else knowing this is what I do in negotiation? Once the negotiations are concluded, would I be willing to have the other party write their account of events and post it on my company website?'. Better the website than publicity as a result of a court hearing.

Outcome

The final link in our negotiation DNA is the outcome. Negotiation is a purpose driven activity and the success of a negotiation is measured by how well the outcome achieves the parties' goals. In some situations a negotiator's alternative may be better than the best possible agreement and so to agree would not be a good result. However, the intent of entering into a negotiation is to find a good negotiated outcome.

Many negotiators (and many negotiation books) express a preference for a 'win-win' negotiation. The essence of this is that both parties gain something from the negotiation and are pleased with their agreement. Being satisfied with the result they are more committed to implementing the outcome fully and will be more positive about the relationship they have with the other party. This will help future negotiations between them. This beneficial negotiation scenario is contrasted with 'win-lose' and 'lose-lose' negotiations where, as their names suggest, one or both parties do not do very well. As a consequence they are not committed to the agreement and are not favourably disposed to the other party. The 'win-win' outcome clearly has more appeal but is it more appealing than realistic?

What, exactly, do we mean by a 'win-win' negotiation?

The distinction between win-lose and win-win negotiating has its academic antecedents in the seminal work of Walton and McKersie (1965) who describe and analyse four sub-processes of negotiation, two of which – distributive and integrative bargaining – form the basis of these two fundamentally contrasting approaches to negotiation.

The core of the distinction, according to Walton and McKersie, lays in the nature of the issue under negotiation. If it is a 'fixed-sum variable-share' issue where one party could gain but only at the expense of the other, then this inherently competitive situation gives rise to a set of strategies (misinformation and commitment) which, if properly applied, result in one negotiator claiming the bulk of the available outcome while the other achieves very little. These negotiations are what we envisage by the term 'bargaining'. They are competitive and leave a nasty legacy for the next negotiation.

By contrast, in some other negotiations the parties' objectives are not in direct conflict; one party might be able to gain and not at the other's expense. In Walton and McKersie's terminology these are 'variable-sum variable-share' 'problems' and should be approached completely differently. The negotiators should exchange information, openly explore options and so find a solution that suits them both. This integrative problem-solving approach provides the basis for future cooperation between the negotiators.

When presented in this way the preference for a 'win-win negotiation' is understandable. However, a genuine 'win-win' agreement is one that neither party can improve on, except at the expense of the other. To get to this position the negotiators will have created some value that previously did not exist (or was not *seen* to exist) when the parties first started negotiating. This is not as easy as it sounds (how it might be achieved will be explored more fully in Chapter 7) and so negotiators often rationalise an outcome after the event, particularly if they have not done very well, and call it a 'win-win' agreement even when it is not.

For example, negotiators might simply split the difference between their respective demands. A shopping centre manager wants each shop to contribute $5000 to an advertising promotion. The shop owners do not want to pay more than $2500 and want a veto over the promotion's theme. The manager proposes a reduced contribution of $4000 provided he has control over the promotion; the shop owners reluctantly agree. Since both parties have gained some concessions from the other they can each regard the outcome as 'win-win' but this outcome can equally be called 'lose-lose' since neither party got what they originally wanted. Similarly, no negotiator likes admitting defeat and even when the outcome is poor a negotiator will seek to justify the small benefits of the agreement. A union official at the end of a long strike where the workers have been unable to secure an improvement in the company's offer might justify the return to work agreement to his members in terms of there being no job losses as a result of the dispute. This repackaging of the outcome is understandable in the practical world of negotiating but the true measure of whether a negotiated agreement was a win lies in the judgement of those who have to implement it, not the negotiators.

Conclusions

This chapter has examined the core of all negotiations through the imagery of the DNA helix. Parties seeking to reach agreement are bound together in a competitive yet cooperative process that involves reciprocity, trust, power, information exchange, ethics and outcome. But negotiation is messy and these essential links in the negotiation DNA do not automatically develop once the parties start negotiating. To be effective a negotiator must carefully build each link in the DNA of their negotiation.

Negotiation is also two-sided and so to be effective a negotiator must ensure the other negotiator is also willing to build the negotiation's DNA. Regretfully the links in the DNA chain can be manipulated. Trust can be abused, information distorted, power can be exploited, and ethics compromised. Careful handling of the negotiation is required and the distinction between the issue being negotiated over and the process by which that negotiation occurs – one aspect of negotiation's complexity – provides an opportunity for a negotiator to achieve this. A negotiator should take a considered, strategic approach to an issue and have a managed approach to the process. These aspects of effective negotiation are explored in the next two chapters.

3 Being strategic

The previous chapter cautioned against assuming that the DNA of negotiation – reciprocity, trust, power, information exchange, ethics and outcome – automatically develops once the parties start negotiating. Negotiators have to work hard to build these elements into their negotiation and guard against their misuse as a negotiation progresses. The distinction between the issue and the process gives scope to developing an effective approach to the task of reaching agreement. This chapter focuses on managing the issue being negotiated and develops a strategic approach to this aspect of negotiation. (The process by which agreements are reached will be discussed in Chapter 4.)

Consider a situation where two negotiating parties have met and thoroughly explored their differences but are still in disagreement over a key issue. They agree to meet again. What should be done to try and break the impasse? The most common response would be to get an agreement that a concession should be made. This almost intuitive response reflects a desire to be cooperative, a preference for agreement rather than conflict. It may well be the correct response to the situation but it may not. How does a negotiator know?

Besides being cooperative and agreement oriented, this instinctive 'we need to make a concession' response to an impasse reflects closed, linear thinking. It is no different from a negotiator who – come what may – says, 'I'm not going to give in on this issue.' This rigid approach to handling an issue ignores two of the practical implications of negotiation identified in Chapter 1; that negotiation is two-sided and that negotiators always have choice.

It is easy to imagine negotiating strategically as playing a game of chess. Strategy is at the heart of the game, particularly through thinking ahead and working out the many options available to the other player for each move you make. Similarly, working through the options from the other side's perspective is an important part of effective negotiating. Pursuing the imagery of negotiation as a game of chess, we should give thought to which piece we might be. The rook and the bishop – both far-reaching pieces – have the limitation that they can only move in straight lines. The most powerful piece, the queen, can move in any direction but again still only in a straight line. Linear thinking is a constraint on a negotiator. In contrast, knights are quite prepared to go this way and that and to jump over obstacles in order to get to where they want to be. So perhaps think of strategic negotiation as being 'the knight's move'.

Strategic choice

The issue choices open to a negotiator

The most profound choice open to a negotiator is to not negotiate at all. Indeed it is sometimes suggested that the first rule of good negotiating is 'don't negotiate if you don't have to'. This choice of walking away from the negotiation – which was explored in the previous chapter – remains an option at all times until agreement is reached. En route to that agreement, a negotiator has a choice of other strategies. The names given to each of these strategies varies between writers but essentially there are four (Table 3.1).

Table 3.1 A negotiator's choice of issue strategy

Strategy	Definition
Contend	To stand firm on the issue and expect agreement to be reached by the other party conceding
Concede	To bring the negotiations to an end by agreeing with the other party
Clear-cut compromise	To split the difference between what you want and what the other party wants so that you both get something, but neither of you gets all that you wanted
Creatively compromise	To find a solution which adds some value to the issues so that both can gain something and not at the expense of the other party
And the non-negotiation option:	
Walk away	To bring the negotiations to a close because you can do better elsewhere

Firstly, a negotiator can stand firm on the issue and keep restating her offer or position without variation (variously called contending, competitive, assertive, and dominating). Secondly, the negotiator can do the opposite and concede, abandon her own position and agree with the other party (conceding, yielding, accommodating, obliging). Thirdly, the negotiators can split the difference between them (which some would call conceding, others a compromise) and finally the parties can create a new solution altogether (problem solving, integrating, collaborating) though here the term creative compromise is used. ('Creative collaborating' may seem a more appealing name for this strategy but although the parties have to collaborate there is still a degree of competitiveness rather than harmonious and unified activity.)

Making the right choice

Pruitt (1983a) and his colleagues developed a dual concerns model of strategic choice which suggests that a negotiator should take into account two factors – concern for self: how important it is for me to get what I want, and concern for other: how important I feel it is for the other people to get what they want. With high or low levels of concern in each case the model indicates which of the four strategies is the appropriate one (Figure 3.1). For example, if it is important for a negotiator to achieve his objective and he has little regard for how well the other party does then he should contend, stand firm on his demands and expect the other

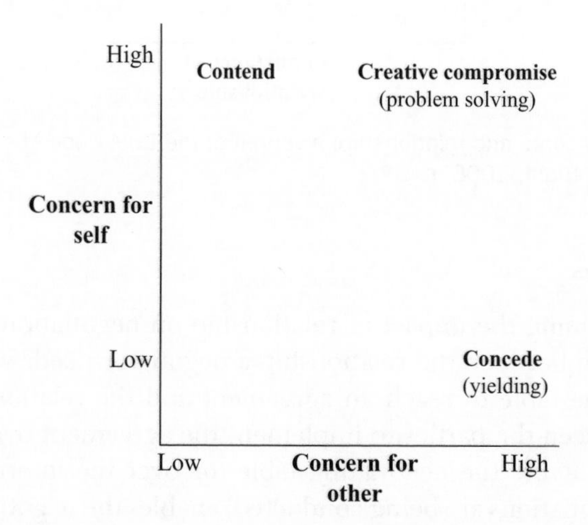

Figure 3.1: Strategic choice: the Dual Concerns Model (based on Pruitt, 1983a)

party to agree with him. If the issue is not important he should concede (Pruitt's 'yielding'). (Pruitt also includes 'inaction' when concern is low on both dimensions but it is not regarded as a distinctive issue strategy here.)

The Dual Concerns Model is intuitively appealing and has been developed by others. For example it became increasingly clear that relationships are an integral part of successful business and so too in negotiation. Hence the Dual Concerns Model has been modified (see Figure 3.2) to suggest that a negotiator should, on the one hand take account of the importance of the outcome, and on the other, the importance of the relationship (Savage, Blair and Sorenson, 1989; Lewicki and Hiam 2006). (As in the Lewicki and Hiam model a midway strategy, their 'compromise', is often included in presentations of the Dual Concerns approach. Their 'avoidance' is again omitted from Figure 3.2.)

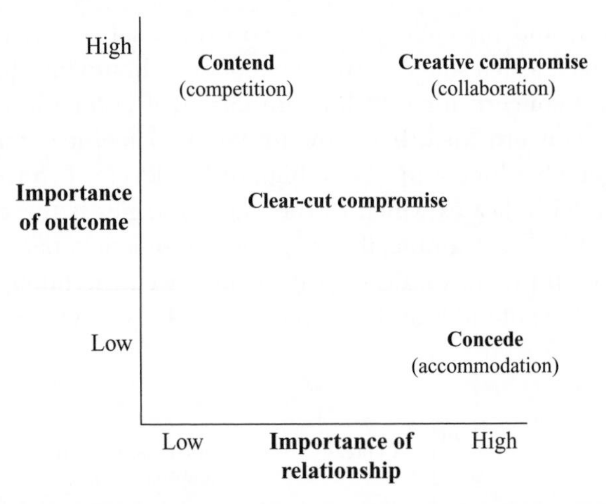

Figure 3.2: Outcome and relationship: a variant of the Dual Concerns Model (based on Lewicki and Hiam, 2006, p. 32)

Relationships

When examining the impact of relationship on negotiation it is helpful to distinguish between the relationship a negotiator needs with the people across the table to reach an agreement and the relationship that is needed between the parties to implement the agreement over time. The relationship across the negotiating table (or over the internet if that is how the negotiations are being conducted) enables the negotiation's DNA to develop – reciprocity, trust and information exchange in particular.

The negotiators don't have to like each other; they just have to have a relationship which permits exchanges to take place. More important for the outcome, particularly in negotiations between organisations, is the relationship between those who have to implement the agreement. These people may not have been at the negotiating table. Good relationships at both levels provide the opportunity for ongoing cooperation between the parties, to their ongoing mutual benefit.

However, we must guard against putting too much weight on the notion of relationship when negotiating. A close relationship can lead to too much cooperation where each party is willing to concede to the other, sometimes without even explicitly discussing the issue. This leads to clear-cut compromises rather than value-added solutions (Halpern, 1994; 1997; Valley, Neale and Mannix, 1995). If friends don't yield to the temptation to yield, they may achieve a better outcome for them both.

A close relationship can also raise expectations. When the Australian government was negotiating with the United States government over a bilateral free trade agreement – something that was important to both – they were doing so in the context of a long-standing strategic relationship, forged during the Second World War and reinforced by Australia being one of few countries to give material support to the United States in the Gulf War. However, when it came down to the final issues in the agreement, one being over beef quotas, the Australian negotiators could not secure the final concession from their American counterparts. As a lead negotiator reflected later, 'it caught us all off guard that our relationship was not worth 30 000 tons of beef.' (*Australian*, 25 February 2004, p. 6). The American negotiators had their own good reasons not to make further concessions on beef imports. The lesson to be learned is that while the parties may well have a strong relationship they are also in a negotiation over a specific issue; the nature of the relationship has to be 'translated' into the negotiation, not presumed.

The presence of a relationship can also be a tactic. The iron ore companies of Western Australia are in a long-term relationship with the steel mills of Japan. Each year the parties meet to negotiate tonnages, price and other issues for the coming year. One ore company negotiator reflected over more than 10 years of negotiations in the early development of the industry and realised that each year, when there was one final issue left on the table, the Japanese would suggest something like 'perhaps you might give on that last point; after all, we are in a long-term relationship, trying to work together', and the Australians inevitably did. He also realised that he could not think of any occasion when the Japanese gave in on the last point 'for the sake of the relationship'. Well done, the Japanese negotiators! The cross-cultural wisdom is that the Japanese value long-term relationships very highly, but an awareness of the importance of a relationship to the other party does not mean it is only one party which has to make all the concessions to keep the relationship going.

What factors should be taken into account?

The two-by-two matrix structure of the Dual Concerns Model has a lot to commend it. It reminds negotiators that they *do* have a choice of strategy and it encourages an analytical approach, which is always a good thing. However negotiation is both messy and two-sided and the Dual Concerns Model may oversimplify the complexity of managing an issue strategy over the course of a negotiation. The way the Dual Concerns Model is presented (though not by Pruitt) conveys the idea of negotiation involving a single strategy choice – that any particular negotiation consists of either contending or problem solving or yielding. The messiness of a negotiation is partly because negotiations are more likely to involve sequential choices of strategy because their levels of concern for self and other will probably change as information is exchanged. One practical implication for negotiators is that they should revisit their analysis during the negotiation to see if a change in strategy is required.

The Dual Concerns Model also portrays a single rather than two-sided perspective. If both parties have high concern for self but not for other then both should contend, in which case there will be no agreement until something changes. Also while a negotiator with high concern for self and for other should engage in problem solving (creative compromise), if the other negotiator is contending then problem solving will not work. (In these situations, it is usually the problem solver who comes out worse off.) A practical implication is that a negotiator should endeavour to raise the other party's level of concern in both dimensions before embarking on a problem solving strategy. Pruitt (1983a) added the notions of feasibility and vigour to the basic model of strategic choice but it would be helpful to give more explicit consideration to the strategic choices of the other negotiator when deciding one's own strategy on the issue.

A dual concerns approach can be strengthened by increasing the number of factors to be taken into account to five: importance of issue to self; concern for other's outcome; expectation of other's strategy; time pressure and quality of alternatives. These five factors provide a framework by which negotiators can chose whether to contend, concede or pursue one of the compromise strategies.

The importance of issue to self

A common feature in all the strategic choice models is the importance of what the negotiator wants to achieve through the negotiation, variously described as 'concern for self' or 'importance of the issue'. The research into the validity of the Dual Concerns Model holds up for this factor, namely that the more important the issue, the more likely it is that the negotiator will stand firm and contend (Pruitt and Carnevale, 1993; Rhoades and Carnevale, 1999; Sorenson, Morse and Savage, 1999). If the issue is not important, then the negotiator is likely to concede and agree with the other party's position (see Table 3.2). (This and the subsequent tables will be combined into the Strategy Framework presented in Figure 3.3 and in Appendix 4.) If the issue is too important to concede fully then the negotiator might seek some common ground. Interestingly – and importantly – the high importance of the issue which can lead

Table 3.2 The effect of importance of issue to self and concern for other on strategy choice

Importance of issue	high	low	low(ish)	high
Strategy choice	contend	concede	clear-cut compromise	creative compromise
Concern for other	low	high	high	high
Strategy choice	contend	concede	clear-cut compromise	creative compromise

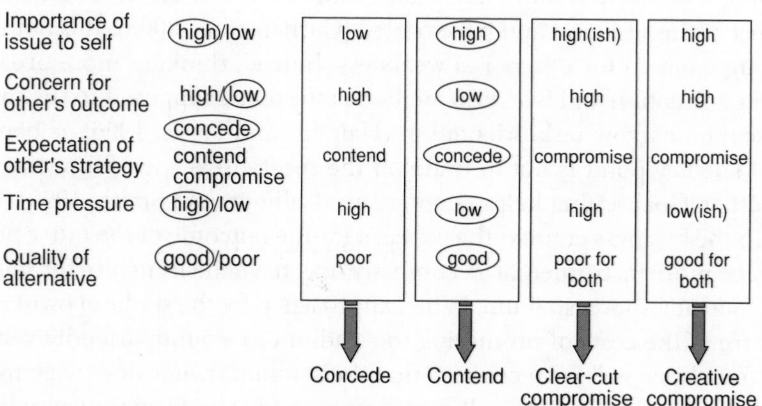

Figure 3.3: The Strategy Framework: the straightforward case

to a negotiator standing firm also provides the opportunity and impetus for negotiators to find other creative ways in which the needs of the issue might be satisfied. Thus one of the antecedents of effective problem solving in negotiation is that the parties stand firm on what is really important to them (Neale and Bazerman, 1985b; Pruitt, 1983b; Roloff and Jordan, 1991).

Concern for other's outcome

A negotiator's concern for the other party's outcome is a significant factor to take into consideration. This concern can be altruistic in that for personal reasons – perhaps liking the other negotiator, perhaps because of one's social or religious values – a negotiator wants the other negotiator to achieve his goals.

Concern for other must be distinguished from the relationship. If the effective implementation of the agreement is going to require an ongoing relationship then the relationship becomes part of the issue being negotiated and so it increases the importance of the issue to self. If the relationship is important to the other party then this will affect their choice of strategy too. Generally speaking an expectation of future interaction leads to more cooperation (Ben-Yoav and Pruitt, 1984a) but, as we have seen, it is important to guard against 'cooperation' being taken to mean 'we must make a concession for the sake of the relationship' – that can lead to appeasement, an approach that has little to commend it.

There is a potential gender effect to be aware of. Female negotiators may be socialised into overestimating concern for others (Song, Cadsby and Morris, 2004) and when they have been found to do less well in negotiation, it seems that they have placed more emphasis on the relationship aspect of the situation and have traded (Curhan et al., 2008). It is not that having concern for others is a weakness. Indeed, thinking more broadly about a situation and who else might be affected, as opposed to the more masculine narrow task orientation (Halpern and Parks, 1996), is beneficial. The key point is not to trade off the substantive issue for a concern for other. Goal setting helps counter this (Calhoun and Smith, 1999).

In the business context the concern for the outcome of the other party may be more instrumental. A company may have the franchise for selling fast food at a sports stadium. When approached by the stadium owner for a share of the costs of promoting the stadium as a family-friendly venue, the franchisee will have concern that the stadium owner does well; more attendees at the stadium will mean more food sales. Many negotiations are based on the principle of how one company can help another improve its value chain and so there is an instrumental concern for the other's outcome in any negotiations between them.

If a shopping centre manager has been instructed to secure a nil increase in cost when renegotiating a cleaning contract to set a precedent for the centre's other contracts, then the importance of the price issue to him is high. If he has little or no concern over whether the contractor does well out of the contract (that is, he is only concerned about the standard of performance of the contract itself) this suggests that he should contend and stand firm on the issue of price (Table 3.2). High concern for the contractor's outcomes as well as those of his own company would indicate trying to creatively find ways of keeping the money value of the contract constant without financially pressurising the contractor.

Expectation of other's strategy

One of the weaknesses with the Dual Concerns Model is its single sidedness. It does not seem to take account of the other party's strategy when determining what stance to take on the issue. This is important because the two-sided nature of negotiation means that the outcome of your strategic choice is dependent upon what the *other* party does by way of response. Negotiators like the idea of standing firm on the issue but this contending strategy is only going to work if the other party adopts a conceding strategy.

Pruitt's (1983a) addition of the notion of 'feasibility' to his model was recognition that a negotiator cannot implement a strategy in isolation. Rhoades and Carnevale (1999) found that negotiators reacted to the strategy choice of others; for example participants in their negotiation research experiments only seemed willing to persist with cooperative problem solving if the other negotiator was responding cooperatively (the reciprocity DNA). Contentious behaviour extinguished attempts at cooperation. If the other party is expected to concede then this (all other things being equal) is a good reason to enter the negotiation (or the next meeting) with a 'stand firm' contending strategy (Table 3.3). Conversely, if a negotiator is absolutely convinced that the other party is not going to concede then the

Table 3.3 The effect of other party's expected strategy on strategy choice

Other's expected strategy	concede	contend	clear-cut compromise	creative compromise
Your strategy choice	contend	concede	clear-cut compromise	creative compromise

only strategy that will get an agreement is for the negotiator to concede herself.

More importantly, the two cooperative strategies of clear-cut and creative compromise both rely on the other party's choice of strategy. It is not possible to engage in either strategy unless the other party is doing the same thing. Consider a simple situation where one party is trying to sell its widgets for $10 but the other party is offering to pay only $6. The 'obvious' or 'mutually prominent' solution (Schelling, 1960) is to settle on $8. This being so, our buyer, trying to be helpful and cooperative, suggests the compromise price of $8 but the vendor responds with the same selling price of $10. Our potential buyer thought he was engaging in the clear-cut compromise strategy – 'meet you half way' – but ended up having taken the conceding strategy. The buyer has now incurred both position and image loss (Pruitt, 1981, p. 23); the negotiating range is no longer between 6 and 10 but between 8 and 10, and the seller can reasonably expect another concession to follow. The critical point, however, is that the clear-cut strategy only works if the other party has also chosen to do it.

As we have seen in the previous chapter, we are all different and negotiators are each disposed towards one particular style that might translate into a preferred strategy. However, this should not govern our choice of strategy; negotiating according to one's personality is not being strategic. Negotiators' personalities may influence how well they implement a particular strategy but should not determine what that strategy should be. An appreciation of the other negotiators' personalities and known negotiation styles will contribute to one's expectation of the strategy they might adopt. Even so, it is important to remember that in most negotiations, personality characteristics will be constrained by other contextual factors.

Similarly, the cultural impact can be significant in the other negotiator's choice of strategy. As will be shown in Chapter 10, it might be expected that negotiators from a high context culture will be more likely to negotiate by leaving stated positions on the table, this being an element in the contending strategy. However, as with personality, the cultural influence is not the only determinant of strategy. A negotiator's understanding of the cultural context of the other party would be considered alongside their estimation of how important the issue is to the other party, the time pressure they seem to be experiencing (being aware that 'time pressure' might mean something very different to people of a different culture) and the negotiator's estimation of how the other party regard the quality of their alternatives. Anything that can be known about the other party is going to help a negotiator make a reasoned estimate of the strategy the other party is likely to adopt.

One factor that does impact on a party's stance and issue strategy is the presence of a constituency. These effects will be explored more in Chapter 9 but it is sufficient for our purposes here to know that the presence of a constituency encourages a contending strategy through higher importance of the issue to self and lower concern for other. Negotiators acting on behalf of others are more competitive and have more difficulty in reaching agreement.

Time pressure

Another factor impacting on negotiation is time. Many negotiations settle just before a particular deadline. US labour negotiation contracts are often finalised after months of negotiation but only minutes before the existing contract expires. Coal exporters in the Hunter Valley reached agreement on better use of port facilities on the evening of the deadline day set by the Australian Consumer and Competition Commission (*Australian*, 9 April 2009, p. 2). A car salesman may well try to instil a sense of urgency into the discussions to put pressure on the potential buyer to decide quickly, knowing that such pressure often induces the buyer to make that last concession to close the deal and buy the car. The time factor might explain why Sorenson's (1999) negotiators, who had low concern for each other, compromised and split their differences, rather than just remain inactive as the model suggests. Knowing there was a timeframe to their negotiations and wanting an outcome, they engaged in the easiest way of finding a solution – split the difference.

If negotiators are not under time pressure then – all other things being equal – they are likely to stand firm, to contend (see Table 3.4), but high time pressure is going to cause them to make concessions (Magenau and Pruitt, 1979; Stuhlmacher and Champagne, 2000) either by conceding unilaterally or splitting the difference through a clear-cut compromise. We might imagine that being under pressure, such as having to find a solution quickly, is an impetus to creativity but this is not what happens in practice (Amabile, Hadley and Kramer, 2002). Negotiators might find a 'creative' face-saving package that enables one or both parties to back down from

Table 3.4 The effect of time pressure on strategy choice

Time pressure	low	high	high	low(ish)
Strategy choice	contend	concede	clear-cut compromise	creative compromise

committed positions, but they need time to find a creative adding-value solution (Carnevale and Lawler, 1986; De Dreu, 2003). However, do not allow too much time because if there is no time pressure to settle, then there is no pressure to settle at all.

As with many aspects of negotiation, what might look to be a constraint on one's negotiating might also be a tactical opportunity. Negotiators who are under more time pressure do less well as they concede more to achieve an agreement, but if negotiators who are genuinely under a deadline tell the other party, this puts the other party under the same deadline and subjects them to the same time pressure (Moore 2004). If both parties are under the same time pressure they are more likely to make mutual concessions (a clear-cut compromise outcome) resulting in a better outcome for the party that initially experienced the greater time pressure. Negotiators should also be aware that if the other negotiator is acting on behalf of constituents then to put them under time pressure to get them to concede might have the opposite effect (Mosterd and Rutte, 2000).

Quality of alternatives

Power is part of a negotiation's DNA and Chapter 2 suggested that one of the most practical ways for a negotiator to assess the power situation is to consider the consequences of walking away from the negotiation. All other things being equal, having a good alternative to a negotiated agreement puts a negotiator into a stronger position but negotiation is two-sided and a negotiator with a strong alternative can anticipate a better outcome only if the other party has a weak one (Pinkley, Neale and Bennett, 1994; Wolfe and McGinn, 2005).

The obvious strategic implication is to try to improve one's alternatives *before* the negotiations start. At the same time be aware of our own almost inevitable overconfidence when entering into a negotiation (Neale and Bazerman, 1985a; Thompson and Hastie, 1990). If strengthening one's own alternative could lead to a better outcome then intuitively, negotiators should do what they can to weaken the other party's alternative, or at least undermine their perception of the strength of their alternative. However, this is not necessarily the case. The research also found that if both parties have good alternatives then provided they see the prospect of a better outcome through continued negotiation they pay greater attention to each other's needs, reciprocity develops (especially through information exchange) and as a result they are able to achieve integrative agreements. So while a negotiator who has a good walk-away

Table 3.5 The effect of quality of alternatives on strategy choice

Quality of alternatives	good	poor	poor both	good both
Strategy choice	contend	concede	clear-cut compromise	creative compromise

alternative might be inclined to contend, if it is found that if the other negotiator also has a good walk-away alternative, the best strategy is not to try to contend even harder but to look to get into a position of trust across the negotiating table to make mutually creative compromise strategies possible.

An example where both parties have good alternatives would be negotiations over a potential joint venture. The business development teams within the two companies will no doubt have scoped many development opportunities so that they both have good alternatives when entering into negotiations with each other. However, the belief that by working together they can create greater synergies and value creating opportunities provides the ongoing incentive to negotiate (see Table 3.5).

In other negotiations, both parties may face poor alternatives. Their failure to reach agreement might have bad consequences for them both. The car manufacturing process is one long supply chain of component suppliers. If a company making and supplying brake shoes can't reach agreement with the metals company which supplies springs for the brakes then it will lose its contract with the car manufacturer. Both the brake company and the metals company would lose, so they both have an incentive to stay at the bargaining table and work together. When facing the pressure of poor no-agreement outcomes, negotiators typically find solutions somewhere between their positions – the clear-cut compromise strategy – rather than embark on a creative search for added-value solutions. The key point is that facing similar quality walk-away options helps both parties to work together. If the quality of the parties' respective walk-away options is unbalanced, this will push the strategy choice to concede or contend.

Practical implications

The five strategy factors and four issue strategies can be incorporated into a broader strategic approach to negotiation that has five elements (Box 3.1). These five strategic elements will be explored in further detail

Box 3.1: A strategic approach to negotiation

- Having clear, considered goals.
- Being constantly aware of one's options.
- Making a considered analysis *before* deciding upon a course of action.
- Considering what might be done in the context to make a preferred course of action more likely.
- Constantly reviewing the situation to take account of changes in the context which might lead to a revision of one's strategy.

in the remainder of the chapter but we start with some general practical points about effective preparation.

Good preparation is essential to negotiate effectively and is built around two key principles. The first is to break a negotiation down into its constituent parts by means of questioning and the second is to do one's preparation from the other party's perspective. Both these principles are embedded in the approach to preparing for a negotiation which has been developed in this chapter.

Taking an 'other-directed' approach to preparation is important because it reflects the essential two-sided nature of negotiation. The author was involved in preparing for some difficult politically charged negotiations involving the very future of the organisation he was working in. In preparation for meetings with the government minister who was dealing with the issue, rather than carefully list and rehearse the key points, the approach taken was to ask 'what will the minister say to us?' and then prepare the response to his points. Similarly, key points should be prepared and rehearsed. It is useful for someone to role-play as a member of the other party to see how your points sound on the other side of the table. List all the other party's possible responses to your points and work out how you will deal with them.

We have noted earlier that negotiation and chess have a lot in common, especially in the need to think ahead and consider all the options. A rather less helpful aspect of the 'negotiation as a game of chess' imagery is its competitive element – strategising a way to checkmate one's opponent is perhaps not the best approach to a negotiation! Unfortunately, this attitude can creep into one's preparation. There is a danger that thorough preparation brings the negotiator to a point where he sees only one solution and thereafter all the planning goes into how the other party can be persuaded to agree to it. From the very start of their preparation, negotiators should maintain the flexibility of 'the knight's move' and carry this attitude through into the negotiation itself.

Having clear considered goals

The good thing about not setting goals is that you always succeed in achieving them! Negotiation is a purpose-driven activity focused on achieving an outcome which can then be implemented and it would be a poor negotiator who sets out with a 'let's just see what we can achieve' approach. Negotiators need to be clear about what they want to achieve and should try to achieve more rather than less. The generally accepted principle of goal setting is that challenging goals lead to better performance (Locke, 1968; Latham and Yukl, 1975). The same is true in negotiation. Negotiators with specific, difficult goals do well (Huber and Neale, 1986; Brett, Pinkley and Jackofsky, 1996), in part because they prepare more fully and are more persistent when negotiating (Roloff and Jordan 1991).

While it is right to set a challenging goal, it must be plausible. A goal which translates into an opening position that appears outrageous to the other party will merely provoke a similarly outrageous response (by virtue of reciprocity), or perhaps provoke the other party to call the negotiations off. How high is too high? A simple test is to ask whether what is being sought is a 'yes-able proposition' (Fisher, 1971; Fisher, Kopelman and Schneider, 1994). In deciding what might be achieved from the negotiation the negotiator, having properly considered the whole situation from his own and the other party's perspective, should ask, 'if I were the other party could I possibly agree to what I am asking of them?' If the answer is 'no' then too much is being expected. However, a negotiator should not negotiate with himself and lower his goals 'to be reasonable' (Bazerman, Tenbrunsel and Wade-Benzoni, 1998).

There is another note of caution about setting goals for a forthcoming negotiation – they can become too positional. The manager of a shopping centre might decide that the centre's advertising needs to be more effective so she asks each shop tenant in turn for an increased contribution to the advertising budget. If she sets herself a challenging goal, a large increase from each tenant, she will probably do better than if she sets a modest target figure. However the original goal of 'what' (more effective advertising) has transitioned into 'how' (increased payments by the tenants) and, as we will see in later chapters, these negotiations are likely to be positional and competitive, missing the opportunity for other creative joint–gain solutions.

It is also useful to have clear process goals. Negotiators often prepare around what they need to achieve at the expense of considering how the process might unfold (Fells, 1996) and so are less able to deal with what occurs (negotiation is 'messy'). While it might seem time efficient and achievement oriented to come to the table and present your proposal of how the issue should be settled, it is quite likely to provoke difficulties rather than a quick settlement. Negotiators should establish an 'end of interaction' objective (Honey, 1976). Rather than having only the ultimate goal of a favourable agreement, it helps to work to more immediate task-related goals. So if the negotiations are expected to last all day, it is useful to ask 'what do we hope to have achieved when we break for lunch?' Perhaps a reasonable expectation is that it will take most of the morning to get a full understanding of the differences between the parties. If so, lunchtime may be given over to each party reshaping any proposals they have in the light of what they have learned during the morning. In this way, negotiators can 'pace' the process and manage it properly. (Managing the negotiation process is explored further in the next chapter.)

Being constantly aware of your options

Negotiators should always remember that there are four issue strategies to choose from. In addition they can always walk away. While this may sound obvious it seems less easy to put into practice when the negotiations begin to get serious. The pressure of the negotiation tends to close one's behaviour and decision-making processes with the result that a negotiator can easily get 'tunnel vision' and feel that there is only one option: 'we can't afford to give on this issue' or 'we really don't have much time so we have to make a concession to get the agreement.' Having 'locked in' to a course of action, the tendency is to then look for information or reasons that justify this decision while discounting anything that might suggest an alternative.

The good negotiator will systematically evaluate each option before deciding. A good way to help remember that there are options is to have them written at the top of one's note pad. It can take some courage to challenge the CEO or lead negotiator when he is insisting that everyone stand firm and suggest that he consider other options but that's what good negotiators do.

Making a considered analysis before you decide

The five strategy factors and four issue strategies can be combined into a decision-making tool. This Strategy Framework (Figure 3.3 and also Appendix 4) requires a negotiator to give full consideration to the other party's strategy choices and so helps counter the tendency to view negotiation from just one's own perspective. This also helps keep a negotiator alert to the fact that the outcome of his strategy is dependent upon how the other party reacts.

The analysis of the strategic factors will indicate what should be an appropriate strategy to take on the issue. The combination of high importance of issue to self through to good quality alternatives, as shown in Figure 3.3, indicates that a contending strategy would be appropriate. The key point is that a negotiator should analyse and consider *all* the factors before deciding on a strategy, rather than just make a hasty and possibly ill-considered decision based on one seemingly compelling circumstance.

Considering changing the context

However, in real life negotiations (in contrast to examples in books!) it is unlikely that all five factors will line up neatly. If the analysis shows a contra-indication for a strategy (time pressure in Figure 3.4) then it would be important to do something about it *before* starting the negotiation. In this case, when all the other factors point to a contending strategy, then something should be done to relieve the time pressure before starting the negotiations.

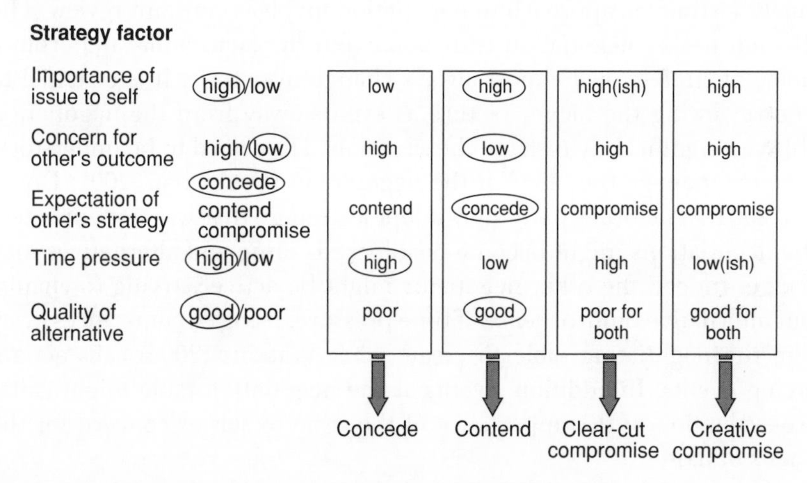

Figure 3.4: Strategic analysis: what might we change?

Analysing the negotiation in this way to highlight what aspects of the negotiating context might be changed is a critical element in being strategic in negotiation. Lax and Sebenius (2002) present negotiation as having three dimensions, all of which should be taken into account:

the process, the potential to create value and the opportunities that exist away from the negotiating table. Similarly, Watkins (2006) recommends that negotiators be alert to opportunities to change the nature of the game not only during the process, but even before the negotiations have started. While much of the literature on negotiation is about changing the game of negotiation from a win-lose contest to a win-win cooperation, these writers are describing something more fundamental. It involves looking at the essential structure of the circumstances surrounding the negotiation and seeing how they might be changed. From the simple expedient of always buying an open-ended ticket when travelling to an overseas negotiation (to forestall being put under time pressure) to undertaking a brand awareness campaign before negotiating with your franchise owners (whose instrumental concern for your ongoing success will now be higher) it is important not to take the negotiation context as a given. Negotiators should always look for ways the context can be restructured to give rise to more favourable strategies and better outcomes.

Reviewing your course of action

Finally, a strategic approach to negotiation involves constant review. The situation in any negotiation is dynamic and the factors that underpin a choice of strategy will almost always change over time. It is essential to keep reviewing the bigger picture as events away from the negotiation table can significantly reshape the situation. They need to be understood to better manage the 'flow' of the negotiation (Druckman, 2001; Donohue, 2004). The other party may adopt a strategy that was not expected. The negotiations might become deadlocked. Time and alternatives may change. Indeed the other negotiator might be actively trying to change your alternatives and/or sense of time pressure, using circumstances away from the negotiating table to create what Watkins (2006) calls action-forcing events. In addition, events at the negotiation table might cause a re-evaluation of the importance of the issue to self or concern for the other's outcome.

Therefore it is essential to regularly review the situation and to reassess one's strategy. Although some elements in the strategy context may have changed for the worse, others may have changed for the better. Questions should always be asked: 'Can we implement our preferred issue strategy in a different way?', 'Do we, in light of these new circumstances, need to lower our aspirations?'

Conclusions

Being strategic means 'to think before you act'. The notion of strategy implies choice and this chapter has reviewed some of the key factors a negotiator should consider before deciding what approach to take on the issue – whether to stand firm, concede or seek some form of compromise, or even to walk away. Being strategic also means 'to think in terms of the other party' and the Strategy Framework requires a negotiator to do this role reversal. The imagery of 'the knight's move' helps convey not only this considered approach to negotiation that is so similar to a game of chess but also the need 'to think and act flexibly'. We have seen from earlier chapters that good negotiators are reflective and so we can add a fourth element to being a strategic negotiator, 'to think after you have acted'. Finally a good strategic negotiator is aware that the issue strategies have to be managed through a complex and dynamic process. It is to an examination of this process that we now turn.

4 The process of negotiation

Whereas Chapter 3 explored the issue strategies open to negotiators, this chapter explores the process through which those strategies are managed. These two aspects of negotiation – having a considered, strategic approach to the issue and being able to manage the process of reaching agreement – enables a negotiator to deal with the complexity and messiness of most negotiations.

No two negotiations are the same, which makes it difficult to describe and precisely categorise the process or provide a clear model for negotiators to follow. Nevertheless, we can identify some phases of activity that constitute the broad flow of negotiation. It is somewhat like travelling on a boat down a river. Having chosen to reach one's destination ('agreement') by river rather than by road or train, the river itself then sets the broad course and direction and there are general rules of navigation which should be followed by all those on the water. In making the journey it is difficult to go against the flow of the river but it is risky just to let the river itself direct the boat. The river has to be navigated – there are times when progress is easy but other times when action has to be taken to stay on course. This calls for an understanding of what might be happening under the surface as well as knowing the course that the river takes.

This chapter will examine the process of negotiation in a number of ways. It will explore the notion of phases, the broad flow of the river. It will review what is known about how negotiators interact. In our river imagery these interactions are the localised movement of water which impacts on how well the boat is placed to handle the next stretch of water. Just as some boat journeys are smoother than others, so some negotiations flow more effectively than others and achieve better outcomes, suggesting that the flow of negotiation through the phases and the patterns of interaction can be managed to good effect. The chapter will draw heavily on the research into negotiation (which might get a bit technical) but will maintain a practical orientation throughout. Chapter 5 will build on this to show how negotiations might be managed effectively. There may be a preferred course down the river but each journey is different as water levels, winds and other factors change. Just as the skipper needs to know the basic principles of navigation and be able to 'read' the river as he journeys along it, so too does the negotiator need to understand the broad patterns of negotiation and be able to manage the interaction to ensure the negotiations stay on course and agreement is reached.

Phases in negotiation

If reciprocity is part of a negotiation's DNA then we should expect there to be times when both parties are matching each other's behaviour. If these periods of matching activity are long enough we regard them as 'phases' in the negotiation. A negotiator might describe a negotiation as, 'we had a fairly robust debate but once we understood each other it was quite easy to reach an agreement.' This would suggest two broad phases in the negotiation – the first broadly competitive and the second being more cooperative. However, if we had a transcript of the negotiation we might find that even when the negotiators were having their 'robust debate' they were exchanging information (which is quite a helpful thing to do) and while 'easily' reaching an agreement, there were times when they were digging their heels in over a particular point. To continue with the imagery of a river, it might be flowing quite fast over rocks and waterfalls as it comes down the mountain and then meanders quite slowly across the flood plain. Yet there might also be some quiet rock pools in the mountain stretch and fast eddies as the river crosses the plain. The negotiator has to be alert to both the overall flow of the negotiation and to the sub-currents.

Competitiveness and cooperation

Table 4.1 lists a cluster of negotiation tactics and behaviours we might label 'competitive' and another cluster which are regarded as being 'cooperative'. Walton and McKersie's (1965) terminology of distributive and integrative bargaining is often used, as are the labels of 'win-lose' and 'win-win'. The contrast is obvious and most negotiators would prefer to be involved in the more integrative approach to bargaining, which is a good choice as the research generally suggests that the integrative approach yields better results.

Table 4.1 Distributive and integrative bargaining strategies and behaviours (after Walton and McKersie, 1965)

Distributive bargaining strategies and behaviours	Integrative bargaining strategies and behaviours
	Probably some climate setting & skills development processes
Limited information exchange, i.e. only information which helps one's case	Full information exchange
Adopting firm positions and making commitments	Open joint consideration of circumstances, interests prior to agendas being established
Threatened alternatives & power plays undermining other's position/party	Absence of power plays
Tense, controlled interaction, concession making to reach a reluctant agreement	Support for other party (even viewing both 'sides' as one)
	Discussion, open interaction
	Emergent consensus

Competitiveness and cooperation – either/or both?

While many people advocate that negotiators follow the cooperative integrative win-win approach to negotiation, it is useful to look more closely beneath the surface to see if this is true. Putnam (1990) described those models which present a negotiation as being essentially either competitive or cooperative as 'separate' models (see Table 4.2). There may be variations in how the strategies are implemented but there is essentially only one 'phase' to the negotiation. However Walton and McKersie (1965) presented their distributive and integrative bargaining not as two separate strategies but as sub-processes *within* the overall process of reaching an agreement. In fact they suggest (p. 165) that the best strategy for negotiators is to engage in integrative bargaining first to increase the size of the pie and then distributive bargaining to get as much of the larger pie as possible. They also note that as well as being the best strategy, it is also the most difficult! Lax and Sebenius (1986) recommended a similar approach in advocating that negotiators should first try to 'create value' then 'claim value'.

This would suggest that negotiation is a sequence of cooperative then competitive tactics. On the other hand Stevens (1963) who, like Walton and McKersie researched management-union negotiations in the North

Table 4.2 Process models of negotiation (developed from Putnam 1990 and from Weingart and Olekalns, 2004)

Type of model	Negotiation strategies implemented
Separate models	
Competitive	Distributive; win-lose argumentation
Cooperative	Integrative, win-win problem solving
Mixed models	
Stage	Distinct and predictable periods of activity, typically issue definition, problem solving and resolution
Episodic	Distinct periods of coherent activity but they are flexible in sequence duration and frequency
Interdependence	An ongoing mix of win-lose argumentation and win-win problem solving throughout the negotiation

American collective bargaining system, suggested negotiators start off competitively and then realise they have to cooperate to get an outcome. However this 'cooperation' may not amount to looking for added-value solutions through full problem solving but a more limited level of cooperation simply because one side cannot get any agreement at all without the cooperation of the other. Recognising that this 'cooperation' might be rather more pragmatic than all embracing, writers such as Pruitt (1981) and Putnam (1994) call this form of the negotiators working together as 'coordination' rather than cooperation. Again is it an example of looking beneath the surface of the negotiation to see exactly what is going on.

Rather than just two phases, Douglas (1957; 1962) suggests that negotiations go through three – essentially competitive to start, then cooperative for a while but becoming more competitive as the negotiators close in on an agreement. Other models increase the number of phases but most models have these three phases at their heart (Holmes, 1992). Models portraying the competitive and cooperative elements of a negotiation as sequential are called stage models (Putnam, 1990; see Table 4.2). The practical implication for negotiators is that there is an underlying sequence a negotiation should go through to reach an agreement, with the further implication that if negotiations *don't* follow this sequence then they will either deadlock or reach a poor outcome.

However, we suggested earlier that negotiation is 'messy' and so another view of negotiation is that negotiators keep switching between competitiveness to cooperativeness but not in a structured way. This means that there are likely to be several episodes of competitive and cooperative interaction before an agreement is reached. Negotiators should therefore expect changes to occur but they cannot be planned for. Finally, Putnam (1990; 1994) suggests what she regards as a more realistic interdependence model of the negotiation process. It reflects a belief that the competitiveness and cooperation seem to feed off each other in a dynamic way as a negotiation progresses. The practical implication of this is that negotiators should give close attention to what the pattern of dialogue is indicating about the progress of the negotiation.

Researchers have presented two contrasting models of negotiation phases. Douglas (1957; 1962) observed three phases when she researched labour-management mediation cases in the United States. The two parties present and defend their respective positions almost to the very end. After a period of sparring and testing the other side, the negotiators begin to look for compromise positions. In Figure 4.1 first the union negotiator, then the company negotiator make tentative proposals. When these are rejected by the other side the negotiators go 'back to their trenches' and restate their positions. In time, negotiators on both sides begin to realise that one particular proposal is going to be the basis of the settlement. Because both parties are reasonably confident of where the negotiations will end up they are able to make formal concessions on their respective positions until they reach a point of explicit agreement.

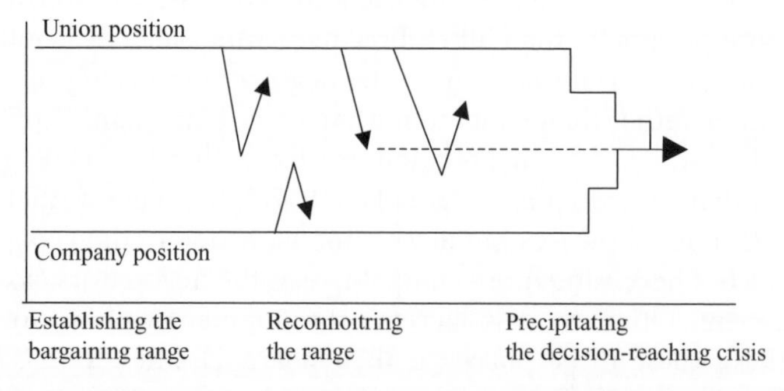

Figure 4.1: Positions, proposals and reaching agreement (after Douglas, 1957)

Fisher, Ury and Patton's (1991) Model of Principled Negotiation seeks to break out of this fundamentally competitive process. Its genesis lay in the experience of nations trying to resolve their differences but it has wider application. Rather than competitively establishing the bargaining range between two 'locked in' positions, the parties should take time to uncover their underlying interests. From this improved understanding of what each party's fundamental needs are, the parties can be far more open

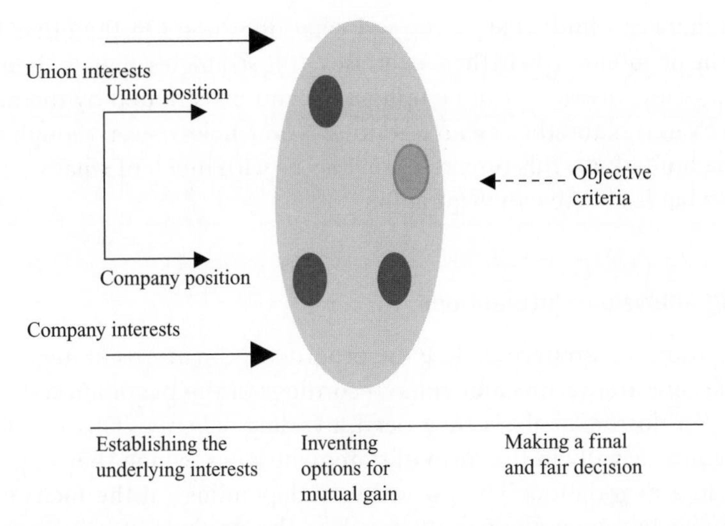

Figure 4.2: Interests, options and criteria in reaching agreement (after Fisher, Ury and Patton, 1991)

and creative, going beyond the range of stated positions to invent options for mutual gain. If there is no one clear solution that meets both parties' interests then a decision can be made by reference to relevant objective criteria. This is a far more cooperative approach (Patton, 2005; Thompson and Leonardelli, 2004) (see Figure 4.2).

A closer look at phrases and phases

If negotiations go through phases, we need to know more about what is going on around the negotiating table to know whether we are in a 'phase' and if so, which one. A phase occurs when the negotiators on both sides are doing broadly the same thing and to find if this is happening we must play close attention to what is being said. So researchers have investigated the content of negotiations with increasing precision. Their findings not only provide practical insights into how negotiators actually negotiate, but by looking at what is going on under the surface helps us understand how the 'negotiation river' as a whole flows towards an agreement.

There is, however, a note of caution as we examine these findings. While some people have researched actual negotiations, much of the research has involved close analysis of carefully constructed negotiation exercises. The strength of this research is that conclusions are robust because they are drawn from repeated negotiations. In particular, the researchers can find what works and what does not. On the other hand what the negotiators do in these exercises – the strategies open to them and the way they interact – can be influenced and constrained by the nature of the exercises and the research setting. Nevertheless, even though there may be limitations, this research provides us with much of what we know about what is effective in negotiation.

Coding analysis of interactions

Negotiation researchers analyse the progress and patterns of negotiation by analysing transcripts and video recordings of the negotiation in great detail. To do this analysis they need a coding schema. This is a list of behaviours, usually in the form of statement types, which they expect to occur in a negotiation. The list will vary depending on the focus of the researcher but generally will be based on the findings of prior research and models of the negotiation process.

An early example of this research was Conference Process Analysis developed by Stephenson and his colleagues (Morley and Stephenson, 1977). It is a complex schema coding not only what sort of information is being conveyed and how it is conveyed but also to whom it is directed (Mode, Resource and Referent in Table 4.3).

Table 4.3 Conference Process Analysis: categories (Morley and Stephenson, 1977, p. 193)

Mode	Resource	Referent
Offer	Structuring activity	No referent
Accept	Procedure	Self
Reject	Outcome activity	Person
Seek	Settlement point: initial, new	Other
	Limits	Party
	Positive consequences	Opponent
	Negative consequences	Both persons
	Other statements about outcomes	Both parties
	Acknowledgement	
	Positive: own and both sides, other side	
	Negative: own and both sides, other side	
	Other information	
	Information	

Box 4.1: Coding scheme (adapted from Weingart et al., 1990, p. 17)

Single offer is made.
Multiple-issue, package offer is made.
Suggests trade off.
Asks for information from the other party.
Shows awareness/recognition/concern for other.
Provides information to the other party.
Negative reaction to other's statement.
Positive reaction to other's statement.
Issue threats or warnings.

Other researchers code negotiations in different ways. For example, Weingart and his colleagues (1990) developed a coding schema of nine tactical behaviours which they found capture most of what negotiators do (Box 4.1).

Just from these two lists – and there are many others – we can see the complexity of negotiation. There are endless combinations of actions and reactions. There is a further complicating factor in that negotiators do not normally negotiate through carefully constructed statements. Reviewing the dialogue of any but the most formal of negotiations will show that as the discussion goes back and forth across the table there are many false starts, half sentences, pauses and repetitions. Added to this, negotiators often talk in 'shorthand'. A union negotiator might explain to management that his members are seeking 'a fair increase in pay and an improvement in conditions'. Since the managers would already know that 'fair' means 'not less than the company down the road' and that the improved conditions the employees were really focused on was overtime benefits, the union negotiator did not spell it out. In a business negotiation one side might suggest leaving 'the financials' to later which everyone around the table would understand to mean the amount of money each side is going to have to put into the project to make it work.

And there are cultural differences too (which we will examine further in Chapter 10). For example, Japanese negotiators have been found to put offers on the table early and they do this as a way of finding out more about the other negotiator's position and priorities. In this way an offer serves a dual purpose of information gleaning as well as providing information about one's party. On the other hand, US negotiators tend to delay putting their offers out on the table until they feel have more insight into each other's situation. They use offers to consolidate what they have learned and understood about the situation between the parties (Adair, Weingart and Brett 2007, p. 1062).

Some practical implications

The details that these researchers have uncovered shows the complexity of the process of negotiation. To be effective, negotiators have to be aware of the preciseness of communication and so must play very close attention to what is being said and how it is being said. Having a separate note taker enables the leader to focus on the other negotiator. Negotiators should never be in a hurry. Sometimes as we listen to other people, we are listening only for when they stop so that we can say what we want to say. Because our mind has been filled with the points we wish to make, we might have listened to the other party but not heard them. The complexity of most negotiation dialogue is why checking our understanding and reflection are so important.

Another practical implication to consider is to make it as easy as possible for the other negotiator. Firstly, this means not interrupting. If someone is interrupted she is likely to react to the interruption rather than listen fully to what is being said. (And in any event, the strength of reciprocity is such that if someone interrupts then before too long they too will be interrupted; and not like it either.) Secondly, it means making one's main points at the start or as the final point (utilising the primacy and recency effects). It is better to make a limited number of points and repeat them – just because you've made a point don't assume that the other party has really heard it or fully appreciates your intent. Make the point again, but in a different way, next time you speak. Taking it steady and repetition are therefore helpful. Finally, particularly in the early stages, don't clutter up your main points with detail. It is not that detail is unimportant, but what *is* important is that the negotiators first grasp the essentials. This then helps show which details are important. Keeping away from detail in the early stages also removes one opportunity for competitive exploitation. If a negotiator wants to undermine your position one of the easiest ways is to pick some detailed points from your presentation and challenge these. The focus then shifts from your main points to your defence of these details and this is not helpful when you are trying to develop a persuasive argument. At the settlement stage, checking the detail is crucial.

Another way a negotiator can help the pattern of interaction is how she interprets what the other negotiators are doing. Just as we have choice of strategy options so we have choice of reaction, so it is not simply a matter of what they say but of how we react to what they say. Honey (1976, p. 80) had yet another categorisation of statements in negotiation. Two of them were 'difficulty stating' such as in 'I can see a problem with that . . . ' and the more explicit 'disagreeing' – 'I can't agree with that because . . . ' We can readily see that to express disagreement though stating difficulties rather than disagreement is going to be more cooperative and helps keep subsequent interaction more open. If the other negotiator rejects your proposal by saying 'that's not acceptable and I'll tell you why: firstly,' then it is preferable to ignore the disagreement and respond to reasons he gives.

This is all the more difficult when the negotiations are being conducted over the internet. Not being able to see the other negotiator has some adverse effects – negotiators are less trusting and are generally more competitive (Citera, Beauregard and Mitsuya, 2005; Naquin and Paulson, 2003). The lack of visual contact and personal interaction can be offset through a prior phone call (or through exchanging some personal information as the email negotiations get started) and generally maintaining small talk during subsequent exchanges (Morris et al., 2002; Nadler, 2004). An advantage of negotiating over the internet is that it leaves a record so the negotiations can easily be reviewed. Some aspects of negotiating other than face to face are listed in Table 4.4.

What does the detailed interaction research tell us about phases?

Researchers have looked ever more closely at what negotiators do. Interviews and direct observations provide a broad understanding of the process, analysis of transcripts and videos provides even closer insight. And the level of analysis has deepened. Researchers get insight from studying the frequency of strategy actions or statement types, from their timing, from whether certain sequences of actions or statements are more common and the ways in which negotiators change from one combination of actions or statements to another. It is necessarily detailed and complex, in part because researchers use different categories for their observations (because they are looking for different things) and in part because the interactions between negotiators are complex (negotiation is 'messy'). Box 4.2 provides some of the many findings. There is clearly a lot going on under the surface of a negotiation! Figure 4.3 summarises the findings diagrammatically to show the broad flow. The research suggests that we can expect an early competitive-looking start to a negotiation, a more exploratory middle period and a focused exchange of offers as the parties position themselves around an emerging settlement.

Table 4.4 Negotiating other than face to face

Negotiating over the phone	**Negotiating over the internet**
The phone is not a leveller, one party can still dominate	The internet is a leveller; no one can easily dominate but nevertheless don't SHOUT
We tend to overdo our strategy and also to be repetitive (because we are not picking up any visual clues as to how much the other person is receiving what we are saying)	The length of communication is not constrained
We tend to be and sound more competitive	There are fewer social protocols; it is not so easy to have a social 'warm up'
We get fewer response cues, especially as to the genuineness of agreement	Bad grammar, compressed words etc. are acceptable; but this leads to mistakes, misunderstandings
Negotiators with a strong case do better over the phone	Interactions are interpreted more competitively
	The 'essence' of email is its immediacy: so we don't read it properly, we just reply; delays in response increase our frustrations
	There is the risk of messages going elsewhere
So:	**So:**
Have a clear 'end of interaction' objective – ask yourself 'want do I what to have achieved by the time I put down the phone?'	If possible, have prior face-to-face or phone contact
Keep your statements short	Include some social chit-chat in the email
Make frequent use of summaries and reflective statements	Spell out your priorities, your reactions fully
	Check your understanding of the email, emailing back to get clarification if necessary
	Make multiple suggestions, explicitly invite suggestions
	If you have to make a difficult response, leave it for a day
	Develop the skill of being 'good on paper', the skill of being able to write a balanced summary of the issues, the pros and cons, the options

Box 4.2: Some research findings on what negotiators do and when they do it

Olekalns, Smith and Walsh (1996)

'Concessionary cues' and 'Rejection responses' are high early (and so help define the bargaining zone) and rise again towards the end (and so shape the settlement) (an example of the same tactics achieving different purposes).

When 'Restructure' (which indicates flexibility and integration) increases relative to 'Positional information' the outcomes improve.

Olekalns and Smith (2000)

'Reciprocating positional information' leads to poorer outcomes than 'Reciprocating priority information' (a common finding).

'Conciliation–contention' sequences may delay a settlement but lead to an improved settlement (that is, some contention helps in finding good solutions).

Kemp and Smith (1994)

'Priority information' led to higher joint profits, but even so, and despite there being little overt competitiveness, preferences were not stated in 40% of the negotiations (that is, as Thompson, 1991, suggested, exchange of priority information is not as frequent as we might expect).

Putman (1994)

Information was provided clearly when negotiators sought to justify their own positions but otherwise the provision of information was 'ambiguous, cryptic and guarded' (analysis of a management–union negotiation).

Olekalns and Smith (2003)

'Priority information exchange' is how two negotiators with a distributive orientation achieve joint gain outcomes; whereas two integrative negotiators or one of each orientation benefit by using 'Process management' (which indicates flexibility).

Weingart et al. (1990)

Negotiators use 'Multi-issue offers' to state their position (rather than to develop tradeoffs) and similarly use 'Providing information' to defend their positions (showing that information and offers can be used competitively as well as cooperatively, as Putnam and Jones 1982 also found) but 'Providing information' contributed to integrative outcomes.

Olekalns, Brett and Weingart (2003)

Negotiators start with a distributive strategy and action (offer-oriented moves) rather than deal in information or be integrative; they turn to information to defend their position, then use information more integratively and then use offers integratively.

However, when negotiators start with an integrative orientation they find they cannot reach agreement and so switch into distributive strategy and action only to then find they cannot get back out of it.

Lytle, Brett and Shapiro (1999)

While negotiators use interest statements throughout a negotiation and increase their use of proposals, they use rights and power statements in the first quarter to explain their position and again in the third quarter (when interest statements and proposals are also high) to explain what is unacceptable.

Morely and Stephenson (1977)

References to 'Other' are the highest in the middle phase of negotiation (indicating exploration).

'Procedure' increases in the last phase (indicating a focus on reaching a decision).

Adair and Brett (2005)

Reciprocal priority information is at its highest in the second quarter of a negotiation, rational argument and offer sequences are high in the third quarter and become more intense in the fourth.

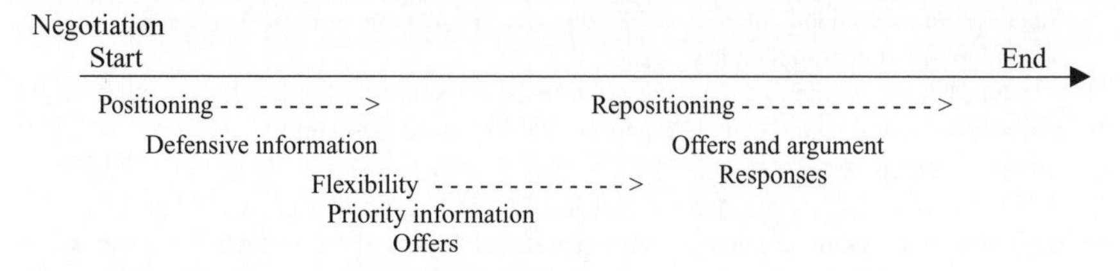

Figure 4.3: Some dominant activities through the course of a negotiation

Making sense of models and research

Both the descriptive models and the more precise interactions research suggest a broad sequence in what negotiators do when they negotiate. There is a certain underlying logic to negotiation and the definition of negotiation follows this logic. That definition, it will be recalled, is that 'negotiation is two parties with differences which they need to resolve, trying to reach agreement through exploring for options and exchanging offers.'

Two parties with differences . . .

If negotiation is about 'two parties with differences . . . ' then it follows that the negotiators need to find out what those differences are. Most negotiations will open with a period when the parties emphasise their differences. This can be done competitively with each stating their positions and endeavouring to undermine the position of the other party. Or it can be rather more cooperative with each party still stating their positions but at the same time trying to understand the motivations and underlying concerns that are driving the other party.

Because negotiators can find out their differences in different ways, it is more helpful to view this as the task of differentiating rather than label the phase as either competitive or cooperative.

What if the negotiators don't take time to emphasise and examine their differences but instead try to be settlement oriented and put solutions on the table? This *may* work but it would be rare for a negotiator to get the best settlement first time. (If the offer is accepted it probably means the negotiator offered too much!) This simply means that if the negotiators don't spend time sorting out what their real differences are at the outset then they are going to have do it at some point later in the negotiation. So we might expect an extended phase of differentiation early in the negotiation and shorter periods again later as the negotiators realise that they have to recheck their understanding of their underlying interests and motivations.

. . . which they need to resolve . . .

If negotiation is about 'two parties with differences which they need to resolve . . . ' then our negotiators need to be sure that they really do need to keep negotiating to resolve these differences rather than invoke their walk-away options. Negotiators who are reaching the conclusion that they need to continue negotiating are not going to create a recognisable 'phase' in the negotiation but may cause an important turning point, particularly if the two parties have been contending. In some cases the question 'do I need to resolve this?' may have been settled in the negotiator's mind before the negotiations began. He has reviewed his situation and knows that, one way or another, he has to reach agreement with the other party. In other negotiations there comes a point when negotiators realise that their initial expectations are not going to be met but the prospect of agreement is such that they commit to finding a solution.

A European airline was in negotiation with an Asian airline about setting up a joint venture to benefit from the growth of air travel in China. The CEOs of the two airlines had recognised the strategic benefits of an alliance and signed a memorandum of understanding (MOU) to that effect. The two negotiating teams built up a good working relationship but they had a major difference over the nature of the operating systems that they could not resolve and so the negotiations deadlocked. However, when the two teams went back home and reflected on the events they realised that although they were two parties with their differences, they did need to resolve them and so, following some third party mediation the negotiations were resumed. In this case, the need to resolve their differences was a positive motivation – the value of what might be created through the joint venture seemed greater than what might be achieved through new projects with other companies. In other cases the motivation may be driven by negatives. Management and union negotiators were sitting around the company's boardroom table at Heathrow Airport in deadlocked silence. One of the airline's planes was waiting to take off from Houston but could not get landing permission at Heathrow because of the dispute. The motivation to resolve their differences lay not in any potential mutual gains win-win outcome but simply because the likely consequences of continued deadlock were so drastic.

In both of these cases the negotiators entered into their negotiations in good faith, looking for an agreement. In this sense they were always motivated to resolve their differences. However, there came a point in each negotiation when they *really* needed to resolve their differences and so needed to do something different from what they had been doing up to that point.

In another major business negotiation, a European telecommunications company was looking to expand internationally and had found a potential investment target. The targeted company saw the benefits of the proposal and so two teams of negotiators worked steadily through the major operational, legal and financial issues to draw up a MOU. In this case the signing of the MOU represented the formal point at which each party made a decision to continue and complete the negotiation. Both before and after signing the MOU the parties had differences they needed to settle. In the early negotiations the differences were around what the structure of the company would look like and if that overall package could not be put together there would have been no agreement. Once the MOU was signed there were still many crucial issues to resolve to bring the MOU into effect. As they worked through the documentation, clause by clause, the negotiations were competitive. Each team of negotiators took great care to ensure that their company's interests were going to be protected in the new entity but the need to reach agreement – because walking away was no longer a realistic option – drove the cooperation.

We should remember that negotiation is two-sided. To reach an agreement, both parties have to put aside the option of walking away and focus on their need to settle. However – and this is an important point in many negotiations – there is nothing in the negotiation process that requires both parties to come to this realisation at the same point in time. If one party is committed to achieving an agreement while the other has yet to get to that point, perhaps because they have a reasonable alternative, the party that needs agreement is in the weaker position and should try to get the other party to see the need for agreement before embarking on any concession making. If not, the concession making will be unilateral.

There is one more point in the negotiation where the question 'do I need to resolve this?' should come back up to the surface. This is just prior to the point of agreement when every negotiator should make one final check of whether what is to be agreed is better than any alternative.

... by trying to reach agreement

If the two parties choose to continue negotiating then there are two ways in which they can try to reach an agreement. They might resolve their differences either through exploring for new options (which are solutions which no one had previously thought of) or through the process of exchanging offers which gradually bring the two parties' positions to a point of agreement.

It will have been noted that the interaction research shows that there is a period of increased flexibility but that the key mechanism is through the negotiators indicating their priorities either directly through providing information or indirectly through the way they start to repackage their offers. The nature of the negotiation tasks which are used for research are focused around pay-off structures where negotiators have different priorities and if they can match these they both get better outcomes. Consequently this exchange of priority information is always going to be important because of the nature of the exercise (Wiengart and Olekalns, 2004, p. 154). Also the way to achieve integrative joint gain solutions is through trading offers which will involve making some concessions around high and low priority issues. This logrolling trade-off is more like the clear-cut than creative compromise though it does add value – a sort of creative clear-cut compromise! This is not to deny the real importance of negotiators searching out different priorities because this *is* a way to create value. However, the nature of the exercises deliberately prevents the participants from 'going outside the square' and so will inhibit some of the more creative aspects of real life negotiations.

So a complete description of the negotiation process should include provision for a more exploratory activity than might be seen in the interaction research. Even so, we should not expect it to be fully open problem-solving and 'brainstorming' creativity. Negotiators don't forgo their underlying competitiveness so in their search for a settlement they might first try exploring options and then exchange offers. (In doing so they follow a stage model, Table 4.2). Alternatively, they might switch between these two approaches (the episodic model) or they might even find themselves doing both at once – the interdependence model. Again, the logic of the task will help unravel this. It seems better to explore options which might create value before resorting to trading offers to narrow down the differences (Lax and Sebenius, 1986; Walton and McKersie 1965).

A model to follow or go with the flow?

Rather than let a negotiation take its course, the logic of what needs to be done to reach an agreement suggests there is a model to follow. In summary, two parties with differences have the task of finding out what those differences are and then deciding whether they need to resolve them through negotiation or whether they can achieve their goals in some other, better way (Figure 4.4). If they continue negotiating they can achieve agreement either through exploring new options and then exchanging offers or by moving directly into the task of exchanging offers. However the simplicity of Figure 4.4 conceals the choices negotiators can make and the complexity of their interactions. While going with the flow of differentiation, exploration and exchange, a negotiator should also be working hard to manage the process rather than be managed by it.

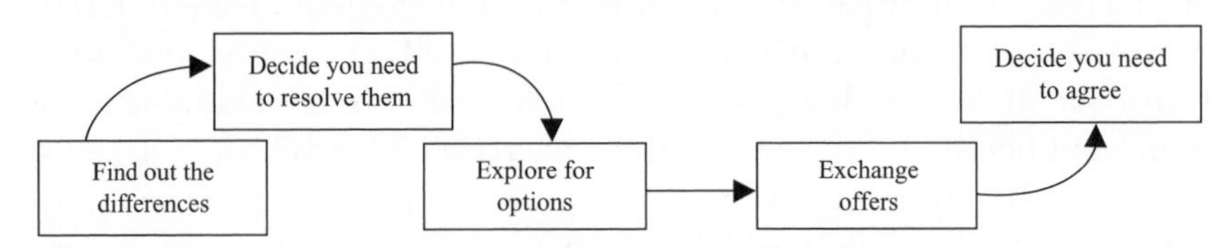

Figure 4.4: Phases and task sequence in the negotiation process

But how? We might be forgiven for thinking that a lot of this research on phases and interactions presented in this chapter is far too complex to be of practical use when stuck in the middle of a negotiation. The findings of the research *are* practical but it is also true that they are complex. There is a way through this. When faced with complex situations we have an ability to simplify them – we develop an expectation or a 'script' of how the situation might unfold. This script then guides what we do next. We build these scripts to help us manage negotiations and the next chapter presents one such script that has been found to be useful. Enjoy the journey!

5 Managing a negotiation

The previous chapter was quite complex. This should not be surprising because negotiation itself is complex but it means that negotiators need something a bit more straightforward to work with when trying to manage their way through a negotiation.

One of the ways used to present the research insights was to talk about negotiation in terms of a river, that has a broad flow and direction but is not constant from headwaters to estuary. In the early stages the water might be running quite fast over rocks and waterfalls; later it slows and meanders and all the while it eddies and forms other currents under the surface. Picturing a negotiation in this way helps a negotiator manage strategies and tactics at any point in the negotiation in the context of the broad flow of progress to an agreement. 'Negotiation as a river' is one image or script. All negotiators intuitively work to a script of some sort – the most common being a competitive one that reflects their understanding of the pay-off structure and tactics of negotiation. These mental models can be teased out by researchers using fairly sophisticated statistical analysis techniques (Van Boven and Thompson, 2003). However, practising negotiators need something more pragmatic, something they can use in real time to guide their negotiating. This chapter explores the idea of a negotiation script as a tool for negotiators to use to get the feel of where they are or ought to be in a negotiation. (An example of a negotiation script is presented in Appendix 5.) It also offers other guidance about managing negotiations, particularly at those times when negotiators look like they're getting into difficulties and when a mediator may seem necessary.

Developing a negotiation script

The imagery of negotiation

One way of gaining understanding of complex processes is through the use of a metaphor or representative image. Metaphors or images help in the process of gaining insights into the totality of an issue or situation – what Heron (1989, p. 12) terms imaginal or intuitive learning. It is a way of taking our experience in one area to explain another and so guide our behaviour in that situation (Gelfand and McCusker, 2002). A metaphor helps answer the question, 'what are we doing here?' Someone who thinks that negotiation is about working together on a problem might conjure up images of teamwork and cooperation. A plan to hold firm and look for any opportunity to divide and conquer conveys the impression that the coming encounter will be more like war than diplomacy, a very different view on how to deal with the 'problem'.

Metaphors or images have been used to convey an understanding of organisations and organisational life (Barker, 1993; Cummings and Wilson, 2003; Drummond, 1998; Morgan, 1986). Imagery has also been used in relation to the process of reaching agreement through negotiation. It has been understood in terms of trench warfare (Axelrod, 1990; Douglas, 1962). Negotiation might be viewed as a dance (Adair and Brett, 2005; Raiffa, 1982) or a sporting contest (an especially masculine characterisation, Greenhalgh and Gilkey, 1999). Negotiators typically expect a negotiation to be a win-lose affair (Bazerman and Neale 1992) shaping their approach to the task, and because negotiation is so often viewed as a sporting contest with winners and losers, Greenhalgh (1987) suggests that even the notion of 'win-win' is unhelpful because it encourages a competitive orientation. Novice negotiators consider that negotiation generally involves more competitive than cooperative tasks (O'Connor and Adams, 1999). Watkins (2004) reports that negotiation typically conjures up images of anxiety but for friends their friendship develops its own conciliatory negotiating script (Halpern, 1997).

These images and perceptions of negotiation constitute the negotiators' script that reflects their expectation of what a negotiation will involve. It is typically self-fulfilling at the negotiation table where the script is played out. For example, if the negotiator's script is a competitive one then a suggestion by the other negotiator that both parties engage in 'side-by-side problem solving to come up with a solution that meets everybody's interests' will be met with suspicion. Clearly, if both parties work to roughly the same script – that is they both have broadly similar ideas as to the purpose of negotiation and what it involves – then this helps them both organise their way through the process more effectively than if they work to different scripts.

In a workshop to prepare for some forthcoming negotiations, a group of management and union negotiators were asked to draw a negotiation. The managers got together and drew a competitive-looking picture – two sides fighting and one coming out victorious. The union representatives drew people sitting around a table having a discussion, a portrayal reflecting their view that negotiation was a consultative process. Both parties had come up with very different scripts or expectations. When each showed the other what they thought the forthcoming negotiations were going to be like, they both realised they had some adjusting to do if they were going to get any sort of reasonable outcome at all.

Lecturers may take the view that their role is to present students with a more cooperative and constructive script. This is, of course, what Fisher, Ury and Patton (1991) have done with their seminal 'Getting to Yes'. They presented a strong contrast between two negotiation scripts – positional and interest based bargaining – and many programs on negotiation have been built around their principled approach to negotiation. Essentially these programs seek to teach the student a new negotiation script. The students in the class may well have developed their own images and scripts of what they think negotiation is all about and these might serve as a filter to the lecturer (or this book's) suggestions on how to negotiate differently.

Competitive scripts

We might envisage a negotiation as something like a boxing match or a test of endurance, or as a round table discussion. We can show a competitive negotiation diagrammatically (Figure 5.1). One party wants more than the other is willing to give. If the parties are negotiating around target points and trying to focus on the other party's resistance point then clearly the negotiation will be a competitive one involving a great deal of pressure and concession making. Given the way the negotiations are set up in the

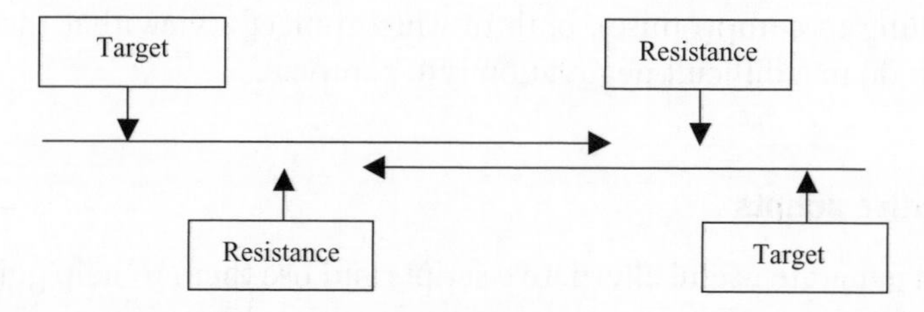

Figure 5.1: Negotiation as competing tension

first place there is not much scope for anything else! It is an outright contest to see who can get the most. If agreement is to be reached then at least one of the negotiators must be 'cooperative' but this does not alter the fundamental competitive dynamic of the process. As Fisher, Ury and Patton (1991) rightly point out, much of what is called cooperative negotiation is simply the soft, conceding side of a hard positional strategy which has not worked.

Alternatively, we can show negotiation as a pattern of more cooperative-looking exchanges where the parties narrow down their differences (Figure 5.2). Even so, this is still competitive. Imagine a lead group of riders pulling away from the peloton in the Tour de France. They need to work together and share the pacemaking to increase their lead but they all know that at some point one of their number is going to try to sprint for the line and win the stage. To be more creative the negotiators need to break out of the existing parameters of the issue and go down a different route all together. (Not permitted in the Tour de France!)

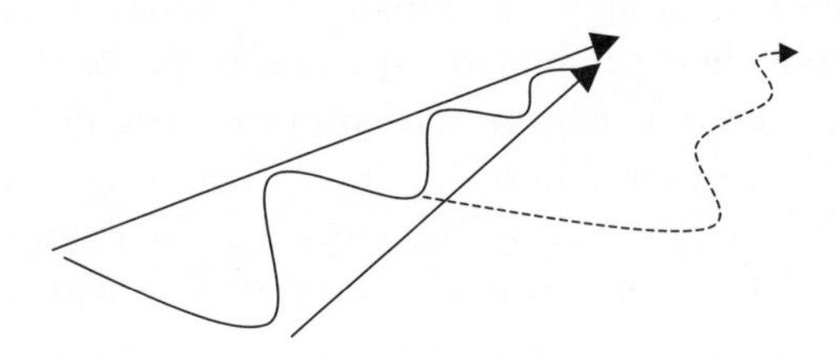

Figure 5.2: Negotiation as cooperative competition

This competitive view of negotiation tends to be our 'default' script because negotiators tend to approach an issue as being a zero-sum (win-lose) issue and negotiate accordingly, that is competitively. They also tend to overestimate the strength of their position and are overly negative about the other party, both of which encourage a competitive stance. Male negotiators are also more likely to pick a sporting analogy for negotiation implying a contest, a winner and a loser. When people feel under pressure, as is often the case in a negotiation, they tend to 'close up' in their behaviour (reveal less information) and harden their attitudes (be less willing to compromise), both of which reflect a view that the safest thing to do in a difficult negotiation is to compete.

Alternative scripts

We can generate useful alternative scripts and use them to help guide the negotiations away from the inherent competitive dynamic.

Watkins (1999) talks about negotiation in terms of architectures – for example, the issue architecture, temporal architecture and the linkages with other negotiations. This architectural perspective suggests an image of negotiation as a building, that the preparation is the foundation, the bricks are information, the windows are potential solutions, the roof beams are points that are being agreed to and the roof is the settlement.

A group of managers developed the idea of negotiation being a jam session by a group of jazz musicians. Orchestra musicians would be rehearsing tightly to a script – the composition as interpreted by the conductor – but jazz musicians are different. They know they have to get their act together for the forthcoming gig and each piece they have selected to play has its fundamental rhythms. Everyone knows the pianist is going to take the lead while the bass player tries to hold it all together but everyone also knows there is going to be a bit of a contest going on as each player draws on their own favourite riffs and tries to carry the piece forward. By pushing to the limits they get creative and every so often it all comes together into something new and compelling. This tension between being individually creative while also working together around a basic format is much like Putnam's (1990) view of negotiation being a process of interdependence between cooperativeness and cooperation, each feeding off the other, much like one jazz player feeding off another, to produce an unexpected but good result.

'Negotiation as Sudoko' is another interesting imagery that sees negotiation as a puzzle – there *is* a good answer but it is not obvious. There are intricate patterns and linkages. Each decision opens up a new insight but there is no guarantee that the puzzle will be completed. Negotiation has also been likened to a roller-coaster reflecting the exhilaration yet tension of not being in full control as events follow one after another.

Negotiation as a train journey

We sometimes talk about negotiations going 'off the rails' or of the need to 'get these negotiations back on track', phrases which invoke imagery of negotiation as a train journey. One such journey is the Indian Pacific across Australia, a journey that involves travelling in a dead straight line for over 470 km, an image suggesting the relatively straightforward linear problem solving approach to finding solutions.

The Nullarbor Model of negotiation (Fells, 2000a) is described more fully in Appendix 5. It endeavours to capture the dynamic of what

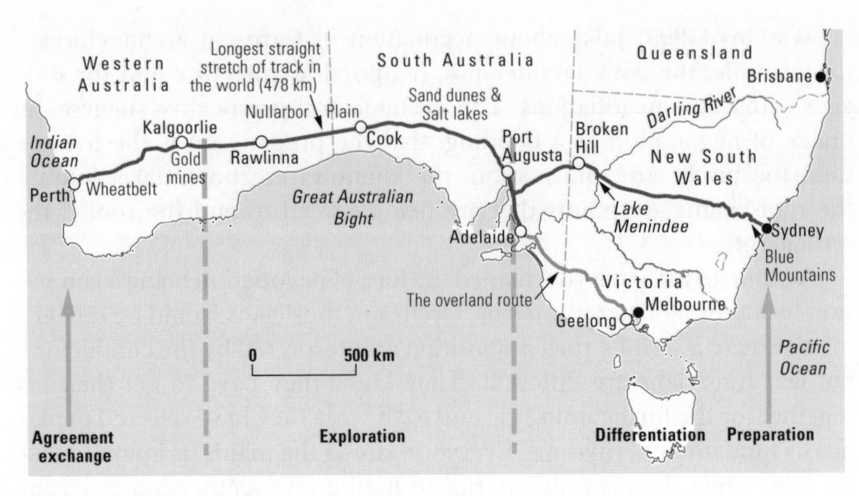

Figure 5.3: The Nullarbor Model of negotiation

is involved in reaching a negotiated agreement by highlighting key points about the process and posing questions to help a negotiator manage that point in the negotiation more effectively. Briefly, the negotiation journey involves starting at Sydney and travelling across New South Wales to Adelaide, which represents the differentiation phase during which the negotiating parties sort out what the real issues and differences are (see Figure 5.3). The train then crosses the Nullarbor Desert, which represents the exploration phase and then, after Kalgoorlie the train heads on down to Perth, which represents the exchange phase. Reaching Perth represents achieving an agreement, and given that Perth is such a fine city, it represents a positive outcome for all the negotiators!

Interestingly, the journey in the other direction also represents a typical negotiation. Starting at Perth, after a bit of competitive sorting out of the issues, the parties get straight into finding solutions (crossing the Nullarbor) only to find they rushed into this too quickly and so none of their 'solutions' seem to work and the remainder of the negotiation (across New South Wales) gets pretty competitive as each party tries to get the best deal possible from what's available. It is better to take time to find out the full extent of the differences. This makes it much easier to find creative solutions which will be acceptable to both parties, though even then there might be some game playing as the negotiators reach a point of agreement.

Managing the negotiations

A negotiation script, such as the Nullarbor Model, provides an imagery that helps a negotiator to navigate the broad flow of a negotiation (to mix metaphors), to 'read' the patterns of interaction as they occur and so have a good idea of what to do next to move the negotiations forward in an effective way. It is not that the research findings presented in the previous chapter are of no use – just the opposite – but a visual image, particularly if the negotiator has developed his or her own, is likely to be a more effective 'trigger' to work out which bit of the research needs to be applied. There are other things negotiators can do to manage a negotiation, particularly at those times when they look like getting into difficulties.

Remember that negotiation is two-sided and messy

Figure 4.4, p. 74 might convey the impression that negotiation is straightforward. We would like it to be so but in practise it is not. The phases might be short or long. (Most time should be spent finding out the differences.) The more competitive of negotiators would tend to disregard the 'explore for options' task altogether. (They can still create value through effective offer exchanges but negotiators generally do well to explore adding value options if they have the opportunity.) The phases may be revisited so the sequence is untidy rather than orderly. This inherent messiness means that negotiators – even good ones – should not expect to fully manage the negotiations down a clear path. Added to this, the other negotiator will also influence the course of events. Nevertheless a negotiator can have a positive influence on the process.

Keep check of the process

Viewing negotiation as a series of tasks helps move away from the broad labels of 'competitive' or 'cooperative' negotiation. If a negotiator labels what the other negotiator is doing as competitive then she is likely to respond in a competitive manner herself. If she labels the other negotiator as cooperative she might respond by making unnecessary concessions. However, if she interprets what he is doing in terms of the task – is he trying to find out differences, explore for options or set up a pattern of offer exchange? – then she can respond accordingly and so help move the negotiations forward.

Because there are different tasks to be worked through and issue strategies to be managed, it is worth keeping a running check on what is happening as it occurs. Without a well-managed process a good issue outcome is unlikely. The simple checklist in Table 5.1 will help a negotiator take stock of both the issue and process dimensions before deciding what to do next. Negotiators often forget that negotiation is two-sided and believe that what they *want* to happen *will* happen. Thinking about what the other party can do encourages a negotiator to think about the other party's perspective before estimating what might be achieved.

Table 5.1 A negotiation management checklist and an example

Issue dimension +	Process dimension +	Action	→Outcome
What are we doing about the issue?	What are we trying to achieve at this point in the negotiation?	How are we going to do it? *What can the other party do?*	What should be achieved by this phase of the negotiation?
Example:			
Contend	Differentiate. Try to find out more about the other party's priorities	Restate our position but ask more open-ended questions:	
		They can: Slowly reveal more information	We should then be able to repackage our offer
		or	
		Continue to simply restate their position	No progress, so restate our position and revisit our best alternative to a negotiated agreement (BATNA)

Make use of deadlocks and manage them effectively

The example in Table 5.1 shows how a negotiation might either make progress or stall depending on the choices the negotiators make. No matter how much planning and training has been undertaken, a negotiation rarely follows a prescribed path (negotiation is 'messy') and often reaches a point of deadlock. Why do negotiations stall? When they do, can they be turned around?

The term deadlock (or 'impasse') has a sense of finality, suggesting the conclusion of the negotiation. There is also a sense that a deadlock is something of a failure. However there are times when walking away from a negotiation is the right thing to do. In contrast, some negotiators are so concerned about loss of face that they would rather walk away than make a final concession to secure a good deal that is on offer.

A more positive way of looking at a deadlock is to view it as merely another stage in the process of reaching agreement (Carlisle and Leary, 1981; Fells, 1986), a period when no evident progress is being made rather than the end of the negotiation. The word 'evident' is important because a lot might be going on in the mind of the negotiator or away from the negotiation table. A classic example is the use of silence which was revealed through negotiations between two of the leading business tycoons of their day. Robert Holmes à Court was asked about some negotiations with John Elliot: 'I understand that there were many long pauses in these conversations', to which he replied, 'It is well known that you always know who is going to win by who has the longest silence.' (*The West Australian*, 20 May 1986, p. 2). There was no evident progress but a lot would have been going on in the minds of the two men.

A deadlock is an opportunity for the events at the negotiation table to be reconsidered in their broader context. Often is it only when they find themselves in a deadlock that the parties truly face the reality of their situation and so, paradoxically, it is the deadlock that provokes further progress. From an issue perspective, the deadlocked parties may decide that their BATNAs are better than the other party's offer. They should then agree to part company as reasonable friends in case they have to negotiate again. If walking away is not a good option, reviewing the Strategy Framework might suggest ways to change the context of the other party so that it shifts away from its contending strategy. In particular are there ways to increase the other party's costs of continuing to disagree or ways of reducing one's own costs? (Chamberlain and Kuhn, 1965; Watkins, 1998). This should all have been explored before the negotiations began but the imperative of a deadlock sharpens the analysis and encourages 'breakthrough' thinking (Green and Wheeler, 2004).

If action away from the negotiation table is not possible, then a change in issue strategy may be required with perhaps some informal or back door communications to 'sound out' the other party. If the process has been poorly managed then efforts should be made to get the negotiations back in phase, perhaps with the involvement of a mediator. If the process has been damaged through inappropriate actions by the negotiators then changed tactics or a change in personnel might enable the negotiations to move forward again.

There is a cautionary note about deadlocks. Because of their power to force change, some negotiators build their strategy around pushing 'the other party into a corner' to provoke a deadlock. This essentially competitive (if not combative) approach is risky because of its one-sidedness. The expectation is that the other party will make a concession but there is no reason to suppose they will inevitably respond in the required manner.

Taking adjournments

As difficulties emerge between the parties, negotiators might feel the need to take an adjournment. This is often the first sign that a deadlock might occur and it needs careful handling. Prior preparation is important. A negotiator should think through what he might do if an adjournment is needed, perhaps determine to restate his main points to give himself time to regroup his thoughts. If negotiating as a team, they should establish clear signals on whether an adjournment should be called.

It is important that calling an adjournment does not give an impression of weakness. A negotiator should first foreshadow that she thinks an adjournment might be useful for both sides. If, for example, the negotiations have been getting heated, foreshadowing an adjournment may be all that is necessary to draw everyone's attention to what has been going on. When an adjournment occurs it is important to make sure that the other side has something to do during the break, otherwise they will simply think you have adjourned to rethink your position and so will expect you to return with a concession. 'I think it's getting near the time for an adjournment but before we do that, can we just summarise the areas of difference we still need to address ... ' or 'we'll take time out to think about what options we might have on the price structure, but can you give some thought to the pattern of deliveries, because that's really important to us.' When the negotiations resume there would then be two items for discussion, not just one.

Be a mediator within the negotiation

One way to overcome a deadlock is to involve a mediator who can rebuild the process and get the parties to reconsider their positions on the issues in dispute. Though many mediators will have been coached in the interest-based approach (Fisher, Ury and Patton, 1991; Boulle, 1996) there are different approaches they can take. These range from being process-oriented and endeavouring to create a climate in which the parties can then find a solution to being issue-focused, using their expertise to secure the parties' agreement to a settlement (described as 'orchestrators' and 'dealmakers' respectively by Kolb (1983). In developing their approach to a case, mediators have to be as strategic as the negotiators. The reader will recognise that the orchestrator or interest-based approaches might be appropriate where the parties have not fully worked through the differentiation or exploration phases, whereas the more assertive deal-making approach might be appropriate if the parties have stalled in the exchange phase.

The role of the mediator is not to fix the dispute but to help the parties fix their dispute themselves (and so be more committed to implementing the agreement). From this perspective mediation is overlaid on the negotiation rather than be a separate process that 'takes over' the handling of the dispute (Figure 5.4). The mediator brings a skills set and experience which the parties might lack and so assists them through the remainder of their negotiation.

The definition of negotiation (Chapter 1) is 'a process where two parties with differences which they need to resolve, are trying to reach agreement through exploring for options and exchanging offers – and an agreement'. This can be rewritten to provide a definition of the role of mediator.

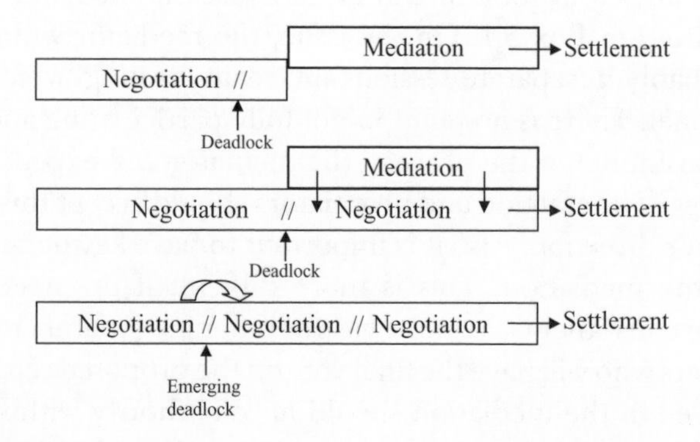

Figure 5.4: Three perspectives on mediation: as a separate process, as an overlay and as a 'within' process

> Mediation is the involvement of an independent person whose role is to assist the parties find a solution to their dispute through helping them clarify their real differences and clarify why they need to resolve them, and through supporting their efforts in trying to reach agreement through helping them explore and create more options and assisting them when exchanging offers, and making sure they are comfortable with their agreement.

It is not the intent here to provide a full description of mediation but instead to note three points from a negotiator's perspective. Firstly, viewing mediation as part of – rather than separate to – the negotiation process provides an opportunity for a negotiator to become a 'mediator' within the negotiation as it unfolds (Figure 5.4). An alert negotiator who is paying attention to the process as well as the issues should see the potential for a deadlock unfolding. Rather than wait for it to occur and suggest third-party mediation, the negotiator can focus on bringing to the negotiation table the tasks that a mediator would have done. As an example, a good mediator will always foreshadow the next steps in the process. She might say 'I'm just going to ask Mr Jones to outline his main concerns and then I'll turn to you, Mr Smith to give you an opportunity to do the same.' This process management gives confidence to the parties and, in this case, Mr Smith would feel less inclined to interrupt (which would raise the level of competitiveness) because he knows his turn is coming. In similar fashion a good negotiator can bring some structure to the discussion (without being controlling). 'Perhaps we could go through our responses to your proposal, and if you agree we can then discuss them together, rather than you respond to them point by point.' Some other process management examples are provided in Table 5.2.

Secondly, if the parties have called in a mediator then there are a number of things a negotiator can do to assist the mediator in his role. These are listed in Box 5.1. On the issue, the mediator will engage the parties (probably in separate sessions) in 'reality testing' which might be confrontational. There is no point in not fully participating and revealing one's true position. On the process, the mediator will expect to manage the sequences of interaction and negotiators should accept this and follow the mediator's direction. Also it is important to have key decision makers present at the mediation. This is more difficult if the negotiators are representing constituents, as in the case of union negotiators representing their members who will have the final vote on the proposed settlement, but those involved in the mediation should have authority within their own side to reach an agreement across the table that has a high probability of acceptance by the constituency group.

Table 5.2 Recognising an emerging critical moment and some recommendations

Dimension	Useful responses
The issue dimension	
Constant restatement of incompatible positions	Summarise e.g. differences
Repeated but failed attempts to repackage the offers	Suggest benefits of an (any) agreement, allude to adverse BATNAs
An 'agreed' proposal or solution gets rejected by constituents	Revert to re-exploration of interests and possible areas of flexibility
The process dimension	
Unwillingness to move beyond stating the issues e.g. long histories of detail, repetition	Talk process. How are we going? How do we feel about how we are going (coupled with forward-looking statements)?
Statements of 'wanting to get this over with' etc.	Emphasise the benefits of a good agreement
Discontinuity e.g. a suggestion or offer in the middle of an explanation of interests	Restate own interests, check understanding that the suggestion was actually a suggestion; if so, clarify Explore if the interests are understood; if they are not then put the suggestion on 'open hold' while restating interests
The action dimension	
Frustration, annoyance	Think what you might be doing to annoy them. Talk process. Adjourn
Withdrawal e.g. less information in replies or even total mental withdrawal	
Increase in interruptions, voice level	Manage own behaviour, summarise

Box 5.1: Some ways to help a mediator help you find a settlement

The issue dimension

Reality testing your core interests:

- give honest information
- reconsider what you really want
- ask yourself 'is our BATNA really so good?"

The process dimension

Taking control of the interactions:

- follow the mediator's lead
- don't give ground easily but be open to suggestions
- take a hint when one is offered.

Thirdly, negotiators who find themselves involved in mediation should be alert to the process being used tactically (Fells, 1999a). The whole thrust of mediation is to help the parties achieve a settlement; in terms of phases and tasks, mediation is an end-game process focusing heavily on exchange. This is often the case but it should not be presumed, particularly if mediation is a mandatory process. Many contracts and legal jurisdictions now require the parties to undertake mediation before their dispute can be listed for resolution though a court hearing. In strategic terms the parties still have an alternative process by which their dispute might be resolved. Rather than the process sequence being 'negotiation–deadlock–mediation–settlement', it is 'negotiation–deadlock–mediation–court hearing–settlement'. This being so, the strategies of the parties in what amounts to a 'mid-cycle' mediation might be completely different (Table 5.3). Many legal cases are settled 'on the steps of the court' so the parties might turn up to the mediation with the intent of using the reality testing efforts of the mediator to find out more about the other party's limits of flexibility, not intending that the mediation will resolve the issue. (Only participation in mediation is mandatory, not reaching a settlement.) Armed with this additional information they would then have a further round of negotiation on the court steps. Even without a court/arbitration option as the next step, negotiators might still see the mediation as a means of gaining information, not settling the dispute. Clearly any party participating in the mediation in the hope of achieving a settlement (and so being prepared to reveal more information and be concessionary) will be disadvantaged if the other party is intent on contending.

Table 5.3 Mid-cycle and end-game mediation (Fells, 1999a)

	Mid-cycle mediation	**End-game mediation**
Prospects for a settlement other than by mediation	Good	Poor
Parties' approach at mediation	Contending strategy	Conceding strategy
Mediator's focus	Process oriented	Settlement oriented
Measure of success	Parties resume negotiation	Dispute resolved

6 Dealing with differences

The previous three chapters considered the issue and process aspects of reaching agreement. Chapter 3 outlined the issue strategies available to negotiators at any point in time – they can contend, concede, compromise in a creative or clear-cut way or they can walk away from the negotiations. Being strategic in negotiation involves analysis before action. Chapter 4 suggested that the process, irrespective of the preferred issue strategy, is going to involve the parties in at least two key tasks: differentiation and exchange, and hopefully a third: exploration. When negotiators focus on each of these tasks for a period of time, they become a phase in the negotiation en route to agreement. Negotiators tend to work to a script or imagery of how a negotiation unfolds and Chapter 5 showed one such imagery – the Nullarbor Model – as an example. The purpose of this and the next two chapters is to fill in the details using the issue, process, action and outcome framework presented at the end of Chapter 4. All three are 'how to' chapters.

Negotiation is a process where two parties with differences which they need to resolve are trying to reach agreement though exploring options and exchanging offers. The negotiators are likely to focus on the task of sorting out their real differences and why they need to be settled towards the beginning of the negotiation. The essence of this task is shown in Figure 6.1. It involves a combination of contending and differentiating as the negotiators establish the parameters for the ensuing discussion. Later, they may find that there were aspects of their differences they had not realised and so they need to return to the task of differentiating. While this occurs the negotiators need to stand firm – contend – on the issues.

The archaeologists on television's *Time Team* love digging up the ground to see what they might find. They probe and dig and survey

Issue dimension +	Process dimension +	Action dimension	→ Outcome
What are we doing about the issue?	What are we trying to achieve at this point in in the negotiation?	How are we going to do it?	What should be achieved by this phase of the negotiation?
Contend To stand firm and maintain one's position in the expectation that, in time, the other party will accept your position.	**Differentiate** To find the full extent of the differences between the parties, particularly their underlying interests. To decide whether to continue negotiating.	**Information exchange** Clear statements, reiterating both 'what' and 'why'. Information 'drip feed'. Checking understanding. *Don't:* Challenge positions. Present solutions.	Each party clarifies its own expectations. Each party has a good understanding of where the other is coming from. Each party has either a realisation of a need to negotiate further or an ability to walk away.

Figure 6.1: Dealing with differences in a negotiation

in all sorts of different ways and places across the archaeology site looking for explanations from the past. When they find something, no matter how small, they want to know how it fits into the overall picture, 'what does it tell us and what does it mean?' and they are usually able to put together a picture of what life was like in the Saxon village or Tudor castle. Except for looking more to the future than the past, laying the foundations for a good negotiation is much like an archaeological dig. Information exchange in negotiation is akin to lots of time-consuming digging (often in the wrong place), turning up fragments and asking, 'what does it mean?' Like archaeologists, negotiators would prefer information about their different interests and priorities to be laid out openly but, desirable though this may be, it is not normally the case and like archaeologists, negotiators have to go digging.

The negotiations should be built slowly. Some people place great emphasis on the negotiators building a personal relationship perhaps through extensive golf and karaoke sessions. While it is important to build a relationship what really matters is what happens at the negotiating table. Negotiation is an evolutionary process; each party will take time to learn and understand the other, talk about issues in general terms, confirm their common understanding of the big picture and what might be achieved, set up open agendas. Take time to do this. No amount of prior golf or karaoke can cope with a solution-oriented or controlling approach once the negotiations start.

In the opening stages negotiators often emphasise the importance of achieving a 'win-win' outcome. This macro-language of cooperation will have no impact if it is not matched by cooperative micro-behaviours such as summarising, being open to suggestions and not interrupting. As the negotiations proceed, it is unwise to assume that because the last meeting was cooperative – a good constructive atmosphere with lots of progress being made – the next one will be the same. Cooperation has to be built and consolidated throughout the negotiation.

The issue dimension

Negotiators should first deal with their differences through contending, which simply means being firm on the things that need to be achieved through the negotiation. If it is important that the cash flow be maintained at a stable level during the life of the contract then this point has to be made firmly – and if necessary often – until the other party accepts that any final agreement will provide for it. The details – not least the amount – would be left until later but the importance of cash flow stability should be made clear from the outset.

The normal advice is to build up the agenda and ask for more than you expect to get – to say, for example, that the stability of cash flow is important when really it is not. Pitching high reduces the chance of a negotiator asking for less than the other party is willing to give. It also gives a negotiator 'room to move' and by appearing reasonable and flexible oneself (even though only giving up on what was never expected anyway) will draw the other party into concessions making. However, too high an opening position increases the risk of a deadlock. Too high a position merely invites a similar extreme position from the other party (reciprocity) making it that much harder to bridge the gap to find a solution. Further, if negotiators are known to ask for more than they expect then making concessions will also be expected and so does not then earn any cooperation dividend. (As usual, these mini-tactics only work on negotiators who have not read the same book of tactics.)

Stating an opening position can lead to the negotiations becoming a 'positional' contest, but it does not have to. The win-lose perspective causes negotiators to lock into their respective positions and even though they know they have room to move they find it hard to do so unless the other negotiator does so first. The difficulty is that the other negotiator is not going to make the first move either! Negotiation then involves pressure, threats and avoiding loss of face, moving straight into clear-cut compromise with little opportunity for creative, adding-value solutions to emerge. Fisher, Ury and Patton (1991) are rightly condemning of this type of negotiation; it is inefficient, it produces poor outcome and it damages relationships. The cause of this problem lies not in putting one's position clearly on the table, but in having a win-lose view of negotiation and being wary of sharing information. Negotiation as a journey is a far better imagery than negotiation as a contest.

Contending need not, and should not, degenerate into competitive positional bargaining. Positional bargaining seeks to deal with differences by eliminating the other party's position. Contending should be viewed as protecting one's interests rather than negating the interests of the other party. It establishes one's own position and demonstrates firmness to the other party. This requires an acceptance by negotiators that there are times when what is needed is simply to go over ground already covered, restating the key points and concerns, not expecting, for the time being at least, that there be any movement on the issues.

The process dimension

Finding out the real differences

Contending will not degenerate into positional bargaining if the negotiators are aware of the process task – differentiation – and if, instead of contending and waiting to see who cracks first, they focus on finding out the real differences which lie behind the positions. The essence of this interest-based approach (which has been popularised through the Principled Negotiation Model of Fisher, Ury and Patton, 1991) is that negotiators focus on the 'why' rather than the 'what' of the issue. An interest is the underlying concern, a motivation or objective that lies behind a particular demand or request. In the earlier example of negotiating a contract, an opening statement to the effect that 'stability of cash flow is really important to me' reflects an underlying interest while 'my minimum monthly revenue requirement is $50 000' may seem much like saying the same thing but is more positional.

For example, in a family court negotiation, the demand for ownership of the family home may not actually be for somewhere to live but as recognition for all the effort and devotion put into making the home into what it was. In a major international acquisition negotiation, it was important to one of the key principals that he be known for achieving a 'billion dollar deal'. This would be the first such deal in that industry in his country; his standing in the business community would be enhanced, giving him greater access to further capital raising (as well as gratifying his ego). The other partner was not willing to put in the amount of cash needed to reach $1 billion but some creative accounting in the area of ongoing management fees boosted the package giving it the billion dollar label.

The pragmatics of interest-based bargaining

If negotiators were completely analytical and rational in their approach to handling information and decision making, they would come to the negotiation table fully understanding their own interests and priorities and would be willing to openly exchange information with the other party. Quickly both parties would be in what the researchers call a 'full information condition' and could work out the best solution for them both. The more realistic situation is one where the parties know what they would *like* their interests to be only to find that they must revise their thoughts on what is really important as they learn more through the negotiation itself. In particular, negotiators have to reconsider and perhaps reorder their priorities as they become aware that they will not get everything they want through negotiation.

A good foundation would be laid if the parties present their key concerns at the outset. A mediator schooled in the interest-based approach would see his first task, after gaining the confidence of the disputing parties, as drawing out from the parties their interests and concerns. These might be written up as two lists side by side on a flip chart so that both parties can see what is really important to the other and what needs to be addressed if there is to be a good settlement.

Negotiators have to do this without the assistance of a mediator who has authority to control the process. Even when both parties openly recognise the need for an interest-based approach, the process of drawing out interests is going to be more pragmatic. Negotiators will continue to state and advance their positions because their belief in the interest-based approach is conditional, 'provided I get what I want on this issue'. Negotiators who have prepared well and so believe they understand each other's interests don't then feel the need to go though the process of thoroughly examining them. In less well prepared cases, the interests might be implicit and it would be unusual for them all to be spelt out at the first time of asking. The critical practical point is that drawing out interests is going to take time.

An example shows the pragmatics of uncovering interests in an inherently competitive situation. The issue concerned access for mineral exploration into a national park in Western Australia. No matter how sophisticated the aerial mapping, at some point a team with a drilling rig has to go to the location and extract core samples to see exactly what is under the ground. The history in this particular national park, which also contained areas of significance for indigenous Australians, was that the drilling activity seemed to be damaging the park and disturbing indigenous sites.

A meeting was called of the four government departments with interests in the situation. The Department of Aboriginal Affairs wanted mining exploration to be kept out of the park. The Conservation Department wanted to maintain the park in its natural state. The Mining Department, not surprisingly, wanted mining companies to have access into the park. Finally the Department of the Premier wanted to promote the long-term government priority of economic growth (and also find a solution rather than have it become a divisive issue in the community).

These opening stances of the four parties can be presented in terms of positions and interests (see Table 6.1). The Departments of Aboriginal

Table 6.1 Mineral explorations in a national park of Indigenous significance – opening stances

Department	Opening stance	Interest	Position
Aboriginal Affairs	No access		Positional
Conservation	Preserve integrity of the land	An interest	
Mining	Access		Positional
Premier	Economic development	An interest	

Affairs and Mining both present positions, the Conservation and Premier's Departments both present their underlying interests.

The first and cautionary point about interests is that you can't negotiate around interests forever; at some point they firm into proposals and then those proposals can begin to look positional. For example while there are many ways to preserve the integrity of the land in the national park, when asked what this meant in practice, the Conservation Department said that the best way to preserve the integrity of the land would be to limit access to conservation staff. This would mean no access to drilling teams. 'No access to drilling teams' is a position. Similarly, the State's economic development was dependent on the mining industry so the Premier's Department's interests were, 'we have to give the miners access'. In negotiation terms this is positional.

The point that the negotiations have now reached is shown in Table 6.2. The issue has now become framed as a win-lose situation where the solution for two parties is to deny access to the drilling rigs

Table 6.2 Mineral explorations in a national park of Indigenous significance – emerging positions

Department	Emerging stance	Interest	Position
Aboriginal Affairs	No access		Still positional
Conservation	Preserve integrity of the land by restricting access	→	Became positional
Mining	Access		Still positional
Premier	Economic development by allowing mining, i.e. access	→	Became positional

but the solution for the other two parties is to permit access. As part of the dynamics of uncovering interests, the parties seem to have done the opposite by becoming more positional. However, when this occurs good negotiators draw on their understanding of phases and tasks within the negotiation process. They understand that negotiation is a journey, not a contest. Rather than challenge the increasingly positional stance of the other party or even try to find ways around it, a good negotiator will endeavour to prolong the differentiation phase. She would try to maintain an even-handed dialogue and encourage more information exchange. As a result, new insights into the underlying interests of the parties might emerge.

In the mineral exploration negotiation, while discussions continued it became clear that when the representatives of the indigenous people were asked what was happening to their sites and routes across the park, they mentioned only one company when they gave examples of sites being damaged. Reframing 'no access to anyone' into 'no access for this one particular company because of what they are doing to the land' revealed an underlying interest in getting everyone to respect the land.

Similarly, a sense of frustration about delay was apparent in the mining representative's comments. Although the industry believed the park to be rich in resources it was not the only area for development. If an application for an exploration permit for a particular area in the park was going to be rejected, could it be rejected quickly so the company could know and move onto another project? When presented in this way, the issue for the mining department is reframed in terms of speed of decision making, not access per se.

Table 6.3 shows these different perspectives on the issue. It can be argued that it would have been far better for the parties to have voiced these specific interests in the first place but we don't negotiate in an ideal world. The essence of good negotiation is to manage the process so that it evolves well, not to assume everyone has been on the right training course. (We will see in Chapter 9, that the presence of constituencies – as in each of the parties here – leads to more positional stances being adopted at the negotiating table.)

The issue facing the parties now can be reframed. Instead of whether to allow mineral exploration in the park – which was a contentious zero-sum issue – the problem (note the change of word) now facing the parties was how to set up a decision-making process on access which (a) was relatively quick and (b) governed the conduct of companies operating in the park. This was the sort of task which government officials are good at and before very long a set of core principles was drafted which enabled each to go

Table 6.3 Mineral explorations in a national park of Indigenous significance – emerging interests

Department	Emerging interests	Interest	Position
Aboriginal Affairs	Everyone to respect the land (no access)	Interests emerge	←
Conservation	Preserve integrity of the land (by restricting access)	Refocus on the interests	←
Mining	Make access decisions quickly (access)	Interests emerge	←
Premier	Economic development by allowing mining but controlled access	Refocus on the interests	←

back and demonstrate to their respective constituents that their key needs and requirements had been addressed.

This example shows two important points about good negotiating. Firstly, it is important to draw out underlying interests so that a good solution can be found. Secondly, the underlying interests are underlying in more ways than one and so may not surface easily. The good negotiator must manage the process to draw them out.

The action dimension

Managing information exchange

While negotiators are stating, restating and explaining their positions they also should be differentiating, getting behind the positions to find the real differences in interests, priorities and motivations. The key activity is information exchange but although this is a strand of a negotiation's DNA, negotiators are often reluctant to offer or reveal information and it takes time for important information and insights to come to the surface. Ensuring that sufficient time is spent on the task of differentiation may involve an element of managing the other negotiator. If the other party seems keen to push forward into looking for solutions it may be helpful to suggest, for example 'Before we get focused on considering your new

Table 6.4 Information exchange: some helpful and unhelpful behaviours

Helpful	Unhelpful
Clear statements of 'what' and 'why'	An unclear mixture of 'shorthand' and detail
Focused statements	Long rambling statements
Repetition	Not revisiting a topic
Drip feed	Not reciprocating
Checking understanding	Interrupting
Summarising	Criticising
Restating	Being in a hurry
Reflecting	

proposal perhaps we might check our understanding of the issues, just to be sure. Would you explain again about . . . ?' (see Table 6.4)

Presenting information: how to contend well

Negotiators should be clear in their statements of their own positions and motivations. To say this is a skill which needs to be developed implies that negotiators are unclear. They are rarely deliberately so but inadvertently can be unclear by being too terse or too rambling. A negotiator might be too terse and not say enough because of the tenseness of the situation which tends to 'close down' our behaviour. Paradoxically, having prepared fully the negotiator may be so familiar with the issues (in itself a good thing) that he then assumes the other negotiator can see the situation equally clearly. As a result, he makes points in 'shorthand' as it were, expecting the other party to readily see the implications of the points being made in the same way that are obvious to the speaker.

On the other hand, talking too long means the other party gets frustrated. They want to make their points too and they so either switch off until they get their turn (eventually!) or interrupt to have their say. Either way, they typically talk for as long as the first speaker (one of the effects of reciprocity) leading to a similar reaction. The pattern of dialogue between the negotiators begins to decay and can lead to a 'dialogue of the deaf' – two parties talking to each other but neither listening.

Another difficulty with a long presentation is that too much detail means the main points get lost. People tend to remember what was said early on or what was said at the end (the primacy and recency effects) but not what was said in between. So a good presentation has the main point first, followed by some supporting points, or leads up to the main point.

Once they've made their main point good negotiators then stop, even though there was perhaps something they missed in their presentation. To go back and cover that lesser point means the main point is now not the last one, and so does not have its full impact.

Gleaning information

The task of differentiation is not only about getting the other party to understand one's own concerns and issues but also to understand where the other party is coming from. Good negotiators will have fully prepared from the other party's perspective and should have a good estimate of what their issues and priorities might be. This will be the case where they have negotiated before or have access to common industry and market information. However, good preparation can lead to overconfidence; what has been inferred about the other party needs to be confirmed at the negotiating table. This should not be rushed.

Getting the other party to be explicit is helped by being explicit oneself (reciprocity), by showing respect, by good listening and by checking understanding. It is also helped by what is not done – not interrupting, not challenging the detail; in fact not criticising anything that is said at this stage in the negotiation.

A negotiator can check understanding by summarising the main points, 'so the key issues for you are . . . '; by restating, 'if I understand you correctly, you want to prevent access to the park because of the damage that is caused by exploration crews'; or by reflecting – which is adding to what has been said, 'if access to the park is stopped then that would stop the damage to the flora and to the sites but the ban would also keep out those companies which we know rehabilitate wherever their crews have been.'

Good negotiators summarise frequently (Rackman and Carlisle, 1978), summarising their positions, what has been agreed or what has still to be agreed. It can be used to slow the process down if the other negotiator is trying to rush the negotiators and it is a useful way to bring the discussion back to the main issues. A negotiator who feels under pressure can summarise and so create time and thinking space to work out what to do next.

Dealing with differences is also helped by what is *not* happening. There should be no attempt to find solutions to the differences as they emerge. If a negotiator is too solution oriented, a critical adverse dynamic can emerge. Two managers are negotiating over how to reorganise production to meet a pressing deadline. As one begins to explain some of his staffing constraints the other interjects, 'you can deal with that particular problem easily! All you have to do is start that work group's shift an hour earlier than the other group.' An instinctive reaction is to think, 'how can he solve the problem when I have not finished explaining it!' and so the suggestion gets rejected. What might have been a good solution has now been turned down, making it more difficult to return to later. While trying to find out the extent of differences, negotiators should keep any potential solutions on hold.

In fact, during a differentiation phase there should be no real attempt to dislodge the other party from their stated position. The reason is the underlying strength of reciprocal behaviour. If one negotiator undermines another when she is trying to explain what is important to her, then he must expect that she will undermine his position while he is trying to explain what is important to him. In these situations, both negotiators 'close up' and explain their positions tightly rather than fully and quickly set up a positional win-lose situation with an overlay of interpersonal antagonism.

Pragmatic information exchange – an example

A small UK-based hi-tech company was working on a new management information system. Although it was still only at a development stage, the company demonstrated its product at a computing technology fair in the United States. Having returned home, a director of the company took a phone call from the Vice President (VP) of management services from a major US-based global company saying that he liked what he saw at the fair and wanted to purchase the system for his company. This was a great sales prospect for the hi-tech company as it would establish its reputation with their first sale. But there was a problem. The phone call was in April; the VP was insistent he wanted it by June but the director knew that the new system was not likely to be ready until November. They put proposals back and forth – all the negotiating was done by phone – and as might be expected, they agreed a compromise timeframe of August (a clear-cut compromise splitting the difference between their respective positions).

There were other issues to resolve so the phone calls continued. As they shared information and got to understand each other more fully it became clear that what the VP had meant when he had said 'we want it by June' was 'I have a budget for projects like this and need to pay for it by June.' The 'it' referred to payment not the product. The negotiators had been too solution-oriented to fully understand where each other was coming from. A better solution for both might have been for the payment to be placed into a trust account in June pending delivery in November.

They continued to contend on other issues but this did not mean that the negotiations were getting competitive. They combined their continued firmness on the issues with spending more time on finding out the 'why?' behind the position rather than just offering ways that the gap between the positions might be bridged. Understanding the why behind their seemingly incompatible positions on product licensing (single versus multi-site) enabled them to create a licensing agreement which accommodated both the VP's underlying need for financial predictability and the hi-tech company's need to set a precedent for future sales.

This example shows again that underlying interests might be very 'underlying' and it is only when negotiators uncover the meaning of words (and remember negotiation is often in 'shorthand') that key underlying facts and perspectives emerge. Therefore it is important to take time to go over and around each issue even though this may not seem very efficient to the solution-oriented. Once a new perspective or insight has emerged it is worth standing back, even if the parties are exploring options, and take time to again differentiate, to fully understand the emerging differences, rather than quickly press on with a search for solutions.

The outcome

When does the phase of dealing with differences come to an end? It ought to end only when each negotiator is confident they understand where the other party is really coming from on the issue. One likely consequence of having a better understanding of the other party is a more realistic expectation of what might be achieved. It might confirm that the goals can be realised through negotiation or that expectations and priorities must be revised or even that the walk-away alternative looks like a better option. The key outcome is that both parties understand what the real differences and interests are and why they need to be resolved.

The difficulty is that often negotiators don't reveal what they really want until new proposals are put on the table which then gives them the opportunity to say what they *don't* want. A good negotiator can learn a lot from the other party's rejections of her proposal. Rather than trying to defend her proposal she will try to find out more about the other party's underlying motives. In terms of the negotiation process this means drawing back from presenting new options and moving the negotiation into another period of differentiation, trying again to explore and understand the differences, Once this is done, then the negotiators can move on again to the task of looking for solutions. There may be several periods during a negotiation where the focus is on the task of differentiating but it is better to do this as fully as possible in the early stages of the negotiation to ensure a more satisfactory outcome.

Box 6.1 provides a practical summary of how to deal with differences and Appendix 6 provides some advice on how to manage competitiveness in negotiation.

Box 6.1: What does it mean, in practical terms, to deal with differences in a negotiation?

Aim

To demonstrate firmness on your key issues.
To gain a full understanding of the other party's perspective on what needs to be resolved and why.

Method

A combination of contending and differentiation.

To do it well

Take your time.
Clearly state your perspective and expectations, that is, the issues and concerns which have to be addressed if there is to be an agreement.
Present your position in a broader context so that it does not look like you are presenting a 'take it or leave it' proposition.
Invite the other party to state and restate their positions and interests; allow them to do so without interruption.
Do your best to outline, albeit a bit at a time, the key drivers behind your position; encourage reciprocity through information drip feed.
Invite the other party to provide background information; reciprocate when they do.
Give attention to building a good working relationship with the other negotiator.
Ask 'why' from time to time (but don't assume you are going to get the full answer the first time you ask that question).
Encourage reciprocity by giving full answers.
Summarise regularly.
Accept that underlying interests might evolve as the parties sort out their priorities.
Take a process perspective: if it seems to be getting positional, view this as differentiation, not closure.
Put any suggested solutions on hold, but try to discern what motivated the suggestion.
Ignore any threats or closing statements from the other party, responding instead with a restatement of your own preferred position and reasons why.

Indicators that the phase is coming to an end

An emerging understanding of the other party's perspectives, priorities on the issue.
Confirmation from the other party that they understand your perspectives, priorities on the issue.

Things to avoid doing!

Talking in 'big picture' generalities with nothing definite.
Saying what you want, but not saying why you want it.
Keep emphasising the common interest (this is an irritator).
Interrupting the other party.
Being judgmental about what the other party says.
Telling the other party what the outcome is going to be.
Making threats, particularly ones you can't implement.
Imposing a false deadline.

Remember

You may need to resort to further short phases of contending and differentiation if it becomes clear that there are aspects of the issues or interests that are not fully understood.

7 Exploring options

When negotiators feel they have a good understanding of each other and of the issues then it is time to move onto finding ways to meet the aspirations of the two parties. Good negotiators will not rush into this solution-oriented phase. If the issues have not been fully understood they will only have to go back and spend more time later dealing with their differences.

The negotiators have the choice of finding solutions through being creative or through the more competitive value-claiming end-game. This chapter deals with how options – ways in which the differences might be resolved – can be created during a negotiation. Again it is a 'how to' chapter. The message of the chapter is that creativity does not come easily. Neat satisfying solutions rarely fall into place as might be implied if the title of the chapter was '*creating* options'. The task is to keep working away until something useful happens, just as Thomas Edison did when inventing the electric light bulb – 99% perspiration, 1% inspiration. The key elements in exploring for options are shown in Figure 7.1.

The foundation for finding new options that might resolve the differences has already been laid – well or poorly – through effective preparation and through time spent in the negotiation itself to differentiate while avoiding a tendency to slip into competitive positional bargaining.

An important part of preparation is thinking what a good agreement might look like. This involves thinking through possible solutions. The more ideas a negotiator has about how the issues might be resolved the better. There is a danger that a negotiator might be so attracted to a particular solution that once the negotiation starts it gets presented as *the* solution and becomes a position to be defended rather than a possible solution to be explored. This is why it is important for negotiators to understand the phases – negotiation as a journey – and so appreciate the importance of timing.

Issue dimension +	Process dimension +	Action dimension	→ Outcome
What are we doing about the issue?	What are we trying to achieve at this point in the negotiation?	How are we going to do it?	What should be achieved by this phase of the negotiation?
Creative compromise To propose or consider new adding-value options. In the expectation that one or more options will accommodate the interests of both parties.	**Exploration** To create an environment where new perspectives and ideas might be suggested and explored. **Differentiation** Continuing to emphasise the differences between the parties.	**Flexibility testing** Examine, explore – what if? why not? Unpack every proposal. *Don't:* Reject any suggestions. Follow one suggestion with. another. Apply pressure.	A possible agreement emerges, perhaps a framework agreement. Or more likely: each party has a better understanding of the possibilities and an improved working relationship.

Figure 7.1: Exploring options in a negotiation

Another practical aspect of preparation emerges from the findings of Rackman and Carlisle (1978). They observed that the more skilled negotiators tended to generate more possible solutions while preparing for their negotiations but they also found that the better negotiators tended to prepare in what we might regard as something of a disorganised way. They did not prepare one topic at a time but tended to prepare for them all at once. We will see later that negotiating one issue at a time is not very conducive to creating value because each issue tends to get 'locked away' (and often as a zero-sum game) and so there is little opportunity to create value by linking one issue to another. How negotiators prepare will influence how they negotiate. If they prepare by looking across all the issues then when they come to the more exploratory phases in the negotiation they will tend to negotiate across all the issues rather than try to deal with them one by one.

The issue dimension

A creative compromise is one that adds value and provides real benefit to both parties. We noted in Chapter 2 the tendency of negotiators to call almost any agreement a 'win-win' because it is better than no agreement at all. However, in looking for a creative compromise negotiators are looking for a solution that genuinely meets their needs and to do this they normally have to find some additional value from somewhere.

Lax and Sebenius (1986) emphasise that value can be created out of differences between the parties, as do Mnoonkin, Peppet and Tulumello (2000). Negotiators can put together mutual beneficial deals that create value out of their differing resources, relative valuations of assets, differing forecast, risk or time preferences. This is why the task of differentiation is so important. Many start-up companies need an injection of capital to get their innovative product to market and they turn to venture capitalists. To the company, an injection of $5 million is – almost literally – like gold dust to them. They would forego the prospect of future profits in return for getting the cash they need now. On the other hand, the venture capitalist is prepared to write off the $5 million(!) and demands a high rate of return if this happens to be the one company out of the 20 or so that he is investing in which becomes a roaring success. So the differences in resources (a bright idea and some capital), needs, risk and time preference all provide the basis for a solution that benefits them both.

Good preparation should reveal these differences before the negotiations start. Indeed, the whole negotiation might be an adding-value proposition. The CEOs of a European and an Asian airline drew up a memorandum of understanding (MOU) committing their companies to further negotiation on a proposed joint venture in the growing China market. They could clearly see the value that could be added to their respective companies if the joint venture went ahead. In this sense, and in many negotiations, the creative compromise was already on the table and the task of their negotiating teams was to turn the prospect of an added-value solution into an actual one (which in this case, they were not able to do). The same process has been observed in international negotiation where a senior politician might make a proposal in a public speech to break an impasse leaving the negotiators to then sort out the details (Druckman, Husbands and Johnston, 1991).

If the parties have come to understand each other's differences, it then seems rather counter productive to keep restating these differences when trying to find new solutions. However it serves the further purpose of challenging the negotiators to find the best solution. It will be recalled that in the Strategy Framework (Chapter 3) one of the factors indicating that a creative negotiation would be appropriate is 'importance of issue to self: high' coupled with high concern for the other's outcome. It is the motivation to meet one's own and the other party's needs that drives the exploration for creativity. This drive for a good outcome should also cause the negotiators to closely examine *any* proposal and ask how it adds value. Some questions are provided in Box 7.1.

Box 7.1: Creating value in a proposal

In what way does this proposal add value?
how much?
for whom?
when will it accrue?
what conditions are necessary for it to accrue?
what are the risks to it?
what can we do to improve this proposal?

Asking what might be done to improve the proposal is an important question but one that is not heard often enough in a negotiation. If a new proposal appears to go a long way to meeting the parties' needs they will be inclined to accept it. Its attractiveness has the effect of encouraging the parties to accept it even though it does not meet *all* their stated goals. This is an understandable reaction; the prospect of agreement makes it seem unreasonable to keep insisting on achieving one's goals. However it is often this very insistence which produces the really good solution, hence the usefulness of the question, 'What can we do to improve this proposal?' The question should be asked early before people around the table get drawn into an agreement mentality. If they are all getting ready to wrap up the negotiation by agreeing to a solution which seems to give them most of what they need, they are not going to take too kindly to someone then appearing to prolong the negotiation and risk the consensus by saying, 'I know we are all happy with this proposal as an agreement but is there anything we can do to improve it?'

The process dimension

Creating an open environment

There are many creative ways to generate new ideas such as brainstorming or even the Nominal and Delphi techniques, all of which are processes for generating options for further consideration. A degree of pragmatism is required because it is not often that two opposing teams of negotiators trust each other enough to openly make suggestions that might disadvantage their own party.

The essence of brainstorming is that any idea which comes to mind should be presented without any critical thought and it should be accepted for what it is – an idea, not a definite proposal. This is important because a negotiator might put forward an idea that, on reflection, does not really work well for his party. He should not be inhibited from putting the idea on the table through fear that he is obliged to accept his own idea to the solution.

The challenge is to get ideas out onto the table in a situation where the negotiators have a lot to lose and will be wary of making risky suggestions. One way negotiators do this is to act at an interpersonal level as well as an inter-party level. (This was the distinguishing characteristic of Douglas' reconnoitering phase). They continue to present their party position, 'the Fleecem Telco Group insists on having two seats on your board if it is going to join with you on this venture' but are more exploratory through an individual role, 'I'll have another look at your proposal of the CEO's appointment instead of a second board position and see what I can make of it.' If the proposal to appoint the CEO turns out to be unacceptable then the Telco Group's formal position is still intact.

If the differentiation has been thorough the parties will have a good understanding of the situation and it may be that the solution has emerged without any explicit 'problem solving'. These tacit solutions (Schelling,

1960) often shape the final outcome and so again negotiators should not rush to come up with new solutions but should reflect upon whether any are already present through good differentiation. If it becomes clear that the emerging solution is significantly different from the opening position of one of the parties then yet more time will be needed to allow these adjustments to take place. Even though the Fleecem negotiators realise that the emerging solution of appointing the CEO is the best one available, it might take them time to agree to it openly.

This points to a role for the good negotiator. In addition to pursuing a good outcome for her party she should pay attention to managing the overall process, perhaps needing to draw the parties back into a period of further differentiation or endeavouring to prolong the exploration phase when the other party is wanting to press onto an agreement.

Joint problem solving

Walton and McKersie (1965), who highlighted some of the major elements in the competitive and cooperative approaches to negotiation, were quite deliberate when they defined distributive (win-lose) items as 'issues' while integrative items were 'problems'. This looks somewhat semantic but the way we place a topic on the table reflects how we perceive it and importantly influences how the other party sees it and shapes their response.

Another element to this 'framing' of the problem is its orientation. Presenting a topic in terms of its past can encourage a competitive overlay to the discussion (particularly if something has gone wrong and the negotiation is about how to fix it). On the other hand, if the negotiators can view their differences with a future orientation, 'what do we need to do next?', they tend to become more focused and action oriented.

In similar fashion, Ury (1991) suggests that negotiators adopt a 'side-by-side approach' where both parties – now working as one – attack the problem together rather than from opposing sides. This way of looking at the task has a lot to commend it, and it is easier to get to this point if the negotiators have done their preparation from the perspective of the other party and if they are both facing common external problems (typically poor walk-away alternatives). However we should also be aware that 'let's work together on this' is a favourite phrase of the 'cooperative inviting negotiator' (see Appendix 6).

A further step in the direction of getting away from the 'them and us' approach is for the negotiators to sit at random around a table rather than in teams on either side. This might be encouraged but should not be forced. Negotiation is 'two parties with differences . . . ' and in most cases – particularly where there are constituencies – they will stay as two parties throughout the negotiation. The author attended a lengthy series of management–union negotiations (Fells, 2000b). The meetings were held in the boardroom and as managers and union representatives came to the meeting they found seats, typically sitting with whomever they entered the room with. Consequently, they were not lined up across the table as management and union. The atmosphere was positive, friendly and open with participation from around the table. However the negotiations reached a critical stage on the question of the wage increase; an offer was rejected. At the next meeting, all the management team were on one side of the table, all the union representatives were on the other and they stayed that way in subsequent meetings. 'Two parties with differences . . . '

Unilateral problem solving

In major business negotiations the parties can also be expected to line up across the table. A telecommunication company sought a strategic investment stake in another that needed an injection of funds for its own expansion plans. It was clear to both parties that by cooperating they could further their respective interests. They also understood that the negotiations should look towards developing a relationship that would need to continue beyond the closing of the initial deal. Mutual respect between the negotiation parties was essential to believing that a long-term relationship between the two companies could flourish. The negotiators met over several days working through technical, legal and financial issues, but despite the context of cooperation it was still a formal affair with lead negotiators on each side doing most of the talking.

How were proposals raised and explored in this context? Firstly, each side did a lot of preparation and so was well grounded in the issues and in their areas of flexibility. This meant that on some issues where there were differences of position, suggestions could be made which proved acceptable to the other side. If the suggestion did not prove acceptable, or some other difficulty arose then the negotiators were careful to make sure they properly understood the difficulty. Typically they agreed to disagree and commit to reviewing the issue later. There was no brainstorming in public. The lead negotiators might suggest a working party be set up which is a more formal example of Douglas' separation of interparty and interpersonal roles. Members of the working party could explore, even brainstorm issues and then report back but they would report back to their own team, not to the joint meeting. Ultimately new solutions were generated unilaterally; that is the creative problem solving took place within each party, not between them. It is not surprising that for every hour the parties spent in joint discussions they spent two or three hours in private meetings, reviewing their positions and generating proposals to overcome their differences.

The more formal the negotiation and the greater the degree of preparation, the less likely it is that the negotiators will generate completely new and creative value-adding solutions while around the negotiation table. This makes it all the more important to create and maintain an open environment through the micro-behaviours of problem solving rather than the macro-language of 'cooperation'.

The action dimension

Making suggestions

It is important that any proposals, particularly those generated within a private session, are put to the joint meeting as suggestions, not solutions. Signalling a proposal as 'perhaps we could look at doing it this way' is preferable to 'we've worked out a solution to this problem.' The first is tentative and inclusive; the second is rather more closing and is more likely to generate a 'no, that won't work' response.

It also helps if the presentation of the proposal is not only tentative but also 'other-directed' by fully outlining the implications for the other party. Even giving consideration to the problems the other party might have with the proposal will help keep the attitudes open and is better than not acknowledging the other party at all.

Making multiple offers helps negotiators identify the best outcomes. Putting just one option on the table invites a closed response. Putting two or three allows for discussion to compare them and so may reveal more insights into preferences and perhaps lead to a better solution. It is, of course, possible to use this competitively – the three-card trick – putting two or three proposals on the table in such a way that they pick the one that suits you. (Any helpful negotiation behaviour – even building trust – can be manipulated for advantage.) Nevertheless putting more than one option on the table is helpful.

Handling suggestions

It is not necessary for a negotiator to generate more solutions – being creative helps but knowing how to handle other people's suggestions is what engenders creativity and better solutions. It is important that each proposal, no matter how unhelpful it seems to be, gets 'unpacked'. Keeping criticism to a minimum – a key element of the brainstorming process – will help create a more open environment, if only by not inviting criticism back when one's own proposals are suggested. However, it is not realistic to expect negotiators to keep themselves wholly free from being critical, especially when they are representing others.

A typical first response to a suggestion you know does not meet your requirements is something like, 'no that won't work because . . . ' This is understandable; it's the win-lose mentality coming to the surface. However it is not the best response. The first step is to clarify exactly what has been proposed. This is particularly important if the proposal has been generated through open discussion – it probably will not have been fully thought through, or be articulated clearly. Also from one's own perspective, we might latch onto the bit we don't like and not 'hear' the rest. So clarifying or checking understanding is a good first response. Note taking helps.

Clarifying also gives the negotiator more time to think through the implications and the opportunity to reflect on the proposal. Reflecting – talking about what the other person has just said – might involve reviewing some of the benefits of the proposal as well as some of the difficulties. Rackman and Carlisle (1978) found that when disagreeing with a proposal, the more successful negotiators tended to give the reasons first. 'Your proposal would mean that we would have to reschedule our delivery schedules – I don't think we can do that' is a better response than, 'we can't accept your proposal because it would mean we would have to reschedule our deliveries.' In the second case the primacy effect means that the proposer would only hear 'we can't accept your proposal' and so be inclined to defend the proposal more strongly with the risk that the exploratory exchanges slip back into positional bargaining. It is often through hearing why a proposal is *not* acceptable that we learn a lot about the other negotiator and what might be acceptable. We tend to be more voluble in explaining why we don't like something than in explaining why we do want something else.

A response to any suggestion should be a mixed message involving some clarification, some reflections on where the proposal might lead and a reminder of what one's own interests are. 'What you are proposing is that we make daily deliveries because this will fit in better with your stock control process. If we were to do that we could possibly combine your delivery with others in the area because each delivery would be smaller, but it would mean we would have to reschedule our deliveries, not only to you but also to these other clients. I'm not sure how your proposal helps us in that regard. As you know our prime concern is to have full-load deliveries; that keeps our costs down and so helps you too.'

Note that at no time did the negotiator say 'no' to the proposal. It is hard not to say 'no' to an unacceptable proposal. If it is not going to be accepted it seems a good idea to have it taken off the table and so allow everyone to move onto another proposal, one that might work. However, it is more helpful to leave unacceptable proposals on the table. There might be an element in it which links with something else later and so becomes useful. Similarly it is helpful – if time permits – to 'park' a deadlocked issue and move onto the next topic rather than trying to force a solution. It may not seem very efficient to leave a lot of loose ends; negotiators like to feel they are making progress and 'tick off' the issues as they are fixed but ambiguity and fluidity are useful. It gives the opportunity to find unexpected linkages and trade-offs (helped by not preparing the issues one at a time). It is really important that someone on the negotiating team takes careful notes of what is being agreed and what is being 'parked'.

Handling rejection

No one likes rejection, not least a negotiator who has put a lot of work into a proposal only to see it turned down by the other side. The first reaction is to go through the proposal again emphasising its benefits – in essence, to contend, stand firm, on the proposal. The critical task, however, is to find out *why* the proposal has been rejected. Often rejections are made in verbal shorthand and are not well explained or they focus on just one aspect and use this to justify rejection of the whole package. So it is helpful to get the other negotiator to explain again their reaction to the proposal; second time around, some more insights might be gained which will help in either reshaping the proposal or in crafting arguments in defence of it.

One way to gain insight into the other party's position when they have rejected a proposal is to ask which part of your proposal they would like you to improve. They will probably respond, 'all of it!' but asking again, 'which part in particular?' might tease out what aspects are of real importance to them.

Handling the process

As in the task of differentiation, summarising, restating and reflecting are useful and constructive activities (see Table 7.1). They help keep the

Table 7.1 Flexibility testing: some helpful and unhelpful behaviours

Helpful	Unhelpful
Tentative proposals	Firm proposals
Other directed proposals	Implications not spelt out
Asking why?, what if? and why not?	Justifying proposals
Open responses to questions	Interrupting
Checking understanding	Criticising
Summarising	Being in a hurry
Restating	
Reflecting	

discussion open. Similarly, interrupting, criticising and generally being in a hurry are counterproductive. They tend to close the discussion down.

Anyone who has seen a video of themselves negotiating will quickly realise that we don't talk in neat structured sentences as if we were reading from a script. Negotiators make a lot of mixed statements (and muddled ones too!). One part of a statement might be firm and rigid; another part might give a hint of flexibility. This provides an opportunity for the good negotiator to respond to the implied flexibility rather than challenge the firmness and so promote openness across the table that might later develop into an opportunity to make and explore new proposals.

This description of the exploration phase presents a different picture of negotiation and how solutions are found to the more normal 'win-win' cooperative, integrative approaches. These other approaches have some validity but we've taken a more pragmatic rather than prescriptive approach. It recognises and seeks to account for some of the 'messiness' of negotiation. As Putnam (1990) suggests, competitiveness and cooperation interact, they seem to feed off each other. And negotiation is two-sided. If one party stands firm and the other party also stands firm this looks to be a competitive positional negotiation. However if both parties stand firm but also stand back and seek opportunities for creative compromise then the competitive standing firm was actually very cooperative. This is why researchers look not only at the immediate reaction to what is said but also to the ensuing frequency of interactions.

An example from a management–union negotiation (Fells, 2000b) will show the difficulty that researchers – and negotiators – have. One issue was the skills allowance for a particular job; the union negotiators had prepared a couple of suggestions which they managed to inject briefly into the debate that was going on across the table. There was no discussion of the suggestions though later one of the management negotiators, while stating his unchanged position, did indicate some openness to the union's points. However, in a later meeting management put forward a revision of one of the union's proposals and this became the basis for settling this particular issue. So one short sentence in the middle of a fairly robust debate, though not discussed at the time, was developed by another negotiator *after* the meeting and turned out to be the most cooperative contribution of the whole session. The critical point is that while it is helpful to talk about cooperation and working together, it is the little things that actually generate cooperation and the solutions that meet the needs of the parties.

The outcome

When does a phase of exploration and creating options come to an end? The negotiators may have found an option that meets both their needs and if so, the negotiations will end with them both fully satisfied. In most cases the negotiators will have found value-adding solutions to some but not all of their issues. Having fully explored a range of possibilities, the negotiators are now much clearer about what they can and cannot agree to; they know the broad shape of the emerging agreement. They know they are not likely to come up with any more creative solutions and realise agreement will come only if one (or both) parties is willing to lower its expectations.

It is easy to see why there is not much 'creative compromise' in negotiation. A negotiator needs to remember – particularly at this point – that achieving one's own goals does not mean the other party has to lose. A good negotiator has to work hard at the micro-level to engender windows of openness whenever they might occur. A negotiator also needs a good understanding of phases – that there are times to differentiate, times to explore and times to exchange.

Exploration phases can decay and be over quickly for three reasons. Firstly, the parties might problem solve unilaterally and come back to the meeting with new proposals. Secondly, as the negotiators begin to see why proposals are being rejected they learn more about the underlying interests which means they might have to go back to differentiating for a while. Neither of these are real difficulties in the process. However, a third way an exploration might end is because one or both negotiators become settlement oriented and defend rather than explore their proposals. This settlement orientation will undermine exploration. It is difficult for one party to keep pushing for openness while the other 'wants to get this settled now'. The negotiator should revisit her strategy and if necessary, revert to contending rather than becoming drawn into conceding.

More positively, if the parties have explored their positions and possible solutions reasonably well, then it will become clear that one of the suggestions is going to 'work'. This mutually prominent alternative becomes the basis for a final agreement. Each party realises that it is going to have to move from its declared positions, a realisation that takes them into the end-game and the task of exchange.

Box 7.2 provides a practical summary of what is involved in exploring for options in a negotiation.

Box 7.2: What does it mean, in practical terms, to explore for options in a negotiation?

Aim

While still having firm commitment to one's underlying interests and needs, to propose new options or openly consider options proposed by the other party.

Method

A combination of exploration and creative compromise.

To do it well

Clearly state what is really important to you (i.e. your requirements without which there will be no agreement) and why it is important.
Invite the other party to state and restate their interests, what is really important to them – without interruption.
Understand what is important to them and show them that you understand.
Search for differing preferences, look for linkages between issues.
Introduce any new proposals as possibilities for consideration rather than as a closing solution.
If proposals are rejected, don't defend them but find out why they are considered to be unacceptable.
Try to build on other people's ideas; clarify and reflect.
If you disagree with another's proposal, give your reasons but don't express your disagreement up front.
Keep all the issues open.
Try to 'fractionalise' the issues, to split them into component parts.
Evaluate any proposal in terms of what you might gain, not what you might lose.
Regularly summarise.
Openly reflect on how you think the negotiations are proceeding.

Indicators that the phase is coming to an end

An emerging realisation that one of the proposals on the table is going to be broadly acceptable to both parties but that more bargaining is going to be required.

To do it poorly; that is, things to avoid doing!

Finding fault in everyone else's proposals, especially interrupting them to tell them.

Telling everyone how reasonable and cooperative you are being.

Using your proposal to 'squash' someone else's (i.e. don't immediately follow another's suggestion with one of your own).

Applying time pressure.

Blaming others for not seeing what's needed to reach an agreement.

Remember

The creativity might be in just one comment from another negotiator; it may not even be a proposal as such.

8 The end-game exchange

Negotiators cannot keep differentiating and exploring forever. At some point they have to make a decision to either reach an agreement or walk away. This is the 'end-game' where much of the exchanging of offers takes place.

In really competitive negotiations almost the whole negotiation may have been an 'end-game' as each side, from the outset, has pressured the other to agree. However, as we have seen, the better negotiators take the process through phases to create value before negotiating over the final outcome. Even so, the 'end-game' is still seen as the business end of a negotiation. This chapter examines how to manage this crucial final and often competitive phase. This is another 'how to' chapter using the issue, process, action and outcome framework from Chapter 5 and concluding with practical summaries of the three closing strategy options: clear-cut compromise, contend and concede. Because of the competitive nature of the end-game, Appendix 6 – what to do if you find yourself in a boxing match – is relevant.

Exchanging offers

Negotiation is a process where two parties have differences that they need to resolve . . . By this stage the parties should have a good understanding of what their differences are and why they need to resolve them. This 'need to resolve' has probably got a lot to do with their walk-away options being less attractive than the prospects of an agreement. Because of this they have been trying to reach agreement through exploring for options and have probably come to a broad understanding of what a final agreement might look like. Their respective positions are on the table. The final task

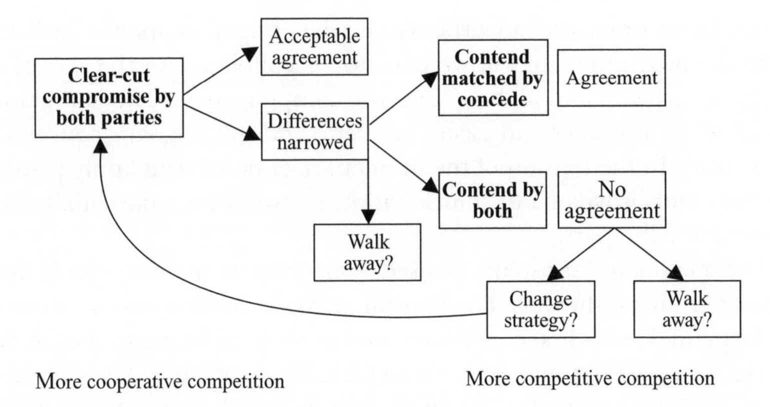

Figure 8.1: Exchanging offers: end-game strategies

is to bring these together through exchanging offers and so achieve an agreement.

The end-game can unfold in a variety of ways (Figure 8.1). Negotiators can move towards the middle ground between their stated positions. This involves an element of cooperation in what is essentially a competitive process, otherwise there would be no *joint* concession making. Clear-cut compromises often result in agreement but sometimes the parties might find that they have only been able to narrow their differences. In this case the negotiations become more competitive. One party decides that it can make no further concessions and puts a final offer on the table. It stands firm – contends – on this final position; agreement will be reached only if the other party concedes. If both contend – another common variant of the end-game – then there is deadlock. However there have been many times when a party has put its final position on the table, threatening to walk away, only to find that it must rethink its position and see again if there might not be some middle ground – another clear-cut compromise – rather than no agreement at all.

In practice, negotiators switch – often instinctively – between contending and looking for a compromise so that the end-game can unfold in many ways. (This is why when looking at the research, the final stage of a negotiation is often less clear than others.) Rather than categorise all the possibilities, the critical point to recognise is that the end-game is seriously dynamic as the negotiators manoeuvre to get the best outcome.

How do negotiators manage the end-game? With great difficulty! The incentive to wrap up the negotiation is strong. Time pressure, the concern about walking away, the need to achieve an outcome given all the work that has been put in so far, all push negotiators towards an agreement.

At the same time, the uncertainty of what might happen – 'will they make the next move or will we have to?' – coupled with the risk of not reaching agreement at all heightens the competiveness. The end-game is a time when mistakes can easily be made and unnecessary concessions given away. In the tension of the moment negotiators can apply pressure unwisely and provoke a deadlock with the result that a potentially good agreement falls apart.

The negotiator must be focused. One step at a time, much like a performer on a tightrope. The tension increases as he steps out from the platform (makes his first concession) and the risks of falling to the left or to the right (being too tough or too conciliatory) are obvious. He is probably being carefully watched as he moves forward, each step making it more difficult to retreat. Of course, he has it much easier than a negotiator – no one is trying to move the other end of the rope!

The issue dimension

At this point, the negotiators will find themselves left with two positions on the table, each party's position being unacceptable to the other. How should they proceed? Firstly, the Strategy Framework (Chapter 3) will help a negotiator analyse the situation. Increasing time pressure and poor walk-away alternatives push negotiators towards agreement. If achieving what was expected is now seen as less important compared to achieving an agreement; if each party's instrumental concern for the other (without whom there will be no agreement) is higher and if each party expects the other to be in the same position, they will work together to find a clear-cut compromise. However, if a negotiator has reached the limit of her flexibility and is prepared to walk away rather than make further concessions then she should contend, particularly if she thought the other party was not interested in a clear-cut compromise. If what is being offered by the other party is better than the walk-away alternative, this suggests a concede strategy, particularly if the other party is expected to contend on their offer.

A negotiator must check two things at all times as the end-game unfolds (Box 8.1). The first is to re-examine the purpose of the negotiation – what was the reason for entering into them? In view of all that has been learned through the negotiation, what is being achieved? The second is to examine what would happen if there is no agreement – what would be the consequences of walking away from the negotiations?

Box 8.1: Taking stock in the end-game

What are our key goals?
Why did we need to enter these negotiations to achieve them?
Does what is now on offer look like a good agreement?
Check your goals
If we walk away now, can we do better than the offer that is on the table?
If our BATNA is so good, why have we not walked away before now?
Check your BATNA

The more cooperative end-game through clear-cut compromise

If the parties are stuck on their respective positions and need to find something else that they can both agree to, Fisher, Ury and Patton (1991) suggest a way that might prevent the negotiation becoming an unhelpful trial of strength. They recognise in their Model of Principled Negotiation that although parties might try hard to invent options for mutual gain they may not fully succeed, leaving some final points of disagreement. To deal with this they suggest that negotiators look to an objective standard. The logic is compelling – both parties can agree with a standard rather than argue with each other.

For example, two companies might agree that it is in their best interests to have a two-year supply agreement but are still in disagreement over prices in the second year of the contract. To agree to review the price might give rise to an unhealthy competitive negotiation in 12 months' time. If they can agree a principle now and write it into the contract that removes the risk of a confrontation later. Clearly a useful objective standard is the consumer price index (CPI) so they could write a clause to the effect that in 12 months' time the supply price will be varied in accordance with CPI.

However, while not denying the power of this approach, negotiators should also be aware of an inherent weakness, namely the risk that the 'objective' standard becomes a proxy for a preferred position. This risk is present because, as Pruitt and Carnevale (1993) point out, there is usually more than one particular standard. In the example above, should the price index be the Australia-wide consumer price index or one based on price trends within the industry? Both are equally objective and their existence would be known by both parties before they entered into the negotiation. So the supplier might well promote the industry index believing it is likely to increase more than the CPI; the purchaser might suggest that the industry figures are not quite so reliable and so they could rely on the Bureau of Statistics' CPI data (which he expects will be lower over the coming 12 months). Even so, negotiators should be alert to the power of finding a standard they can both agree to, particularly if the negotiators have to report back to constituents – 'we were deadlocked but to go with a CPI increase seemed fair.'

Alternatively the negotiators might just split the difference between their two positions, which is relatively straightforward if dealing with money issues. If there are several issues remaining, it might be possible to trade one issue for another. Reciprocity and notions of fairness become important because negotiators are likely to reject an offer, even if it actually benefits them, if they think the outcome will in some way be unfair.

The more competitive end-game through contending (or conceding)

If a negotiator can make no further concessions then he can only achieve an agreement if the other party makes more concessions. To achieve this he has to adopt a contending – standing firm – strategy to force the other party to concede, which raises the level of competitiveness in the negotiations. There is one more end-game scenario. If it becomes clear that the other party is not going to make any further concessions then to get an agreement, he has to make the final concession himself.

The process dimension

The more cooperative end-game through clear-cut compromise

The critical point about the clear-cut compromise strategy is that it will only occur if *both* parties undertake it so part of the process is in ensuring mutuality. Trust and reciprocity – two links in negotiation's DNA – are really important at this point. The trust is not the generalised trust of whether there are commonalities and mutual understandings but the more calculative situation-based trust – if I make a concession can I trust the other negotiator to reciprocate? It is therefore important to set the process up rather than make a concession and hope the other party follows suit. 'Talk process' (Box 8.2) before making any moves on the issue. In the end-game of one negotiation (Fells, 2000c, p. 111) with the parties' different positions on pay firmly on the table, one of the management negotiators informally sounded out one of the union officials. Both agreed the negotiations were deadlocked, neither wanted industrial action and both thought somebody had to do something to move the negotiations forward. There was no discussion of the substantive issues but by the end

Box 8.2: What does it mean to 'talk process'?

Sounding out

Talk about what you think should happen next in the negotiation; talk about the need to look for some sort of compromise solution (keep it a bit vague) and look for an indication from the other party that they also think the negotiations are at that stage.

Making a move

If by their response you get the impression that the other party also thinks that the negotiation has reached a stage where both parties need to find some middle ground, *then* you can propose a compromise solution.

Trying again later

If their response suggests they are still expecting you to make all the concessions, then just stand firm and restate what is important to you, i.e. continue contending.

After some further exchanges, test out again whether they are ready to compromise but don't make a move on the issue until you believe they will reciprocate.

of the conversation each knew that a compromise offer would not be greeted by a contending strategy from the other party.

Negotiators are more willing to make a concessionary move if they know where the process is likely to end and that they won't get drawn into making unexpected concessions. Having confidence that both sides are moving on the issue reinforces a negotiator's sense of having some control over the outcome. In this regard some of the advice on concession making – such as that it is usually productive to concede on a minor issue but better not to concede first on a major one (Hendon, Roy and Ahmed, 2003, p. 81) – emphasises the competitive orientation of the end-game and seems to forget that negotiation is two-sided. If both parties follow this advice they necessarily continue deadlocked on the major items.

A negotiator can protect his position while seeking a compromise solution by making 'if you, then I' offers. A human resources manager is seeking to limit the payment of overtime to the weekend and stop the present arrangement of overtime being paid after 38 hours worked during the week. The staff representatives are apprehensive of any change which might impact on their earnings but are prepared to be a bit flexible and so suggest a compromise in a conditional way, 'if you are prepared to pay overtime after 40 hours worked then we might look at that.' Should the HR manager indicate that 40 hours might be a solution, then the staff representatives can be more explicit about their proposal, confident that they won't get drawn into yet more concessions.

However, if the HR manager responds by still insisting that overtime be paid only for the weekends, then the staff negotiators should simply restate their position of no change. By holding to their respective positions both parties would be contending, expecting the other to concede. The ensuing deadlock should cause them to review their walk-away alternatives, which might be quite drastic for both parties. Only then, and as a last resort, should the staff representatives consider making a unilateral concession and formally propose that overtime be payable after 40 rather than 38 hours.

Making offers

As the previous example has shown, it is during the end-game that the negotiators are faced with the stark choice of reaching agreement or walking away. Up to this point the BATNAs, the walk-away alternatives, have been almost theoretical. Threatening the other party that you will go to court always sounds a good alternative until the moment you are faced with closing the negotiations down and relying 100% on your lawyer.

It follows that a negotiator should focus on presenting the benefits of an offer, particularly if it is a final offer, in comparison with the costs of walking away. Negotiation might be viewed as a process of restructuring the alternatives negotiators believe they have open to them. It is in the end-game that these alternatives become clear and so the points of comparison become important as is shown in Figure 8.2.

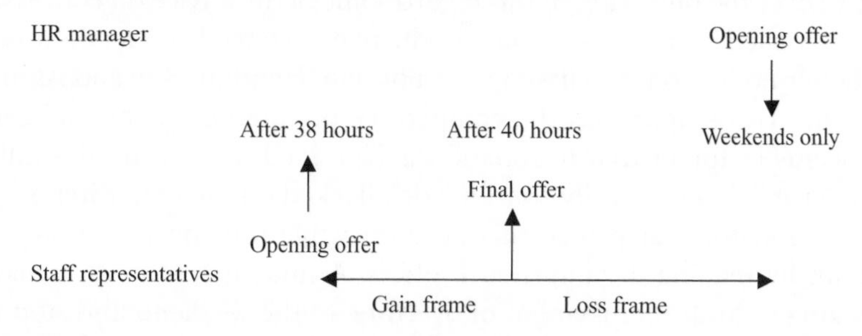

Figure 8.2: Framing in the end-game

Returning to our staff representatives who are trying to get the HR manager to agree to their final offer of overtime after 40 hours, there are two ways they can make this offer. To do it in these terms: 'I know you wanted weekend-only overtime but the most the staff will agree to is 40 hours', immediately focuses on the 'loss' the HR manager would be making – a loss frame (see Figure 8.2). Alternatively, to put the offer as: 'you know it has always been 38 hours and that is what we told you when you first asked for our position but we think we can extend it to 40' places the emphasis on how much the company is gaining and so makes it easier to accept. Shaping an offer in a 'gain frame' generates more concessions than a loss-framed offer (particularly if the negotiator can have been made to feel positively disposed towards you earlier in the negotiation). We tend to feel our losses more (Carnevale, 2008).

When presenting an offer it also helps to refer to what has been achieved so far in the negotiation and, if relevant, to the transaction costs of having to start all over again with another party. The benefits of reaching an agreement (however small) should be emphasised. The intent is to convey the impression of both parties working together to get the best deal in the circumstances. This working together aspect can be emphasised by pointing to the benefits for both parties in reaching agreement and to the cost facing both if there is no agreement, rather than just pointing out the other party's costs if they fail to agree. Similarly presenting an offer in relation to the other party's walk-away point (or what you believe it to be) leaves them with the choice, rather than feeling they are being forced to accept something.

The more competitive end-game through contending (or conceding)

If a negotiator plans to make a final offer, then it is critical to check that if the offer is not accepted then the walk-away alternative is better than anything which might be gained from further negotiation. Secondly, the offer must be final and be seen to be final. The whole intent is to present to the other negotiator a choice between just two options – the offer on the table or the consequences of no agreement. Walton and McKersie (1965) suggest that making an external commitment helps. A CEO making a final bid for shares in another company might convey a degree of finality 'My final offer is $5 per share. I just happened to meet a finance reporter and he's written a short piece about my offer. Should be in the paper today so there it is in print for all to read. You can't expect me to go beyond that.' (However, if he had finished with '. . . you can't expect me to go beyond that today' the potential vendor might just wonder if the price might be different on another day.)

A first offer tends to become an 'anchor' for the negotiations and so going first has an advantage (Galinsky and Mussweiler, 2001; Magee, Galinsky and Gruenfeld, 2007) (though we should note that these offers are in the context of an experimental negotiation, not case studies). So what if the other party has made the first offer? The research suggests that to focus on walk-away options or one's own objectives will tend to counter the anchoring effect of the other party's first offer. In essence, put something else on the table to talk about so that the discussion does not focus on the other party's offer (keep the negotiation two-sided).

Conceding is never easy but there are times when it has to be done. The critical point is to be clear on what is being agreed to and that it *will* conclude the negotiations. Some negotiators like the 'disappearing concession trick' whereby when agreement is just about to be achieved they put another small issue on the table or revisit a point that has previously been agreed. As always, the walk-away alternative is the reference point when deciding how to respond.

The action dimension

Managing concessions

The end-game can be a difficult time because by this stage it is obvious to the negotiator that he will achieve less than he had set out to do but equally compelling will be the prospect of not reaching agreement at all. However as the end-game unfolds it is necessary to guard against the risk of the process getting its own momentum and leading to hasty decisions. Two ways to counter this are clarity and checking. This is not the time for loose ends. Being clear on what is said, offered, rejected or agreed to is vital, which means being clear oneself and checking your understanding of what the other negotiator is saying, offering, rejecting or agreeing to. Checking helps slow the negotiations and guards against hasty reactions in the tension of the moment. Taking time to write down offers as they are presented – even though you may have discussed something like this offer many times before – is useful. Summarising what is being agreed is another useful way of taking the pace off the negotiations (see Table 8.1).

Table 8.1 Concession making: some helpful and unhelpful behaviours

Helpful	Unhelpful
Making clear statements	'Fudging' concessions and agreements
Positive framing	Reiterating what is being given up
Referring to both parties' BATNAs	Making unsustainable threats
Checking understanding	Being in a hurry
Summarising	Blaming the other party
Allowing reactive behaviour	

It is important to recognise that making concessions is not an easy thing to do. When making concessions negotiators incur both position loss – they will achieve less than they hoped for; and image loss – they seem to lack firmness and so might make yet more concessions (Pruitt, 1981). Image loss is important vis-à-vis both the opposing negotiator and any constituents. So, rather than an explicit, 'we agree to your position' the concession might be a quietly spoken 'no problem' or 'we'll look at that' with the item being dropped off the agenda for the next meeting (Fells, 2000b). Negotiators must be alert to these muted changes in position and not cause the opposing negotiator to lose more face than is necessary. If the negotiator has been resolutely arguing for a particular outcome but is now going to have to agree to something less, he may feel the need to vent his disappointment and get a bit of history 'off his chest' or say a few home truths about your company and how you do business. This is not the time to react but to let him work through it and make the concession that you want him to make.

The outcome

What should have been achieved is an outcome that meets the needs of both parties. More realistically the outcome will be accepted because it is better than walking away. The outcome should not leave one party feeling that they have lost, intending to claw back that loss during the life of the agreement. Neither of the parties should have agreed to something is that is inferior to what they might have achieved through some other means. As we have seen the final negotiated outcome will be achieved though either a cooperative process of compromise or a competitive process of contending and conceding. Figure 8.3 and Box 8.3 summarise the compromise route to an agreement while Figure 8.4 and Boxes 8.4 and 8.5 summarise the main elements of the more competitive end-game.

The final outcome of the negotiation is not the agreement itself but the way in which the agreement is implemented and whether at the end of this time, both parties feel that they had achieved all that they expected to achieve when they shook hands at the negotiating table.

Issue dimension +	Process dimension +	Action dimension	→ Outcome
What are we doing about the issue?	What are we trying to achieve at this point in in the negotiation?	How are we going to do it?	What should be achieved by this phase of the negotiation?
Clear-cut compromise To find some middle ground in the expectation that agreement will then be achieved on some if not all the issues.	**Exchange** To reach agreement.	**Joint concession making** Make clear 'if you...then we...' statements. Emphasise benefits of proposed agreement relative to no agreement. Check the detail. *Don't:* Agree to what you can't deliver.	A possible agreement. Or at least, a smaller agenda of unresolved items.

Figure 8.3: Exchanging offers in a more cooperative end-game through clear-cut compromise

Issue dimension +	Process dimension +	Action dimension	→ Outcome
What are we doing about the issue?	What are we trying to achieve at this point in in the negotiation?	How are we going to do it?	What should be achieved by this phase of the negotiation?
Contend To stand firm in the expectation that the other party will now agree with you.	**Exchange** To reach agreement (or walk away).	**Concession making (by the other party)** Make your position clear and final. Emphasise the benefits of the proposed agreement relative to no agreement. *Don't:* – gloat over concessions	Agreement. Or a confident decision to walk away.
Concede To reduce one's demands in the expectation that the other party will find them acceptable.	**Exchange** To reach agreement.	**Concession making** Make the concession clear. Emphasise the extent of the concession for the benefit of agreement. Check the detail. *Don't:* Agree to what you can't deliver.	Agreement.

Figure 8.4: Exchanging offers in a more competitive end-game through contending (or conceding)

Box 8.3: What does it mean, in practical terms, to seek a clear-cut compromise?

Aim

Having explored as many possible solutions as seems reasonable but without complete agreement, then to set up a process by which each party can indicate that it is prepared to reduce its claims and work towards a compromise solution.

Method

Clear-cut compromise and exchange.

To do it well

Clearly state what is really important to you and why it is important.

Restate what you believe is important to the other party.

Talk process, talk about the need for finding compromise solutions and ensure the other party also sees the need for making a compromise.

Emphasise the benefits to both parties of an agreement and the costs to both parties of not reaching agreement.

Make your proposal clearly, preferably 'if you will ... then I will ...'

Allow the other party to backtrack over old ground or make extreme demands (particularly if they are negotiating on behalf of others) as part of the process of coming to terms with the need to accept a lesser outcome.

Be clear on what you are agreeing to.

Check any emerging agreements against your BATNA.

Indicators that the phase is coming to an end

Agreement.

One (or both) parties being clearly resistant to making any further concessions.

To do it poorly; that is, things to avoid doing!

Making a concession in the hope that the other party will do the same.

Making lots of threats knowing you can't carry them out.

Blaming the other party for not being reasonable.

Making lots of rapid offers and trades, losing track of what is being agreed to.

Adding new issues onto the table in the hope of getting a bonus.

Remember

It takes two to reach a compromise.

Box 8.4: What does it mean, in practical terms, to secure a concession?

Aim

Having reached as many compromise agreements on issues as seems possible, to bring the negotiation to a close by requiring the other party meet your final position, failing which you will walk away (essentially end-game contending).

Method

Contending.

To do it well

Clearly state your final position, making it clear that it is final.

Check your BATNA.
Emphasise the benefits to both parties of achieving an agreement.
Allow the other party whatever rationale they chose ('new' information, the bigger picture, the future etc.) to justify their concessions even though you might not believe it to be valid.
Allow the other party to backtrack over old ground or make extreme demands (particularly if they are negotiating on behalf of others) as part of the process of coming to terms with the need to accept a lesser outcome.
Apply pressure, but steadily though reiterating your closing position.
Leave the other party with the final choice of accepting your offer or of walking away.

To do it poorly; that is, things to avoid doing!

Making lots of threats.
Keep on referring to your win or even to a 'win win' situation (doing this becomes an 'irritator').
Drawing attention to the fact that they are now accepting something they had previously said was unacceptable.
Blaming the other party.
Telling them that you are a better negotiator than they are.

Remember

You can win this particular negotiation but there is no need to make an enemy as well.

Box 8.5: What does it mean, in practical terms, to concede?

Aim

Having reached as many compromise agreements on issues as seems possible, to bring the negotiation to a close by agreeing with the remaining demands of the other party.

Method

Conceding.

To do it well

Check that what you are about to agree to is better than your BATNA.
Clearly state what you are agreeing to.
Emphasise the benefits to both parties of agreement being achieved (i.e. that your concession is a positive contribution).

To do it poorly; that is, things to avoid doing!

Blaming the other party for forcing you to concede.
Agreeing to whatever they want just to end the negotiation.

Remember

That the light at the end of the tunnel – the prospect of an agreement – may be a train!

9 Negotiating on behalf of others

Negotiation is made even more complex when negotiators act on behalf of others as delegates from the group or as formally appointed agents. Few negotiate solely on their own account – two business development teams negotiating over a potential joint venture represent their respective companies as does an IT manager negotiating to acquire a new system for her company. A union official negotiating a new enterprise agreement represents the membership. A delegation to the local council seeking a change in the parking regulations represents their neighbours up and down their street. When the CEO of Air Berlin negotiated over lunch and then shook hands with the CEO of Airbus on a $7 billion deal to supply airplanes, both had complete authority but both were representing their companies and all their employees (Newhouse, 2000, p. 40). In these situations negotiators can find themselves acting as a bridge, spanning between the two sides and forming a channel of communication and accommodation.

This chapter will consider the practical consequences of having to negotiate on behalf of others – whom we call the constituents – rather than for oneself. The general proposition is that these negotiations are typically more competitive and positional than negotiation between two individuals. This chapter will examine why this is so and suggest what might be done about it. Much of the research into collective negotiation has been drawn from the workplace and management–union bargaining but the principles apply in all contexts. Appendices 7 and 8 add some further thoughts about managing workplace and business negotiations.

The structure of constituency negotiations

The most obvious and important point about the presence of constituencies is that there will be three negotiations, not just one. In addition to the

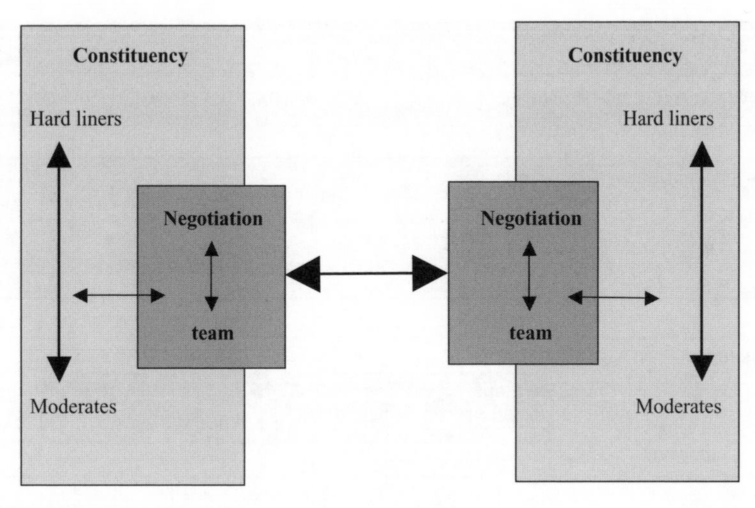

Figure 9.1: Two parties: three or more negotiations

negotiations across the table *between* the parties there will also be negotiations *within* each party (Figure 9.1). The remit given by the constituency to their representatives is important, and then there will be yet more negotiation within the teams as they prepare to meet each other.

Any group planning to send someone to negotiate on their behalf first has to give their representative some direction. There is no reason to presume that the group will be of one mind (negotiation is 'messy') so there will probably be a lot of negotiation within the group itself to come to a collective point of view which the representative can then present to the other party. For example, a group of residents meet, intending to send a delegation to their local council about difficulties in parking their cars when football games are being played at the local stadium. They all agree that they want to have space reserved outside their own homes but they do not agree on whether it should only be on match days only or also when there is a local music concert or permanently because there is often a parking overflow from the local shopping centre.

Not only do the neighbours differ on what they want the council to do, they also have different views on how their case should be presented. Some 'hard liners' want to present a firm strong position while others (who see themselves as 'moderates' but as 'weak' by the hard liners) are prepared to present the problem, trusting the local council to come up with a good solution. Before they can meet with the council the group has to reconcile these differing views on both the issue and the process. Consequently they

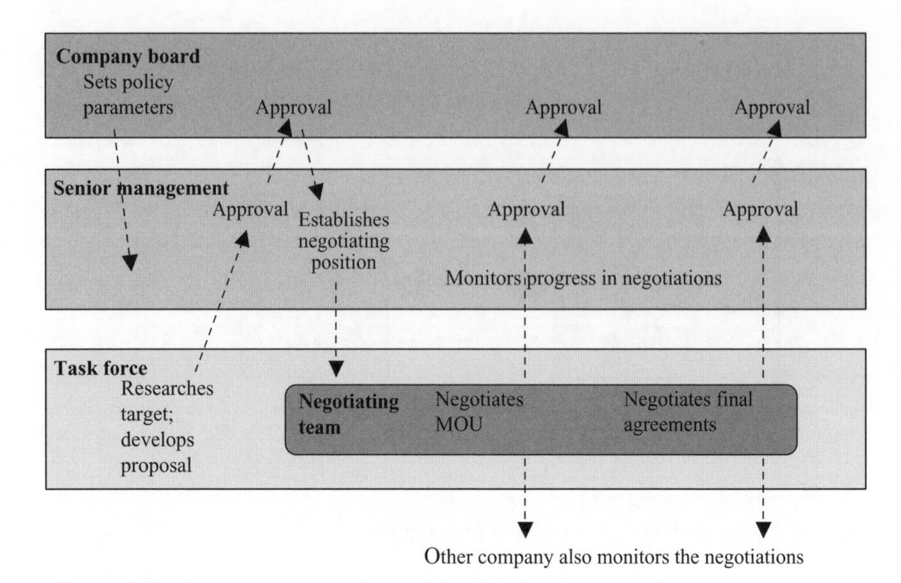

Figure 9.2: Business negotiation: some layers of decision making

will find themselves going through the phases of negotiation – differentiation, exploration and exchange – to get to a point of agreement on what their representatives should say to the council. These representatives (if there is more than one) will discuss – even negotiate – between themselves to agree on the best way to proceed and just how much emphasis to place on the points they have to negotiate over. They may even find themselves in negotiation with those they are going to represent before setting off to meet the other party.

Similarly within the council there will be those who are sympathetic to the residents' situation but others who take the view that football has been played at the stadium for many years and all the residents knew of the problems when they moved into the area. So the council will also have to negotiate within itself to formulate a coherent response to the residents' petition and their representatives will have to agree amongst themselves – another negotiation – about how best to proceed.

In another example, Figure 9.2 shows the main elements of internal and external negotiations in a formal business negotiation such as over an acquisition or joint venture. The terminology differs from Figure 9.1 but the essential elements of where one group is negotiating on behalf of another are present. Although the company constitutes one party to the negotiations it comprises several layers. The company board has established its policies on business development; potential acquisitions or joint ventures will be researched until a target company is identified that meets the parameters set by the board. Once a formal proposal has been developed and approved, a negotiation team will be established to pursue the proposal. The first stage in negotiation would typically be a memorandum of understanding (MOU) covering the main elements of the proposed agreement. If approved by both companies this MOU would be signed and negotiations would resume to finalise the detail and prepare the necessary legal documents for final approval and signing. The level of authority given to the negotiating team would vary between companies depending on their management structure but generally the team would need the authority to negotiate, referring back to senior management only when critical issues impacted upon their negotiating limits.

The public nature of constituency negotiations

Figure 9.3 provides another example of how complex the structure of negotiations can become. This portrayal of an enterprise negotiation for a group of employees in a public hospital shows that reaching agreement across the negotiation table is not the end of the process. Although employed by the hospital, the outcome of the employees' wage negotiations was subject to third party approval (the government) which, incidentally, had also set the policy context for this and all other public sector wage negotiations. This complex process has its private sector equivalent when a large company sets a central wages policy for all its operating units and then delegates the task of negotiating agreements to each unit.

There is one contrast between these business and workplace examples. The former would have been done as quietly as possible, not in the public eye. (The unpredictable effect on the companies' share prices could change the valuations which are at the heart of the negotiation, as happened when the proposed Qantas–British Airways merger negotiations became public, *Australian Financial Review*, 4 December 2008, p. 61.) However many constituency negotiations are far more public from the outset and, as in the case of the hospital negotiation, include a public approval process. Agreements reached in the international arena are often subject to ratification by the elected representatives in government. Those seeking to negotiate free trade agreements have to understand the influence producer groups can exert over the United States Congress or the political pressure of farmers in many parts of Europe. Once a community or environmental issue gains public attention (which may have been the result of the campaigners' pre-negotiation preparation) far more people become interested in the outcome. The larger audience makes it more difficult for either party to back down from public statements and often the realisation

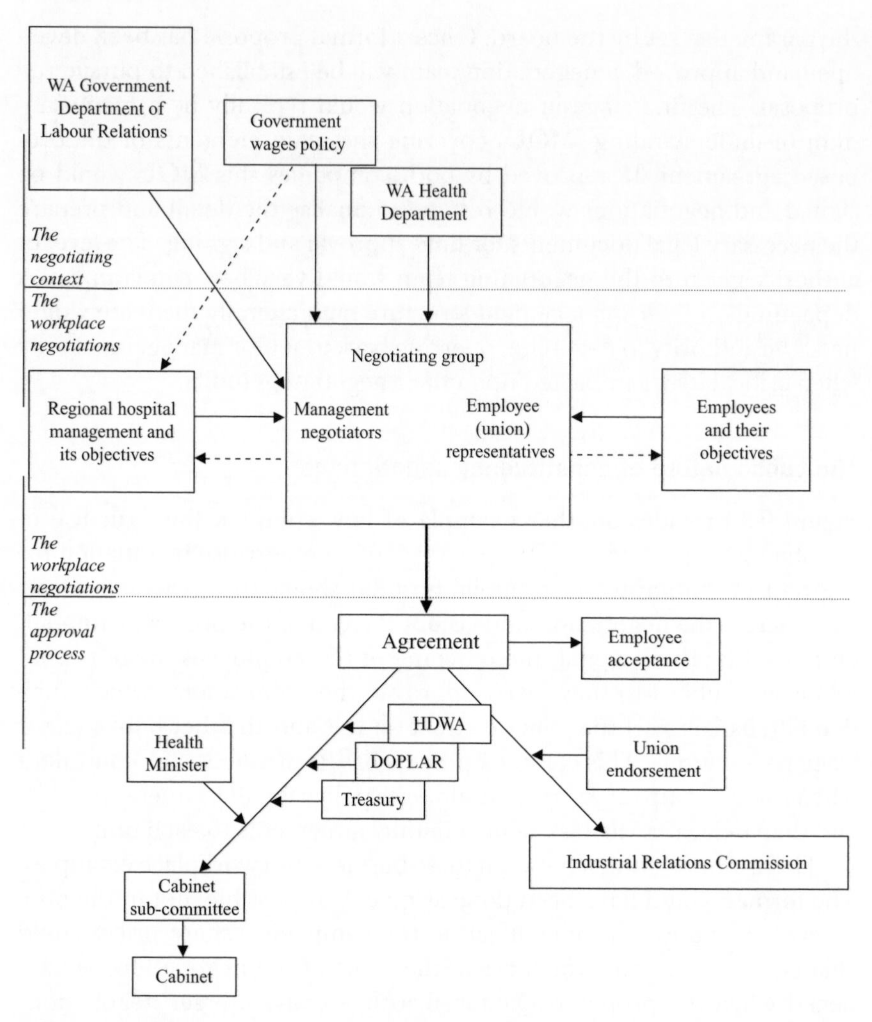

Note:
HDWA – Health Department of Western Australia
DOPLAR – Department of Productivity and Labour Relations

Figure 9.3: The agreement-reaching process at a regional hospital (Fells, 2001)

that any agreement will set a precedent for subsequent cases only adds to the pressure to stand firm.

The public nature of these negotiations highlights an important point when negotiating with someone representing a constituency group – the task is not to convince the person sitting across the table but to convince them (and then help them) to convince the people they represent. Any problems that one negotiator may have moving their constituents towards a point of agreement are problems for both sides. Negotiators should not leave themselves open to the final plea from their opponent that 'you have to give me something to go back to my people with'. However, they should be alert to shaping proposals in a way that will help the representatives when they present them to their constituents, or even perhaps increasing their own competitive stance to assist the other negotiator to convince his constituency group that no more concessions will be forthcoming.

What does this complex structure do to the DNA of negotiation?

When negotiators are acting on behalf of others the two strands of the negotiation DNA are 'fatter' and more complex, each containing within it another negotiation DNA. The other elements of the negotiation DNA are also present in both the intra- and inter-party negotiations (Table 9.1) but the inter-party negotiations are made more difficult because the people who will be making the decisions on the issue – the respective

Table 9.1 How the negotiation DNA is complicated by the presence of constituencies

Negotiation DNA	Constituency effect
The two parties	The strands of the DNA are now much larger and each strand contains a negotiation DNA of its own
Reciprocity	Reciprocity between those at the negotiation table is still present but there is no basis for reciprocity between their respective constituents
Trust	Trust still needs to be built between those at the negotiation table but ways of building trust between their respective constituents are limited
Power	Power is still best understood in terms of walk away alternatives, but those of the constituents, not the negotiators
Information exchange	Information is still a critical factor but the constituencies are likely to have different and probably less information than their negotiators
Ethics	Ethical behaviour is still a critical element
Outcome	The focus of the negotiation is still the agreement and how it will be implemented but implementation will be by people other than those at the negotiation table

constituents – are not at the negotiating table. They do not gain as much insight into the priorities, limits and non-negotiation alternatives of the other party as do their negotiators. They do not build trust so easily and so are less willing to consider new proposals. The fundamental dynamics – the issue strategies and process tasks – remain the same; though the exploration phase may be even more constrained and the whole negotiation is likely to be more competitive (see Box 9.1). The real difficulty is that the strategies and tasks have to unfold across three negotiations at once!

Box 9.1: Reasons for increased competitiveness in collective/constituency negotiations

The difficulties in developing the party's stance to take into the negotiations; it is easier to get broad support for a position than it is to get endorsement to a broad statement of interests.
The need to convey an image of representation, that the negotiator does actually represent the constituents' views; this tends to lead to high opening positions being developed as these will have broad support.
The need to report back induces firmness at the bargaining table, not only as a tactic but also in order to avoid loss of face with the constituents.
The constituents generally expect their negotiators to act 'tough'.

The role of the negotiation representative

There are two good reasons to appoint a negotiation representative in addition to the practical one that the constituency group itself is too large to meet directly with the other party. Firstly a carefully selected representative, particularly if a professional, such as a union official, a lawyer or a diplomat, will bring expertise to the negotiation. This expertise should comprise a broader knowledge of the issues and of what settlements are possible together with experience in knowing how to best manage the process. In addition, representatives can establish trust – at least a working relationship – across the table, one professional to another, even though they might be stridently arguing over the issues. This interpersonal trust can help the negotiations over sticking points and not least at the points when trust is really needed: is the information being provided to me true? Can the representative be expected to reciprocate? And will he do what he says he will do?

The second reason for appointing representatives is that they tend to be tough negotiators and can get good outcomes for their party. Early research suggested that to get the best outcome, the representatives should be appointed rather than elected (elected representatives feel they have been given a free hand) from outside the group and be required to report back (Klimoski and Ash, 1974; Klimoski, 1972; Breaugh and Klimoski, 1977; Ben-Yoav and Pruitt, 1984b, Klimoski and Breaugh, 1977). These all cause the representatives to contend more strongly on the issue and so achieve better results (though at the increased risk of deadlock). 'My hands are tied' can be an effective closing commitment tactic (Friedland, 1983).

However, negotiating on behalf of others is not easy. If the representative is too tough, then a deadlock might result even though the constituency group was prepared to settle for less. On the other hand being too flexible in searching for a solution can result in 'agreements' being rejected by the constituency and the reputation of the representative being damaged. Representative negotiators experience the tension that arises from the mixed-motive nature of negotiation, the tension between striving to fully achieve the constituent's stated goal and being prepared to accept a lesser outcome rather than none at all. The implications for how the process is managed are explored below.

A further consideration is whether the interests of the negotiators align directly with those they are representing. House agents act on behalf of the seller and will supposedly get the best price because their fee is based on the sale price but their personal interest is in closing the deal and moving onto the next (Levitt and Dubner, 2005). Managers regularly assert that union officials are only playing tough because soon they will have to face their membership for re-election to keep their jobs, the implication being that the members are more moderate and reasonable than the elected officials. (The research findings cited above suggest that what is more important in determining a contending stance is the requirement of the union officials to report back and have the potential outcome voted on.)

For the best way to manage the relationship between a principal (an individual or group) and their negotiation representative, Fisher and Davis (1999) suggest the 'agent' (their term for a representative) should have no authority to settle an issue but should be given discretion as to how the negotiations are to be conducted. She should focus on the underlying interests and priorities rather than be settlement oriented. As the principal gains a greater understanding of the other party (through their agent engaging in good communication with them about the negotiation) they should give their agent more flexibility to explore and make recommendations. Final decision making should always reside with the principal.

The effect of constituency on the process

The three parallel negotiations each involve differentiation, exploration and exchange and the key tasks of information exchange, flexibility testing and concession making. In a one-on-one negotiation there is no reason that both negotiators should automatically progress through the phases and tasks in parallel, hence the need to manage the negotiations and to work as much as possible to a similar script. This element of pace and progression through the phases becomes more important when there are negotiations in parallel, making the task of managing them more difficult.

The tension representative negotiators face arises because they are in a boundary role position (Druckman, 1978; Walton and McKersie, 1965). They have to be advocates for their constituents and yet be responsive to the other party – and persuade the constituents to be responsive too – if agreement is to be achieved. Consequently constituents might find their representatives negotiating more with them than with the other party! Walton and McKersie (1965) outlined some of the tactical possibilities for representative negotiators, not the least being to try to moderate the demands of the constituents before presenting a position to the other party. However, to convey an image of strength the constituency has to be 'solidly behind' their representatives when their opening position is presented. This is just one of many tactical dilemmas faced by representative negotiators.

As the negotiations progress the constituency groups' expectations may have to be negotiated downwards even further by their representatives. The more diverse the constituency the more mediation skills are needed by the representative negotiator, particularly in international negotiations where the constituency might actually be a number of government departments, each with its own committed stance on the issue under negotiation (Druckman, 1978; Fisher, 1989). In the workplace, particularly on the workers' side of a negotiation, leadership is needed to bring the constituency to a point of agreement (Fells and Savery, 1984; Friedman, 1994; Walton and McKersie, 1965; Warr, 1973). Warr's in-depth study of a lengthy management–union negotiation shows that when the negotiations started the membership were solidly behind their opening position but thereafter and throughout the negotiations there was a broad spread of opinion – some in favour, others opposed to – the latest management position (Warr, 1973). Another aspect of leadership is providing the constituency with a clear rationale, both for the state of the negotiations and for what is being agreed (Morley, 1992). Only when the emerging agreement 'makes sense' to the constituency group are they likely to commit to it. This is why union negotiators need the confidence and authority to manage membership meetings and why management negotiators should realise that when they present their offers they have to be framed with the employees in mind, not just the board of directors.

The Forth Bridge in Scotland provides a useful image of a negotiator acting on behalf of others. The bridge – the first major steel bridge in the world – works on the cantilever principle, the extended arms of the towers balancing out across the river. The towers need to be on a solid foundation – the skill and experience of the negotiator. Each tower has to be constructed in two directions at once, back towards the firm ground – the solidarity of the party the negotiator is representing – and equally reaching out towards the other side – another negotiator (who is in a similar position). If too much is built on one side rather than the other – too much attention paid to one's own party or too much flexibility offered to the other – the tower will topple over and the negotiations collapse. Only when our negotiating towers of strength have carefully reached out in both directions is the link between the two parties – successful agreement and implementation – complete.

'Separation' in constituency negotiations

The changing dynamics between the joint negotiations and the constituency can be viewed in terms of cohesion and separation (Figure 9.4). At the start of the negotiations the constituency and their representatives will be as one, solidly behind the position being put to the other party.

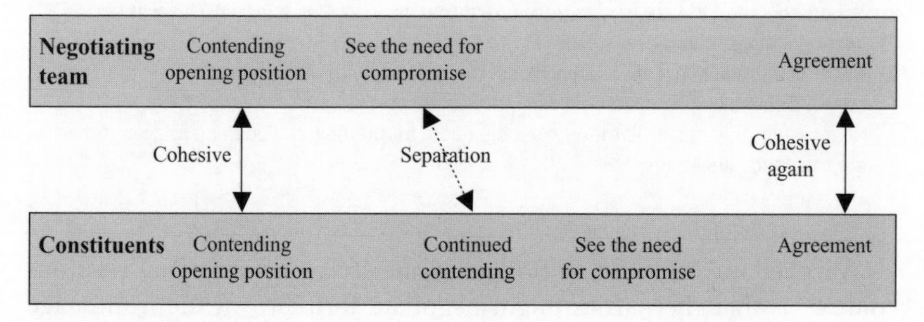

Figure 9.4: Constituency–negotiator separation in positional bargaining

As the negotiators gain a greater understanding of the differences, the other party's priorities and BATNA, they realise the need for compromise but the constituency – not having been present at the negotiations – will still feel justified in maintaining their original position. At this point, the negotiators become separated from their constituents until through communication (and negotiation) with their constituents the latter also come to the realisation that compromise is necessary. At some point, constituency support will coalesce around a final position that can be agreed to by both parties.

The more competitive the opening stance of the parties, the more difficult it will be to bridge the separation. If the representatives are to find creative or clear-cut compromise solutions while their constituents are still set on contending, they must build a bridge towards the other party. Some ways negotiators manage this are shown in Box 9.2. One way is the interpersonal exchanges as identified by Douglas (see Chapter 7) where negotiators indicate their own views ('I might have a look at that proposal') while maintaining the integrity of their party's position, should the negotiations not move forward ('Our position on this issue is unchanged'). In one negotiation (Fells, 1998a) both management and union negotiators, in their party roles, contended on the pay issue and expressed the difficulties they would have in getting their party to accept a revised position. Concurrently they sounded each other out through interpersonal exchanges on how work performance would be linked to pay (which might be a way to bridge their incompatible pay positions).

Box 9.2: Managing separation in constituency negotiations

Negotiators may at the same time be both standing firm yet looking for solutions.

Negotiators may stall in the negotiations in order to give themselves time to organise their own party around a new negotiating position.

Negotiators may begin to make distinctions between their own views and the policies or views of those they represent.

Negotiators, and the key negotiators in particular, may develop informal links with opposing negotiators to find new solutions.

Negotiators will begin to re-emphasise the constituency group position as the final concession-making process unfolds.

Negotiators may raise their level of 'toughness' as the negotiations close, even if they are the conceding party.

Another way of building bridges, again from the industrial relations context, is that the parties might negotiate formally on the front stage while talk informally on the back stage (Friedman 1994). This 'back stage' might be a quiet discussion between key negotiators during a coffee break or a more considered approach through a third party. This two-track negotiation is also evident in international negotiation and in the business world where formal negotiations are supplemented (or even rescued) though 'chance' meetings at conferences or other public events. For example, the trigger for another attempt at a merger between British Airways and Qantas was a conference speech by the BA Chief Executive (*Australian Financial Review*, 4 December 2008, p. 1).

Negotiators must be alert to these process complications and allow them to be worked through. If the opposite negotiator has just come from a difficult meeting with his constituents he may well take a harder line in the joint meeting but this does not necessarily mean that the negotiations are going backwards. Flexibility around the process is preferable to making concessions on the issue to break a deadlock caused by the process being too rigid.

However, negotiators should also be alert to the tactical opportunities within constituency negotiations. Negotiators can use the 'my hands are tied' ploy to fend off pressure to make further concessions. There is no difference – in a negotiation sense – between the union official saying, 'I can't take this offer back to my membership' and the company negotiator saying, 'there is no more money in the budget'. In both cases the negotiators are using an away-from-table event (the membership endorsement of the earlier claim; the management's previous budget meeting) as a constraint on their negotiating flexibility.

The practical implications for the representative

Walton and McKersie (1965) rightly pointed out that the more strongly a negotiator negotiates with his own team to keep their demands to moderate proportions, the easier is it is to reach agreement with the other side. It may not be possible to influence the constituency position but a negotiator should be aware that the negotiations start in the preparation meeting, not when facing the other party. These pre-negotiation negotiations should be handled carefully (see Box 9.3). Indeed, attitudes could be shaped even before the formal planning starts by providing information which might then pre-empt a groundswell of hard-line views taking hold at the constituency meeting.

The more authority negotiators have the easier it will be to bring together a coherent and moderate (perhaps even interest-based) opening position to put to the other side. This does not mean control or imposing

Box 9.3: Some recommendations when negotiating on behalf of others

Have pre-negotiation negotiations
Provide prior information to the constituents
Ensure open discussion of the issues
Ensure some 'other directedness' in the discussion
Provide an understanding of the likely process of negotiation (the script).
Maintain communication
Have clear discussions with your own constituency
Start bridge building with negotiators on the other team.
Maintain trust and authority
Have a strong influence over the process
Ensure your negotiating instructions are clear.
Manage the process
Accept a slower pace
Help the other negotiating team with their constituency.

one's views. The critical point of any negotiation is how the agreement is implemented and in a constituency negotiation it is the constituents who have to agree and then implement it. (Negotiators on *both* sides need to remember this). Thompson, Peterson and Brodt (1996) found that teams achieved better outcomes than individual negotiators – there was more exchange of information within the team and, as we know, information is a key to finding a value-adding solution. So a representative negotiator needs to draw out all the information (differentiation) from the constituency group through open discussion; a viewpoint put forward by one of the quieter people in the group may be something that becomes really important later in the negotiations. Similarly, tightly structured issue-by-issue discussions might inhibit creative linkages (Rackman and Carlisle, 1978) so allowing the discussion to flow from one topic to another is important.

When a group gets together to discuss an issue, particularly if they have a grievance or want to bring about change, it is easy to forget that negotiation is two-sided. The negotiation representative should endeavour to have some 'other directedness' in the discussion to get the constituency group to give some thought to what the other party wants from the negotiation and *why* they want it.

Ensure everyone is working to the same script

Another important contribution a negotiator can make through the preparatory discussions is to build a reasonable expectation of the forthcoming negotiation by taking time to discuss how the negotiations might proceed. The fundamental script of negotiating still holds but, as we have seen, the most difficult part is exploration. It is too easy to envisage negotiation as a trial of strength and final reluctant concessions (hopefully by the other side). The script needs to be balanced, accepting competitiveness through differentiation but sowing the seeds for exploration.

On one occasion a company–union negotiation ended in serious conflict. When their agreement was due for renegotiation they met and undertook a 'lessons learned' exercise to see how they might avoid getting into that same situation again. As part of this process they developed an alternative negotiating script. A one-day workshop does not reshape ingrained behaviour and they started the substantive negotiations as they had always done, according to their old, comfortable, competitive and positional script. As usual, they reached a deadlock but at this point, rather than continue to apply pressure as they had done before, they stood back, and remembered the more exploratory negotiation script they had talked about previously and then agreed to move forward in this different direction.

Maintain communication

It is important that negotiators maintain regular communication with their constituents. Constituency briefings and preparation meetings should be scheduled just as carefully as the joint meetings. Each of these becomes a negotiation in itself, preparing the negotiator for the approach to be taken in the next joint session.

A critical issue for the two teams of negotiators to sort out is how much feedback should be provided after each negotiation session. Some prefer relying on agreed minutes of the meeting but these can take time to prepare and so leave an information vacuum. Often it is sufficient merely to agree on the key points that the negotiators will convey to their constituents, so a good negotiator, in drawing the session to a close, will ensure that the feedback points are clear. If the negotiators cannot trust each other to report back openly, there are more difficulties in the negotiation than can be overcome by relying on formal minutes (which themselves might become another source of dispute). Employers are often unwilling to give their employees time to talk through the issues when a major negotiation is in progress, perhaps unaware that when time to discuss is limited the more contending position is easier to accept.

A good negotiator will try to build a working relationship with negotiators from the other party so that the process may be maintained even though the parties are in conflict over the issues. At least one negotiator on each side should be preparing the ground should an informal 'back door' approach be necessary to bridge an impending deadlock.

An option in the more public forms of constituency negotiations is to attempt to convince the opposing constituency direct. Employers can communicate directly to their employees, not simply though the negotiation process; the local council might call a community meeting to broaden the issue beyond the interests of the petitioners from a particular street. These opportunities to communicate, and in some cases take unilateral action, provide one party with more strategic opportunities than the other (Fells, 1998b). The presumption behind direct communication is that the constituents are more moderate than their negotiators but this is not always the case (see Figure 9.4 above) and if the communication is perceived as an attempt to undermine (manipulate) the negotiation process, attitudes can be hardened.

Maintain trust and authority

A negotiator (or negotiating team) must earn the trust of those they represent. Part of this trust is built on the negotiator's experience. An obvious source of mistrust – that the negotiator will negotiate something behind the backs of the constituents – can be dealt through clear instructions on the issues and how much flexibility the negotiators have. Only they have the 'feel' of the process and they should know best how to implement the chosen issue strategy and how best to respond to the other party's manoeuvrings. The negotiator should therefore determine when and how particular positions, suggestions and concessions are made in joint session. The constituents, if they want a good agreement, should commit to considering any alternative proposals their negotiators might bring back to them. Equally they should not think their negotiators are letting them down if they recommend that a concession is necessary. The final decisions on the issues should always be with the constituents.

Managing the process

Negotiators can help or hinder the process of bringing their constituencies to a point of agreement (Table 9.2). Bringing the three negotiations together takes time so periods of no obvious progress should be accepted, even anticipated. Allow for the fact that the other negotiating team may feel additional constituency pressure; this can happen at any time during the negotiation, but particularly in the end-game. Negotiators should

Table 9.2 Constituency negotiations: some helpful and unhelpful behaviours

Helpful	**Unhelpful**
Extensive, open, other-directed preparation	Allowing a single, extreme position to be developed
Making provision for regular consultation with constituents	Misrepresenting the progress of the negotiations to the constituents
Allowing for periods of strong contending, even when exploring options	
Allowing time and behavioural flexibility during the closing stages of the negotiation	Undermining the authority of the opposing negotiator
	Pressing for a quick settlement

be alert to hints at flexibility or attempts to set up informal communication and respond positively but cautiously, not trying to push open the flexibility offered into a major breakthrough. Finally negotiators should remember that final agreement lies with the constituents, not with those sitting across the table, so to force a table settlement may not lead to a good outcome.

10 Cross-cultural negotiations

On a business trip to Manila the author's first meeting was to be hosted at a restaurant. Establishing business relationships in the social environment of a restaurant is what one expects – it is a recognised characteristic of doing business in Asia. On another occasion he went overseas to discuss a possible joint venture and was hosted at a restaurant. Not in Asia but New Zealand. What then of the Asian characteristic of doing business in a social environment – how 'Asian' is it?

A senior executive from an Australian engineering company was on time for his morning appointment in Lagos with the CEO of a Nigerian company interested in a joint mining venture. He was kept waiting all day in the reception area without even being offered a coffee. Africans supposedly have a different notion of time – the advice is 'be punctual, even though you may be kept waiting' (Acuff, 2008, p. 289). Eventually the Australian was invited into the CEO's office. Should he complain at having to been kept waiting all day? Should he even have waited all day? If the African CEO ever came to Australia, should he be kept waiting all day too? He has a different notion of time, so isn't that what he would be used to?

It is easy to make mistakes when negotiating with someone with a different cultural background. The difficulties are real. Although the essential DNA, the strategic considerations and the tasks of negotiation are unchanged, the script seems to be different. This chapter will examine ways people from different cultures approach the task of negotiating an agreement. It will also offer a different perspective through images of negotiation as rock and roll and as a banquet. The purpose in understanding cross-cultural negotiation is two-fold: to manage these negotiations more effectively and, equally important, to draw from the diversity to improve one's own way of negotiating.

How do cultures differ?

One important point can be made at the outset. Most of the difficulties in cross-cultural negotiation arise because negotiators ignore the fundamental fact of *all* negotiations: that it is two-sided. Failing to take into account the perspective of the other negotiator will always lead to problems.

It is easy to stereotype and presume that all people from one culture behave similarly – the John Wayne versus Charlie Chan fallacy (Sebenius 2002a) – but a moment's thought of just a few from one's own culture will show that there are as many variations within as there are between cultures. As Fang (1999) points out, when negotiating with someone from China it is important to know whether they are negotiating as a Confucius gentleman, a Sun Tzu strategist or Maoist bureaucrat. Perhaps a mix of all three!

As the negotiations unfold, it is easy to attribute any behaviour – particularly different behaviour – to culture and so ignore many similarities. Salacuse's (1998) survey of negotiators from a number of countries indicated that one's professional background influences conduct, including one's approach to negotiation. As they meet to negotiate a business deal, a lawyer from Europe and one from Asia might find their training and the role they are expected to perform as lawyers mean they have a similar approach irrespective of their European or Asian mindsets. Globalisation, particularly in education and business practice, and generational change are having a moderating effect on culturally specific behaviour though the core values remain (Tung, Worm and Fang, 2008).

In making judgements about others we implicitly believe our way to be better which, of course, is not necessarily the case. Our own biases begin to show, particularly in attributing adverse factors to other negotiators and to their culture. These biases are not likely to be extinguished by paying undue attention to points of etiquette. Indeed they may even be reinforced if the negotiator feels that he is the one making all the attempts at cultural adjustment with no reciprocation from the other party (reciprocity being one of the strands of negotiation's DNA).

Negotiators should also be alert to cultural differences being overemphasised as a tactic to secure further concessions. Those from cultures known to have a relatively fluid understanding of time may use this to deliberately delay meetings with the intention of making a more time-focused negotiator feel uncomfortable and so be drawn into making unnecessary concessions. Similarly negotiators should be aware that doing what comes naturally, such as getting right down to business as soon as the meeting starts, may be viewed by others as an attempt to control the proceedings and gain advantage.

Dimensions of cultural difference

A culture is a shared value that shapes behaviour. Typically steeped in history and beliefs, culture is reflected in all aspects of life, especially one's view of what is important. As with other aspects of negotiation, our understanding of cultural variation emerges from a number of sources, each providing particular insights. Writers with extensive experience in international negotiation provide useful country-by-country checklists that blend cultural and business practices (such as those by Acuff, 2008; Gesteland, 2005; and Requejo and Graham, 2008). A second source is the findings of experimental research such as that by Professor Brett (2007) and her colleagues, which provide insights into how cultural difference might account for variations in negotiation behaviour and outcomes. Communication and conflict resolution specialists and the marketeers also make a contribution, again often providing useful country-specific guidance (Ghauri and Usunier, 1996; Hendon, Hendon and Herbig, 1996; Leung and Tjosvold, 1998; Schuster and Copeland, 1996a; Usunier and Lee, 2005).

Many of these writings draw on the work of cultural specialists such as Hall (1959; 1960; 1983), Hofstede (1980; 1991; 1994) and Triandis (1995) who provide insights into the fundamental distinguishing differences between cultures. Some of these dimensions of cultural difference are summarised in Table 10.1 (which draws on the review provided by Usunier and Lee, 2005). (This table might serve as a preliminary cultural awareness checklist – of oneself as well as of the other negotiator as part of one's preparation for a negotiation. See Appendix 9 for a more comprehensive checklist.) As in all bipolar categorisations it should be remembered that it is a question of degree between the two contrasting descriptions.

Given the embeddedness of culture it is not surprising that some of the attitudes and behaviours listed in Table 10.1 could easily appear under more than one dimension or are mutually reinforcing. For example, the masculine characteristic of a results-oriented competitive 'win' might also be a typical characteristic of individualism. High individualism tends to be associated with a low power difference; similarly high uncertainty avoidance with a high power distance. Those from high uncertainty avoidance, high power difference or high context cultures (see below) seem more disposed to trust (Johnson and Cullen, 2002 p. 353); the degree of individualism or collectivism is a less clear indicator. As noted in Chapter 2,

Table 10.1 Some dimensions of cultural difference

Individualism

Degree of self reliance rather than reliance upon others. This flows through into confidence in making decisions, in the ability to get things done and assessing success or failure.

Individualism is often contrasted with collectivism which places an emphasis on subordinating one's position within the group; this flows through into behaviour within the group and towards the out group.

High (individualism)	*Low (collectivism)*
Draws on own motivation, own reasoning	Draws upon contextual support in decision making and action
Can achieve mastery over events	Tendency to be fatalistic, accepting
Events (outcomes, achievements, mistakes) attributable to the individual	Events attributable to the context
Expressive of attitudes, opinions	Passive, inscrutable, not willing to appear different from the group
Acknowledges the presence of conflict; will actively seek to resolve the difference and move on	Expresses disagreement only indirectly, prepared to let a difference 'sit'

Power distance

Level of acceptance of inequality as legitimate. This flows through into how relationships are organised, decisions are made and power is exercised.

Low (egalitarianism)	*High (hierarchical)*
Hierarchy present, but not overt; more egalitarian	Hierarchy strong and visible
Has a sense of empowerment, able to contribute to decisions	Power to make decisions is at the top
Authority is recognised but may be challenged	Authority is deferred to

Uncertainty avoidance

Attitude towards risk. This flows through into evaluations of situations and proposals.

Low	*High*
Willing to take risks	Prefers stability
Encourages change	Prefers consistency
Innovative	Cautious

Table 10.1 (*Cont.*)

Masculinity	
Attitudes of self and others. This flows through into how individuals relate.	
High	*Low*
Actions are with others	Actions are for others
Assertive	Passive
	Others' achievements are considered
Results oriented, competitive 'win' orientation	Relationship oriented
Precise outcomes which should be upheld	'Understandings' as outcomes, which might evolve
Temporal perspective	
Attitude towards time – short- or long-term perspective. This flows through into evaluations of situations and issues and influences how tasks might be approached.	
Short term	*Long term*
The future is 'bigger and better'	The future is shaped by the past
Early returns valued more highly	Longer-term benefits are more important
Conscious of emerging difficulties or 'downsides' and will want to address them	Less impacted by pressing 'downsides'
Linear perception of processes or approach to a task	Circular view of processes
Focused on the immediate task, action oriented	Discontinuous, fuzzy action
Conscious of time, 'time is money'; tendency towards monochronic (punctual, agenda driven, one task at a time)	Not impacted by time, tendency towards polychronic (operates by 'rubber time'; engaged in multiple tasks)

any predisposition (or otherwise) to trust is tempered by the need for situation-specific acts of trust in the context of the negotiation.

These cultural dimensions reflect different ways of viewing the world, relating to others and approaching tasks – all of which are important when negotiating. Communication and negotiation researchers have tended to focus on individualism and collectivism as being a key dimension that flows through into negotiation, influencing how negotiators define what they want to achieve (the issue) and how they interact with others (the process). Researchers also consider the impact of power distance (egalitarianism/hierarchy) as this can influence how decisions are made and how conflict is dealt with. Finally, the temporal perspective is seen as an influence on how issues are defined and the process is envisaged.

High and low context communication

Another measure of difference between cultures is how they communicate and convey information; important because information exchange is one of the strands of negotiation's DNA. Hall (1976) identified differences between low and high context communication. The former is explicit and direct, intending to minimise any scope for ambiguity. High context communication relies on the physical context and the person who is communicating as much as through what is actually being said. The listener is also expected to infer meaning from what is *not* said. It also reflects a broader attitude of wanting to understand the whole context before reaching any conclusions, whereas people from low context cultures are prepared to learn more through making decisions.

There are two royal universities in Sweden – Lund and Uppsala – and naturally they vie for the position of premier university. Uppsala holds any meetings between the two universities in their senate room where pictures of the Kings of Sweden – all of whom studied at Uppsala – hang on the walls. This example of status and scene setting – both important when relationships are being built – alerts us to dangers in stereotyping as Scandinavian cultures are generally recognised to be low context communicators. The differences between high and low context approaches to communication become even more important in the exchanges over the issues under negotiation. In replying to an offer to purchase, a high context negotiator might respond, 'we like your package overall and would like to accept it. Some other companies have put in offers to us which place a higher value on our product. We'd like to discuss your offer further.' This means, 'please increase your offer.' A low context negotiator might have responded, 'you will have to do better than that; we had expected you to offer around four million, not three.'

Some of the distinguishing characteristics of high and low context communication (listed in Table 10.2) are consistent with the individualist – collective dimension in Table 10.1 above. This is not surprising as the way we communicate is in part a reflection of how we view ourselves and the world around us. The way we think influences how we communicate (Drake, 1995; Hofstede, 1994; Kumar and Worm, 2004). An analytical approach – associated with the individualistic West and most comfortably

Table 10.2 Low and high context communication (adapted from Hall 1976; Gudykunst, 1998)

Low context communication	High context communication
The meaning and intent will be conveyed primarily through the spoken word	Much of the intended content will be conveyed in the physical environment and by who is participating
Statements will be precise and relevant	Statements will be broad ranging, indirect
Statements will reflect opinions, feelings, and reactions	Statements will be reserved Communication will be in a way that maintains harmony within their own group
Information will be sought through questioning	Information will be sought through inference and through indirect means e.g. through reactions to offers made
Silence will be filled with words	Silence conveys meaning

done through direct communication – leads to an emphasis on factual presentation and rational argument, a search for an ideal solution and perhaps a persistence to find such a solution which becomes more important than the people involved. In contrast, a holistic approach (regarded as being more of an Eastern characteristic) might present an argument in an abstract way, perhaps through analogy and would be accepting of two concurrently competing perspectives. (The analytical approach would require finding which of the two was 'better'.)

Decision making, power and the management of conflict

The hierarchical nature of some societies seems to stand out more than the egalitarianism in others. Senior people – senior by rank or age – are granted respect and are looked to for guidance; their preferences are accommodated and their decisions accepted. Nothing is done which might look like disagreement. Thus although negotiating as a team, the team members will follow the lead of the senior person and will not easily express a conflicting opinion. In contrast, in an egalitarian society there is a greater acceptance of open participation, discussion and challenge, though we should not think that democracy prevails – the CEO is still the boss!

The hierarchical or egalitarian characteristics of societies and organisations impact on some key aspects of negotiation – how decisions are made, how power is exercised and how conflict is managed. Negotiators face many unanticipated decisions during the course of a negotiation–should we reveal this information at this point? Should we break for an adjournment? Should we say that we like their new proposal? We would expect members of a negotiating team with a more equitable form of organisation to be more comfortable in making on-the-spot decisions and be more willing to take a new position on the issue before referring it back to their principals. In contrast, the negotiators in a more hierarchically influenced group would not want to act outside of their superiors (who may not be present but will have given clear guidance) with the consequence that they may appear inflexible and unresponsive and, so far as the issue is concerned, always contending by not giving even a hint of flexibility.

Power is an important link in negotiation's DNA and in Chapter 2 power was examined in terms of BATNA, the best alternative to a negotiated agreement. This is an analytic conception of power, abstracted from any broader relationships. The BATNA is invoked by negotiators in egalitarian cultures only as a final power persuasion tool (Adair, 2003; Brett 2000). Negotiators from hierarchical societies – where power is based on relationships as well as alternatives – are found to use not only BATNA-related arguments but also social persuasion (Adair et al., 2004; Tinsley 2001). In hierarchical societies those in a superior position are granted power by virtue of their position (they probably also have better alternatives) and this flows through into a negotiation. The expectation will be that the benefits from any agreement should be distributed on the basis of the parties' relative status. It is therefore important in any negotiation to make an assessment of relative power early. However, as an example of the difficulties in discerning the effects of culturally based strategies Adair et al. (2004) found that the insights gained through using power arguments can be used either to create joint gain in the case of Japanese negotiators or to enforce a competitive outcome as in the case of Russian negotiators.

These differing approaches to decision making and the use of power also flow into how conflict situations might be managed. Those from a more hierarchical culture will generally be less comfortable than those from an egalitarian one to express disagreement or to react openly to disagreement from across the negotiating table. Rather than try to work through a difficult situation it might be postponed to be managed through a third party or perhaps just through the passage of time. In this, as in other practical outworkings of hierarchy and egalitarianism, there are some affinities with collectivism and individualism.

Different meanings of time and their effect on negotiation

Our attitude to time reveals a lot about our approach to life (Hall, 1983; Brislin and Kim, 2003). 'Every year is getting shorter, never seem to find the time' is a line from Pink Floyd's best selling album *Dark Side of the Moon.* From *Time*, a song about the relentless passage of time and the pressure we allow it to place on us, it is a reflection of those cultures where the immediacy of time and the use made of it is important. Time is money. Carpe diem – seize the day! Negotiators from these cultures will be punctual, not have too much time for social chit-chat but instead start working through the agenda, one item at a time, totally focused on the issues and finishing on schedule, all reflecting a monochronistic approach to time. Future planning is important so as not to waste time doing things that are not necessary. Milestones feature and are kept to; deadlines generate activity to meet them. Commitment is shown by getting on with the task. At the negotiating table we can expect linear thinking, task-focused activity and low context forms of communication.

In contrast, some cultures (broadly termed 'polychronic') seem to place little value on time – a wristwatch may be a fashion statement but is not something to live by. Present events are part of life's broader canvas. There is no imperative to seize the day because another will come. The 'now' will occur again as part of the cycle of life. So they have time to build relationships – which are important to them, and once formed they are expected to endure. Meeting times are part of the flow of the day (particularly useful if living in a city where the traffic is bad!) and it is acceptable for other people or events to interrupt a meeting or for plans to change. The present is measured against the past so time will be spent talking over the history and the broader context of any topic, which leads naturally to talking about a lot of things which are not strictly on the agenda (if there is one). High context communication is another reflection of this broad approach. Negotiations will be lengthy with attention given to building relationships. The passage of time will be used to test one's sincerity and commitment.

It would appear that there is a broad divide between those cultures with Anglo-Saxon or North European roots who are generally monochronistic and people from the rest of the world who are more polychronic (Mayfield et al., 1997) though, as always, the broad generalisation must be evaluated in the context of the specific negotiation.

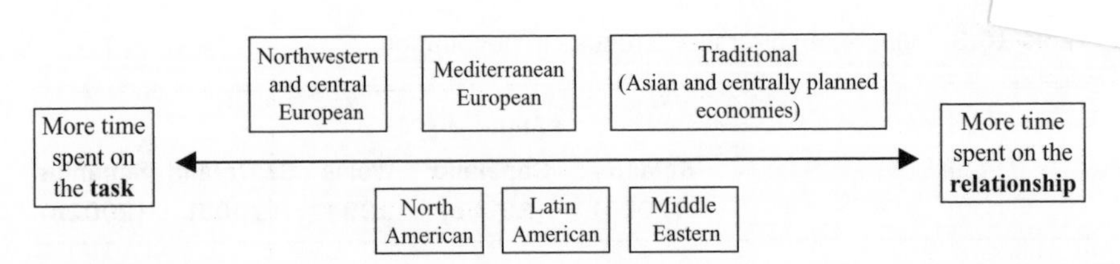

Figure 10.1: Culture Classification Model (adapted from Schuster and Copeland, 1996b)

Making some sense of this cultural complexity

The multifaceted nature of culture makes it difficult to classify cultural differences in a way that offers practical guidance. Contrasts provide insights though it must always be remembered that this approach misrepresents a characteristic as either/or whereas in reality it is a question of emphasis and, in some circumstances the characteristic is dominated by the context and so is not even relevant. Schuster and Copeland (1996a; 1996b) suggest the key distinguishing factor is the balance of time (as an indicator of importance) spent on relationships relative to time spent on the task (see Figure 10.1) and they identify 10 implications for how people communicate. Gesteland (2005) also regards being deal or relationship focused as the most significant distinguishing characteristic. Having a contract or a relationship heads Salacuse's (1998; 2004) list of 10 factors by which a negotiator's style might be assessed. Weiss (1994) has a list similar to Salacuse's. Sebenius (2002b), drawing on the works of Hall and Hofstede, suggests four key areas to consider: the underlying view of the process, the approach to building agreement, the form of agreement and its implementation. The similarities between different writers' insights into cross-cultural negotiation can be seen in Table 10.3.

In contrast to these broad 'deal-making' perspectives on negotiation, the research of Professor Brett and her colleagues has focused more on negotiation behaviour and so takes a different approach to classification. However, they also find a starting point in whether the negotiator's emphasis is on resource distribution or relationship building. This, they suggest, is likely to be driven by a broader individualism (independence) or collective (interdependent) orientation. Adair and Brett's (2004) summary of their research (see Table 10.4) is useful in recognising that both individualists and collectivists can each be either competitive or cooperative in a negotiation. This is preferable to an implicit assumption that it is the individualists who are competitive and the collectivists who are cooperative. (Collectivists are, but only within their own group.) Finally, Brett

Table 10.3 Aspects of cultural differences in negotiation

	Salacuse (2004)	Schuster & Copeland (1996b)	Weiss (1994)	Gesteland (2005)	Sebenius (2002b)
General orientation and objectives					
Contract or relationship	√	√	√	√	
Ongoing or sporadic contact, implementation		√			√
High or low time sensitivity	√		√	√	
High or low risk taking	√		√		
External or internal basis for trust			√		
Specific or general agreement	√	√	√		√
Win-lose or win-win approach	√		√		√
Approach to the negotiation task					
Bottom up or top-down approach	√				√
Direct or indirect communication	√	√	√		
Form of reasoning & persuasion		√	√		
High or low emotionalism	√			√	
Negotiators					
Skill or status-based selection			√		
Group- or leader-oriented organisation	√	√	√		
Formal or informal style	√	√	√	√	
Business or individual commitment		√	√		
Personal disclosure or social topics		√			

and Gefland (2006) review the assumptions which lie behind the theories of social action in the negotiation context (Table 10.5) and note that much of the research seems dominated by 'Western' ways of thinking (as this book might also be). They suggest that a greater understanding of other cultures provides insight into one's own culture and offers

Table 10.4 Culture and negotiation processes (based on Adair and Brett, 2004)

Independence	Interdependence
Leads to resource distribution as the primary goal.	Leads to relationship building prior to resource distribution
Is associated with low context communication	Is associated with high context communication
If competitive, then will seek to secure individual gain through rational influence, substantiation or reference to alternatives	If competitive, then will seek to dominate through the use of affective influence, persuasion based on status superiority or the relationship
If being cooperative, will then seek to enlarge joint gain through direct information sharing, indicating interests, comparing positions and clear responses to offers	If being cooperative, then will seek to develop trust and do so through indirect information exchange through offers, particularly multi-offers

Table 10.5 Responses to problems in negotiation (based on Brett and Gelfand, 2006)

	West	Non-West
Motivation		
How should we evaluate the outcome of the negotiation?	Economic	Relational
Communication		
How do I get the information I need about the other party's interests and priorities without giving up too much information about my own interests, thereby making myself vulnerable to exploitation?	Through questioning	Through offers
Persuasion		
How do I get the other party to make the concessions necessary to reach my desired end point?	Rational argument	Emotional appeals
Attribution		
Why did this event occur?	Dispositional	Situational
Confrontation of conflict		
How do I manage conflict?	Direct confrontation	Indirect confrontation

the possibility that there are other ways of doing things that are just as effective.

Summary – an agreement-focused perspective

A way through these diverse insights into the effect of culture on negotiation can be found by taking the raison d'être of negotiation as a starting point. The whole purpose of a negotiation is to see if an agreement can be achieved and then – importantly – to have that agreement implemented effectively. So envisage the agreement the other party might want – 'what would a good agreement look like from their perspective?' They might be seeking an agreement that specifically addresses all the points at issue or one that records only the broad parameters on the understanding that points of detail will be addressed later as the need arises. These outcome preferences reflect and reveal two different broad approaches to the task of reaching an agreement through negotiation.

If we consider why some negotiators want an agreement which covers all the details and contingencies it is probably because they view it as the mechanism to ensure the proper implementation of what has been agreed. The agreement will also provide ways to ensure that any changes in circumstance during its term are dealt with equitably. They feel they have to rely on the agreement because they do not envisage much beyond a pragmatic working relationship being developed with the other party. Since the detail of the agreement is significant it follows that communication and negotiation is likely to be direct and task focused. This typically leads to an issue-by-issue approach that easily becomes a series of mini win-lose encounters in the broader context of the negotiation as a whole.

Those seeking a more general agreement will probably not enter into an agreement at all unless they reach an understanding of the other party as being a partner. In this case the partnership will be a living relationship with the implementation of details and responses to changed circumstances being sorted out as necessary when the situation arises. Since points of potential conflict do not have to be addressed in advance, the discussions can be open-ended and – seemingly – 'win-win'.

Managing a cross-cultural negotiation

Preparation is the key for any negotiation. It is naïve to enter into a business negotiation in another country without first having thoroughly researched the situation and developed a sound business case. The appraisal must extend beyond whether the proposal is technically and economically sound to consider the full context in which any eventual agreement will be implemented including the risks involved. No amount of cross-cultural sensitivity training is going to compensate for agreeing to a supply contract without knowing how the local financial system operates (who is the person who actually authorises any payments out of the country?). It will not compensate for being unaware that your agreement with a local manufacturer to produce your product under licence also requires approval from the local government authority (why is that approval being delayed?). In short, any proposal requires an understanding of the local business system. This will take time and almost inevitably will involve establishing local connections.

The techniques for developing sound international business proposals are beyond the scope of this book. From a negotiation perspective the preliminary encounters with a potential business partner will be an exploration to establish whether there is any prima facie prospect of a deal (deal prospecting is described in Appendix 8). The foundations of any subsequent negotiation are being laid during this time. As in all negotiations, it is necessary to consider the issue, process and behavioural dimensions.

The issues dimension

Good preparation for any negotiation requires questions to be asked and the preparation to be done from the perspective of the other party (see Chapter 3). The difference when preparing for a cross-cultural negotiation is that we probably know far less about the other party. Recognising one's relative ignorance is not a bad thing. At the same time, it is important not to succumb to transference – assuming they think like us, or to stereotyping – assuming they all think and act the same. The uncertainties of cross-cultural negotiation simply place greater emphasis on preparation and on the need to manage the differentiation phase, regarding it as a period to learn and confirm as much as to inform. It places a greater emphasis on early relationship building, if only as a means to gathering information.

The Strategy Framework (Chapter 3) is designed to enforce an 'other directed' perspective by requiring a negotiator to estimate the other party's strategy. This can only be done by evaluating all the strategy factors from the other negotiator's perspective. Box 10.1 gives some broad indications of how a negotiator should be alert to different perspectives.

Box 10.1: Strategic analysis: some cultural dimensions

Importance of issue to self
The more collective their orientation the more likely they are to view the issue broadly and in a longer time perspective; the underlying motivation may be far deeper than appears on the surface.

Concern for other's (i.e. your) outcome
An individualistic orientation would give rise only to an instrumental concern for your outcome; a collective orientation is concerned only with the welfare of the in group; concern for other (that is, you) should not be presumed until a relationship is established and you are thus part of their group.

Expectations of other's (i.e. your) strategy
The more collectively oriented negotiators will expect individualists to want to achieve an outcome and so will expect them to make concessions.

Time pressure
The more collective and polychronic cultures would be less impacted by potential deadlines and so not 'feel' the pressure as much as in individualistic cultures.

Alternatives
Similarly the broader perspective of collective or hierarchical cultures might not regard 'poor' alternatives so negatively.

An example will show how people might feel the pressure of time differently and also highlights the danger of transference, transferring one's own thoughts and attitudes to others. The example involves a factory where stocks of a crucial component will run out by the end of the week, resulting in the factory's temporary closure if supplies cannot be found. In this situation, time *does* matter whatever your culture; nothing can be done to change the fact that Friday is four days away. The component supplier has an individualistic, monochronic perspective and so believes the factory manager would feel under pressure because of the impending crisis and would want to secure supplies of the components as soon as possible. The supplier would expect an urgent negotiation and quick agreement; he would expect the manager to pay a higher price for a special delivery. However, a manager from a more polychromic culture might be prepared not to reach agreement until later in the week. He might use the time to explore alternative sources while at the same time, arguing with the supplier about the need to keep prices down for the sake of the relationship. He might even be prepared to allow production to stop for a few days – the dislocation would not have too much of an impact in the long run. So, instead of negotiating with an eager buyer, our component supplier might find that the Friday deadline was not pushing this particular manager into a conceding strategy over delivery terms.

The process dimension

Earlier chapters have used imagery to convey an understanding of negotiation and to develop an appropriate script to manage the process effectively. Adair and Brett (2005) develop the imagery of dance in suggesting that negotiation, like dance, is a sequence of steps that draws on the cultural context. Compare the restrained Viennese waltz and the expressive intensity of the Spanish flamenco (both dances being opportunities for courtship) as reflections of the Northern European and Mediterranean cultures and their approaches to negotiation. Negotiation as sport and as family are two other metaphors to capture the essence of US and Japanese negotiation respectively (Gelfand and McCusker, 2002). At the risk of complete oversimplification – and being fully conscious of dividing the nearly seven billion population of the world into just two groups – we can suggest two images that convey the essence of 'Western' and 'non-Western' negotiation.

The rock and roll approach to negotiation

Western civilisation has given us many wonderful things – parliamentary democracy, soccer and (perhaps not quite so wonderful) pop celebrity culture and the paparazzi – but one of the most defining characteristics of western culture is rock and roll music and the electric guitar. This provides the visual imagery of our model of Western negotiation.

The body of a standard guitar widens, narrows, then widens again. The widening of the body reflects a Western negotiator's desire to get on with the task straight away, lay everything on the table and open up all the issues. The volume controls will be turned on full because rock and roll music has to be loud; not that our negotiators will be shouting but they well certainly be intent on getting their message across, full of emphasis with not too much subtlety or concern for relationship building and trust.

Following some pretty intense discussion the negotiators begin to see the key issues which need to be addressed to reach an agreement. Perhaps there are six of them (the six strings). The key point is that the issues are identified and worked upon. The differences do indeed seem to be narrowing efficiently and quickly; agreement is expected. However, we then find that the body of the guitar widens again reflecting that through our haste to look for the solutions we have missed some broader aspects that should have been considered. It may seem we are getting further apart rather than making progress. However we need an agreement so we take this in our stride and then focus again on the core issues (the strings), working through them step by step and overcoming each hurdle (the frets) in turn. The tension increases as the negotiators bring the issue to a head and endeavour to tie off the loose ends. At the last minute there will be some final 'tweaking' or fine-tuning to get the agreement precisely right.

Negotiation as a banquet

The great Chinese civilisation has given us many things that we now take for granted, not least paper and ink, the game of chess and kung fu movies. Not only have the Chinese given us the ubiquitous Chinese takeaway restaurant but also the Peking duck banquet. This banquet provides a good image of what negotiating is like in Asia and in many parts of the non-Western world.

When participating in a banquet the whole point is not the food but the social interaction. It is the same with an invitation to negotiate. The primary purpose of the invitation is not to seek your involvement in a formal business meeting, but to participate in an opportunity to understand each other.

At the beginning of the banquet the chef brings out the cooked duck for everyone to see. There has been a lot of preparation of the food to get to this point and this is the same in a negotiation. Our Chinese negotiators will be fully prepared and – as is reflected in our imagery with the whole duck being presented at the outset – they will have a good grasp of the big picture.

During the banquet the courses are presented in small stages, typically one dish at a time, not like a Western feast where the main course would be offered as meat and a range of vegetables to be eaten together. The duck is not presented all at once; some parts are used in one course, other parts form the basis of another dish. Towards the end of the banquet – and you never really know when it is going to end – a soup is presented which may well have all the remaining duck in it. This is a reflection of how information is often conveyed in a Chinese negotiation with some talk about the big picture, the possibilities and the prospects for the relationship and then separate details and insights being offered from time to time, not as a neat information package.

When the banquet ends, you will have made some friends. You probably will have not actually eaten very much but will feel reasonably full, only to feel hungry again soon after.

This is much like negotiating with the Chinese. A relationship may have been built and lots of discussion will have taken place. While some things may be understood you are left wondering what, if anything, was actually agreed, but it will all be sorted out in due course.

The action dimension

Creating images and scripts offers a way of understanding the broad flow of a negotiation. The detail within a script leads us to consider how the three tasks of information exchange, indicating flexibility and managing concessions might be done differently. Comparisons can be made between those with a collective orientation and who tend to be most comfortable with high context forms of communication and those who have a more individualistic orientation and prefer to communicate in a more direct low context manner. This again risks dividing the world's negotiators into two broad categories of 'the West' and 'the non-West' but it is a workable division suggested by the cultural and negotiation research presented earlier in the chapter.

Exchanging information

We have seen that all negotiators need to differentiate, to establish what the real issues are. We have also seen that people from different cultures may well have different perspectives on the same issue – one viewing it narrowly, another seeing it as part of a far broader perspective. (It is the negotiators with a more individualistic orientation who are less able to see the integrative potential in a situation (Gelfand and Christakopoulou, 1999; Ma et al., 2002).) Negotiators convey essential information about their priorities and also seek information in different ways, which is why there is less joint gain in cross-cultural negotiations than in intra-cultural ones (Brett and Okumura, 1998; Lituchy, 1997; Natlandsmyr and Rognes, 1995). This simply makes the task of differentiation all the more important, which in turn makes building effective relationships between the negotiators an early priority. Finally, negotiators should always remember differences in cultural background may cause objective information to be interpreted differently (Tinsley, Curhan and Kwak, 1999).

The process of exchanging information (and with it the task of building relationships) will start from the first encounter, not necessarily at the first formal negotiation meeting. Table 10.6 presents some contrasts in the way two broad groups might disclose their objectives, interests and other information surrounding the issues under negotiation. Only if taken to the extreme will either of the two lists in Table 10.6 undermine the general behavioural requirements for effectively managing the differentiation phase presented in Table 6.4, p. 98 and Box 6.1, p. 102 of Chapter 6. Some further recommendations are provided here to deal specifically with having to exchange information with someone whose preference is to do it in a different way. Those from high context cultures seem able to adapt to a

Table 10.6 West meets the rest: information exchange and differentiation

Non-West	West
Lengthy build up to the negotiation	Direct and to the point, efficient
Lengthy discussion, time not an issue	Deal with the present
Will present a range of open, long term possibilities	Will outline the history and context only to explain the present situation
Will include a relationship dimension	Will use PowerPoint for impact
An occasional 'this is what we want you to do'	Will encourage open discussion
Will expect the other party to infer priorities etc. from the weight of discussion and equally from what has been glossed over	Will, ideally, outline interests, priorities and seek reciprocal information
Will expect the other party to infer from the authority of the speaker	Will use rational arguments to explain linkages, goals and priorities
Will make statements that are intended to relate back to earlier ones	Will ask open, priority questions
Will, in time, respond to direct requests for information	Equally possible, will take positional approach and be hesitant in information exchange
And to be helpful:	**And to be helpful:**
Will give clear emphasis to important points	Will present issues broadly, not in detail
Will respond as directly as possible to questions	

more direct (low context) form of information exchange (Adair, 2003) so those who recognise themselves as being from low context cultures need to pay even more attention to the diverse ways information may be being communicated by their high context culture counterparts.

The task of exploration, indicating flexibility

In many negotiations the exploration phase is limited. Negotiators are generally more comfortable working around and exchanging offers and generating new workable solutions in their private sessions. Finding potential solutions requires flexibility and trust (which implies some risk taking) and so is even more difficult for those in collective, hierarchical cultures. They find it difficult to 'go out on a limb' and make a new suggestion, or make a first response to a proposal; they are much more comfortable conveying the standard party line. Using Douglas' (1957) terminology, they will prefer inter-party rather than interpersonal exchanges. Further, high context negotiators might prefer to put an offer on the table early and work around that, an action which might be regarded by a low context negotiator as 'anchoring' the issue and precluding any further exploratory discussion (Adair, Weingart and Brett, 2007). This offer-driven approach would seem to a low context negotiator to push the negotiation into the end-game.

The broad behavioural requirements for effective exploration (Chapter 7, Table 7.1, p. 114 and Box 7.2, p. 116) apply irrespective of cultural context but from Table 10.7 it would appear that negotiators from the West are the ones who drive the exploration process and so feel frustrated when this is not reciprocated, while those from the non-West are searching for new solutions in a different way.

Table 10.7 West meets the rest: exploration, indicating flexibility and creativity

Non-West	West
Will take proposals away for consideration rather than respond to them	Will want to 'unpack' any suggestion Ideally, creative solutions will emerge from an interest-based discussion
Creative solutions will emerge, if at all, through information being presented differently	More likely: unilateral problem solving leading to a new proposal
And to be helpful:	**And to be helpful:**
Will make preliminary responses to proposals	Will regard positions or offers as opportunities for discussion rather than for debate or challenge
Will recognise their desire to see progress	Will recognise their need to consult and take their time

The task of exchange, managing concessions

The 'end-game' of any negotiation can get competitive and Chapter 8 (Table 8.1, p. 126 and Box 8.3, p. 130) presented a number of ways to manage this critical phase of the negotiation effectively. The competitiveness emerges primarily because one party is saying 'no' to the other party's settlement proposal. Culturally based differences can be seen in three important aspects of the end-game: how offers are put, how they are reacted to and how any emerging conflict is handled (see Table 10.8). As indicated above, negotiators from high context countries will view making offers as a way of gaining insight and so will start this process early, requiring Western negotiators to view the offers as information rather than a closing 'end-game' move.

Table 10.8 West meets the rest: exchange, managing concessions and conflict

Non-West	West
Will be prepared to let the negotiations 'sit'	Will want an outcome
Will indicate broad principles of what is agreeable, unless it is a major financial item in which case it will be specific	Will make detailed proposals Expectations of the other party will also be spelt out
Will repeatedly make multi-issue offers	Limits clearly stated ('we can't do that') with justifications
Will press for variations around a theme	
Will place the offer in the context of the ongoing relationship	
Will not reject a proposal but offer an alternative or restate a previous one.	Unacceptable offers will be rejected outright; will outline alternatives (BATNA)
Disagreement will be avoided, will be handled by changing topics etc.	Will be comfortable with differences; any disagreements will be expressed at the negotiating table until addressed
And to be helpful:	**And to be helpful:**
Will recognise that saying 'no' to a proposal (and giving reasons) will not affect the relationship	Will prepare for a slow change in positions rather than rapid trade-offs at the negotiating table

Some practical implications

As would be expected, the research suggests that negotiations between cultures are less successful than negotiations within cultures – at the general level, not operating to the same script, and at the behavioural level, misinterpreting what the other party is trying to do. However, if each understands the other's approach they can help each other improve the

Table 10.9 Some ways to be a cross-culturally helpful negotiator

Non-Western ways to be helpful	Western ways to be helpful
Information exchange and differentiation and give clear emphasis to important points.	Present issues broadly, not in detail.
Respond as directly as possible to questions	Regard time spent on exploring the 'big picture' as a positive
Explore, indicating flexibility, and creativity make preliminary responses to proposals	Regard positions or offers as opportunities for discussion rather than for debate or challenge
Recognise their desire to see progress	Recognise their need to consult and take time
Exchange, managing concessions and conflict	Prepare for a slow change in positions rather than rapid trade-offs at the negotiating table
Recognise that saying 'no' to a proposal (and giving reasons) will not affect the relationship	

negotiation process to their mutual benefit. Some ways this might be done are presented again in Table 10.9.

The hierarchical, collectivist, high context perspective of non-Western negotiators helps them take a broad view of the situation and so by working through, over and around the issues they can help more issue-focused negotiators see the broader possibilities. On the other hand, these same cultural characteristics tend to inhibit open creativity and make it difficult to put new exploratory proposals. This makes the non-Western negotiators seem passive and reactive (if not stubborn) which can lead to frustration in Western negotiators. The passivity and unwillingness to express disagreement can make not agreeing look like agreeing, with resultant misunderstandings later. Also the Western negotiators can easily sense that they are making all the moves, doing all the work and will only get agreements if it is they who make the concessions, leading to any agreements then being seen as 'unfair', a value which is important to them.

So early in the negotiations the Western negotiators should not try to rush things and be accepting (and attentive) to the alternative ways of putting issues in their wider and historical context. Similarly, they should try to broaden their own presentations. At the same time non-Western negotiators could contribute by bringing emphasis to their key points, perhaps through summary and checking understanding and by responding with direct information. As the negotiations progress, Western negotiators can maintain an exploratory approach by viewing positions and offers as opportunities for discussion while the non-Western negotiators should be willing to give their reactions to proposals, confident that they will only be taken as preliminary reactions (and, equally important, confident that their own party will not see this as disloyal).

The egalitarian, individualistic and low context approach of Western negotiators brings different benefits and difficulties. They find it easier to be openly creative and explore what might be achieved. This at least provides the opportunity for the more constrained non-Western negotiators to have some new avenues to discuss in private sessions later though it would be better still if they could enter into some exploratory discussion there and then. However, the West focus on getting an outcome can be frustrating for non-Western negotiators who will want to take more time to consider issues and proposals, particularly within their broader goals. The Western negotiator can learn from this and take an opportunity to slow down and reflect. The willingness of the Western negotiator to express disagreement to a proposal (seen by her as a positive aspect) can easily be taken by a non-Western negotiator to be a rejection of the negotiation relationship itself. 'Reasons first' would be a constructive behavioural technique and given the high context ability of the non-Western negotiator, the phrase, 'I'm sorry, but I can't agree' will probably not be necessary.

There is one more important point to help overcome the potential difficulties in cross-cultural negotiations. Show respect to the other negotiator. Showing respect to the person across the negotiating table is a far more personal commitment than a broad cultural sensitivity to relationships. Similarly, no negotiator should be so task focused as to ignore the humanity of other negotiators. A negotiator should be consistent in personal behaviour and act with evident integrity. 'Do to others as you would have them do to you' is wise advice. Respect will then be earned as well as given and in a climate of mutual respect an unintentional cultural faux pas will be seen for what it is – unintentional. That a negotiator should show respect is a golden rule – the only one in this book.

Non-West and West – is there a single global script?

If negotiators learn the effective behavioural skills of other cultures, will we get to the point where there is one global negotiation script? Or to put it another way, will negotiation involve playing a bit of rock and roll while having something to eat as the negotiators journey across the Nullarbor?

There are obvious similarities between the Nullarbor Model and 'negotiation as rock and roll' revealing an underlying Western approach to negotiation. Indeed, focusing on the tasks of negotiation (Chapter 4) in an attempt to get at the core of reaching agreement may itself reflect a Western bias. The counter position, that negotiations are about relationships, does not seem sustainable unless the relationship leads somewhere – so that at some point the parties to the relationship will need to explore options or at least exchange offers to achieve even the loosest of agreements. If rather than starting from Sydney, the train journey was from Beijing we might find that the 'Eastern' context of the negotiation journey would show some differences. It might take far longer to decide whether to actually take the journey at all. Rather than being one of those things you 'must' do – a true Australian experience for oneself – it might be viewed more broadly: where would such a trip fit within our family's heritage? Would those close to me also benefit? I might be concerned to find out who else would be travelling before buying my ticket. Once on the train, the question to ponder may not be so much 'do I want to get to Northbridge (Perth's Chinatown)?' but 'when I get to there, will I want to spend time with the people I'm meeting on this train?' If I'm not sure then I will get off and wait for the next train and resume my journey. I will appreciate the time the journey is taking, not like some of my fellow passengers who seem to be getting a bit impatient. I will, like everyone else, have travelled across New South Wales (differentiation), crossed the Nullarbor (exploration) and travelled down the Avon Valley (exchange) but when I get to Perth, I'm not likely to 'sign off' on my journey (agreement) at the station. I will probably want to meet my fellow passengers again because there might be one or two more points about the agreement that I would like to discuss.

Conclusions

Do cultural differences change the essence of negotiation? If a negotiator is strategic in her thinking, prepares from the perspective of the other person, is fully alert to the other person thinking quite differently on the issue and allows a lot more negotiation time to build relationships and to unravel/decode information, then perhaps she will find that there is not so much difference at all. The script might seem different but since the essence of negotiation is unchanged the main storyline can be followed without too much difficulty – if one pays attention. At some point the parties have to differentiate; this is going to take some time but information rarely flows freely, even in the most open of negotiations. They have to explore options but in most negotiations (even the 'win-win' ones) this is mainly done unilaterally, so it is always important to present proposals openly and to maximise what can be learned from them (or from their rejection). Finally offers have to be exchanged and concessions made (which no one likes doing) to get to a point of agreement. This too may take longer than expected but if both parties need an agreement, then one will be reached.

Appendix 1: A preparation checklist

Preparation is vital in any negotiation. The questions below, which are based on the definition of negotiation provided in Chapter 1, are a useful starting point in developing a broad understanding of what a forthcoming negotiation might involve.

Two ***parties***:
who are the parties involved?
are there any constituencies in the background?
is anyone being left out of the negotiations?
can we usefully change the structure of the negotiation?
With ***differences***:
what are the conflicts of interest?
where are *they* coming from?
what do we *really* want from these negotiations?
why?
what don't we know about the negotiations but would really like to know?
Which they need to ***resolve***:
what are the alternatives to reaching an agreement?
for us?
for them?
Trying to reach agreement:
how will the negotiations be handled?
how might trust and reciprocity be developed?
Through exploring ***options***:
what are some possible creative solutions?
And exchanging ***offers***:
how will any closing tensions be managed?
And an ***agreement***:
what will a good agreement look like?
are there any other negotiations which are consequent upon this one?

Appendix 2: A negotiation review checklist

If preparation is vital before any negotiation, then reviewing the negotiation once it has ended is equally important. The definition of negotiation again provides a simple framework for such a self-reflection. Integral to the answer to each question is another question: 'how could we do this better next time?'

To strengthen the review it would be helpful to compare your answers to these questions after the negotiation with your answers to the preparation questions (in Appendix 1). It would also help to compare your reflections on different negotiations; some instructive patterns may emerge.

Two ***parties***:
how well did we understand the other negotiators?
did the structure of the negotiation 'work'?
With ***differences***:
how well did we get to understand the extent of what were the critical differences which needed to be addressed?
Which they need to ***resolve***:
did we overestimate the quality of our walk-away alternative?
Trying to reach agreement:
what were the critical incidents in how the negotiations were handled?
did they trust us?
did we trust them?
when was there a sense of us working together rather than working against?
if so, when and how did that develop?
Through exploring ***options***:
how well did we manage the process of developing some creative solutions?
And exchanging ***offers***:
how well was the closing tension managed?
And an ***agreement***:
how does the final agreement compare with what we said we *really* wanted from these negotiations?
has this agreement made any forthcoming negotiations easier?

Action commitment:
What am I now going to do differently when I next negotiate?
Why?

Appendix 3: Self-reflection tools

It is important to have a realistic assessment of one's own approach to negotiation and there are many useful self-reflection tools. The Thomas-Kilmann Conflict Mode Instrument (Shell, 2001) enables negotiators to make an assessment of their preferred style. (It relates to the Dual Concerns Model which is explored in Chapter 3.) Robinson, Lewicki and Donahue (2000) have developed a Self-reported Inappropriate Negotiation Strategies (SINS) scale – which enables a negotiator to check out their ethical standpoint (and practice).

Deutsch (1990), whose advice we are following to 'know thyself', suggests that negotiators can evaluate themselves across six dimensions:

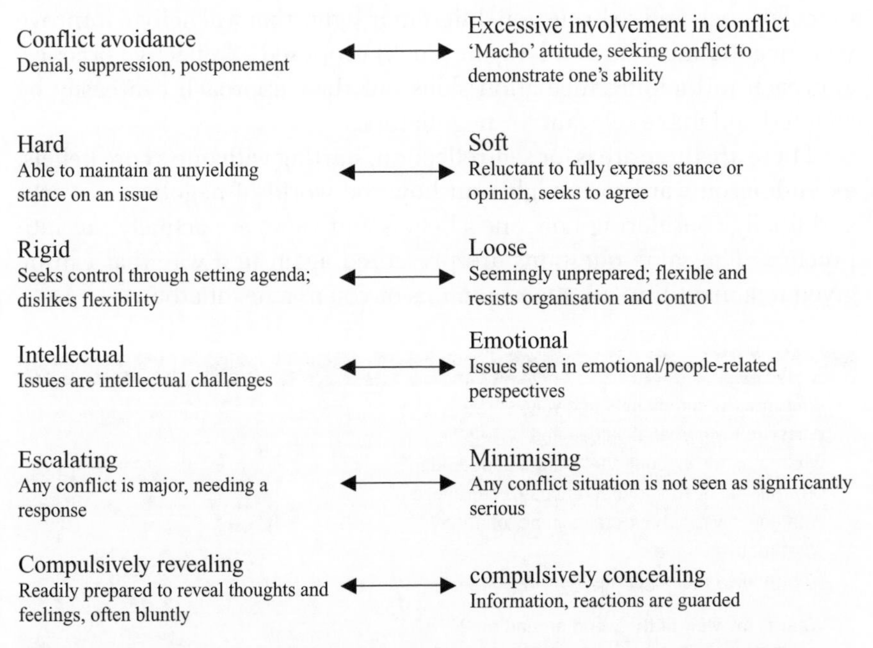

Figure A3.1: What is my approach to negotiation? (based on Deutsch, 1990)

Salacuse (1998) provides a list of 10 negotiation factors that he suggests can be used to assess other cultural approaches to negotiation (see Chapter 10) but they can equally be used for a self-assessment.

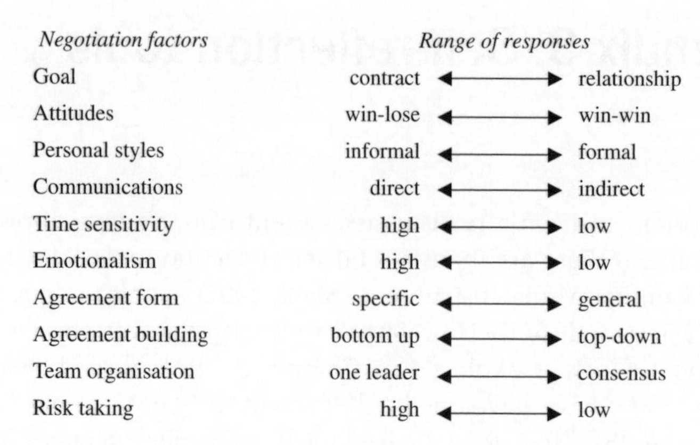

Figure A3.2: What are my negotiation preferences? (based on Salacuse, 1998)

Checklists, such as those in Figures A3.1 and A3.2 above are a useful way to start assessing one's approach to negotiation. The next step is to be rather more contemplative. This is more time consuming but can go much 'deeper' and so bring you different insights that will help to improve your negotiating. Lang and Taylor (2000) proposed a 'reflective practice' approach to building mediation skills but their approach can easily be adapted and made relevant for negotiators.

There are three areas for self-reflection, starting with one's core beliefs, extending outward to thoughts on how the world of negotiation works and finally considering how one's beliefs and views are actually put into practice. The same questions are presented again in a way that can be given to a mentor to ask their opinions of you as a negotiator.

Self-reflection checklist

What are my core beliefs and values?

What are my personal values and beliefs?
What is my view about conflict and cooperation?
On what basis should differences to be resolved?
What is my view about ethics in negotiation?
What motivates me?
What makes me negotiate the way I do?

What is my view of the world around me?

How do people behave in situations of conflict/disagreement? Why?
How do people reveal information (or not?)
How does trust work?
How does fairness work?
How does power work?
What makes an outcome 'good'?

How do I interact with others?
What words describe my typical reaction to a situation where there are differences between participants?
How do I behave when facing difficult choices or situations?
How do I handle critical incidents in negotiations?
What actions by others give me difficulty? Why?
What actions by me give rise to unhelpful reactions by others?

Action commitment
What one thing am I now going to do differently the next time I negotiate?
Why?

Mentor's perceptions checklist

From what you have seen me do when I negotiate, what do you think are my core beliefs and values?
What makes me negotiate the way I do?

From what you have seen me do when I negotiate, can you tell . . .
How I expect people to behave in situations of conflict or/disagreement?
How I expect others to reveal information?
What I think about trust?
What I think about fairness?
What I think about power?
What sort of outcomes I am trying to achieve?

From what you have seen me do when I negotiate
What words would you use to describe my typical reaction to a situation?
Where there are differences between participants?
How do I behave when facing difficult choices or situations?
How do I handle critical incidents in negotiations?
What actions by others give me difficulty?
What actions by me give rise to unhelpful reactions by others?

Action recommendation
What one thing do you suggest that I do differently the next time I negotiate?

Appendix 4: The Strategy Framework

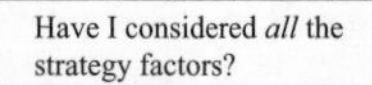

Strategy factor	
Importance of issue to self	*high/low*
Concern for other's outcome	*high/low*
Expectation of other's strategy	*concede/ contend compromise*
Time pressure	*high/low*
Quality of alternative	*good/poor*

Are there any strategy factors which can be improved?

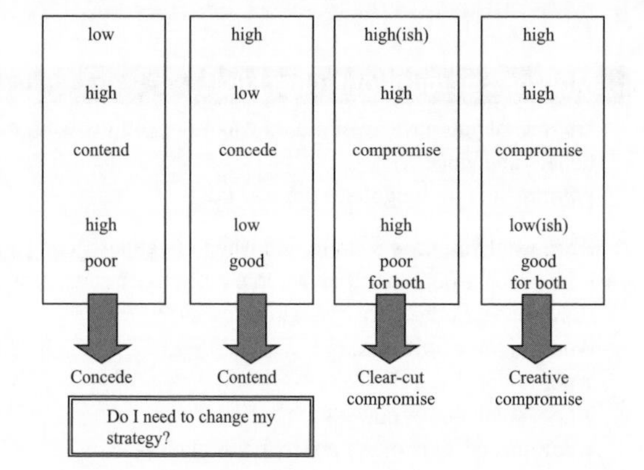

Appendix 5: The Nullarbor Model

The trans-Australian railway, which runs from Sydney to Perth, opened in standard gauge in 1970. The journey is 3961 km, making it one of the world's great train journeys. Known as the Indian Pacific, it takes three days. What makes the route distinctive is that it has the longest length of straight track anywhere in the world – 478 km in a dead-straight line (see Figure 5.3, p. 80, Chapter 5). It is this straightness that forms the basis of the imagery for our prescriptive model of negotiation.

A prescriptive model describes what ought to happen for a good outcome to be achieved. It may be a bit idealistic but if it also has a degree of realism – which this one does – then it can help us negotiate better.

The Nullarbor Model recognises the competitiveness of negotiation but seeks to emphasise the importance of moving a negotiation through phases and to spend as much time as possible in cooperative problem-solving activities. The underlying premise is that if the right steps are followed then the process of cooperating in finding solutions is quite straightforward and *will* yield a good quality outcome to meet the needs of the parties. However it is not an idealistic 'win-win' model; the journey to Perth might not be completely straightforward.

We start the journey at Sydney.

The Nullarbor Model

Getting started: preparation

The Indian Pacific is not the only way to get to Perth. You can drive(!) or go by plane. This reminds us that even before sitting down to negotiate, it is important to consider your alternatives and decide whether you have to negotiate at all.

Negotiation point
The importance of *alternatives* and the non-negotiation option.

Managing the negotiation
Do I really need to negotiate?
What will happen if I don't?

Getting started: at the negotiation table

Leaving Sydney the train has to work its way through the Blue Mountains, which isn't easy. This represents the fact that early in the negotiation there is often some unexpected conflict. We can't expect negotiations to go smoothly and so we need to manage this conflict without overreacting or letting it affect our approach on the issues.

Negotiation point
The role of *conflict* and the effort needed to overcome it.

Managing the negotiation
Does the conflict coming across the table indicate the approach that the other party is going to adopt or is it that we are just going through the Blue Mountains and it will settle down?

If so I should just work my way through it rather than develop a reciprocal response to what they are doing.

Continuing at the negotiation table

Even when you have got as far as Broken Hill, you can still get off the train, go back to Sydney and get on a plane to Perth. This reminds us that even when involved in a negotiation, and making progress, we still have other alternatives. They are becoming increasingly costly but they are still available to us.

Negotiation point
Alternatives remain but are increasingly costly.

Managing the negotiation
Now I'm getting to understand the issues between us better and what might and might not be achievable, is it still worth my while negotiating?

Needing to cooperate because they need to settle

In our Nullarbor imagery we are saying that as the train travels across South Australia the passengers stop leaving Sydney and start going to Perth. Of course, they are doing both for the whole journey but at some point (and not necessarily halfway) they start thinking more about the destination than the place they have left. This represents the period in a negotiation where *both* parties realise that they are going to have to work with the people across the table in order to reach an agreement. What's more, by the time you get to the edge of the Nullarbor Plain, you really don't have any alternatives – you can't get out and walk! In negotiation terms, you get to a point where your only realistic alternative is to cooperate with the other side.

Negotiation point
The *joint* need for agreement –> *cooperation.*

Managing the negotiation
Am I *really* sure that they are willing to look for genuine compromises or are they still expecting me to make all the moves?

Do I need to 'talk process' before giving any more information or making any suggestions?

Finding solutions

But what does 'cooperation' mean in practice?

It's quite straightforward. Firstly, analyse the issues you now face recognising that you have a joint problem, not an individual one. Then exchange as much information as possible and explore the different perspectives which this new information reveals. Finally, invent new and different options to resolve the problem.

Negotiation point
Cooperation means rational *problem solving.*

Managing the negotiation
Are they likely to see any proposals I suggest as being firm commitments?

Can we keep this as tentative and exploratory for as long as possible to see what might develop?

We should be aware that all sorts of things can go wrong in a long train journey – the track can flood, the Indian Pacific can get stuck behind a slow freight train; perhaps some of the passengers are showing signs of frustration at how long the journey is taking.

Finding solutions, even while endeavouring to be cooperative, might still involve some competitive trading of offers and some periods of slow, or no progress.

Keeping going

The next big stop after the Nullarbor is the gold mining centre of Kalgoorlie where you can get off the train and fly or drive to Perth. In terms of our image of negotiation this tells us that having worked through various options we still have to check whether the agreement we are putting together is better than what we might achieve by walking away and pursuing another alternative. However, a proper application of the problem-solving approach should result in an outcome that clearly adds value and so is better than any alternative. So you keep negotiating.

Negotiation point
Alternatives exist but are not attractive.

Managing the negotiation
We've come up with some potential solutions but are they better for me than walking away from this negotiation?

The end game of negotiation

The final run into Perth follows the twisting course of the Avon Valley. Often just when you think you have an agreement in your sights, conflict resurfaces, perhaps over an issue that had been overlooked, or because one party tries to extract some extra value out of the agreement. The premise of the problem-solving approach is that the negotiators will have found a high quality agreement which meets the needs of both parties. This being so the best way to overcome any last minute difficulties is to emphasise the benefits of the agreement rather than make any last minute concessions just to wrap up the deal.

Negotiation point
The high quality of the potential agreement overcomes conflict to bring closure.

Managing the negotiation
Does this final competitive pressure from the other party mean they are fundamentally unhappy with the outcome?

In which case, do we need to go back and travel across the Nullarbor again or is it an end-game play and I should just stand firm?

The agreement

Perth is a great city and while the journey there might be enjoyable as well as challenging, what is important is how visitors enjoy themselves while there. It is the same with negotiation. Achieving an agreement may have been both challenging and satisfying but what really matters is how well that agreement is implemented.

And just as the visitors to Perth may well take time out to reflect on their journey so too should negotiators see what might be done better next time.

Developing your own image of negotiation

The railway imagery may not 'work' for you. If so, then try to develop another imagery that you can use. It needs to be something that involves a sequence of events and activities rather than a single or short activity. For example, if you go sailing – perhaps a yacht race; if you like classical music – perhaps your favourite symphony; if you like cooking (and eating) – perhaps the process of preparing (and eating!) a meal. Or maybe consider negotiation as constructing a building; as a game of chess; as a marriage or a dance. (In Chapter 10 images of rock and roll and of a banquet are used to describe cross-cultural negotiations.)

Use your imagery to identify some of the key points in negotiation. This may need a bit of creativity but don't try to 'stretch' your image too far or the imagery will not work for you in the heat of a negotiation. It is not necessary to have everything covered in your image; it simply needs to bring to mind the key features of negotiation. Perhaps try your imagery out on a colleague or friend for their ideas and suggestions. Then try it out next time you negotiate and refine you imagery over time.

A route to agreement

The usefulness of creating an image of the negotiation process is that it helps us evaluate how much progress is being made and how well the process is being managed. It helps keep the negotiations 'on track'. The image of a negotiation as a trip across Australia provides a checklist of negotiation points to consider when you are sitting in a negotiation wondering 'what's going on here? Where exactly are we in these negotiations?'

The Nullarbor Model of negotiation - a summary

The importance of *alternatives* and the non-negotiation option:
We are still in Sydney – do we really need to negotiate at all?

The role of *conflict* and the effort needed to overcome it:
Are we still going through the Blue Mountains? There's some conflict but it's OK, we should expect it.

Ongoing alternatives but increasingly costly:
Are we at Broken Hill? We are not making much progress – can we get off?

The *joint* need for agreement–> *cooperation*:
Are we going through South Australia?
Are we ready to work with them to find agreement?
Are they ready to work with us?

Cooperation means rational *problem solving*:
We are crossing the Nullarbor — Are we cooperating fully?

Alternatives exist but are not attractive:
We are at Kalgoorlie. We've explored some possibilities but are they good enough?

The *high quality agreement* overcomes conflict to bring closure
We are in the Avon Valley.
We are experiencing some last minute problems.
We must focus on the benefits of the agreement.

Remember: this is a view of what *ought* to happen, not what *does* happen.

Appendix 6: Managing competitiveness

It seems a good idea to use negotiation tactics which give you a competitive advantage except for the fact of reciprocity, which means the other negotiator will then try the tactics back on you.

We should note, though, that being competitive in the sense of wanting to do well is a positive, not a negative. The negative side surfaces when the negotiator stops being strategic and allows the desire to do well to drift into a desire to 'do better out of this negotiation than the other party'. This is a polite way of saying 'we must beat them so that they don't beat us'. It reflects the imagery of negotiation as a sporting contest.

Here are some competitive 'hard ball' tactics and some advice on how to handle them (the inference is that good negotiators will not resort to these tactics themselves). Since negotiation is about an issue and involves a process, competitiveness can be found in either dimension.

Competiveness on the issue

Negotiators can adopt a number of competitive issue strategies.

The tough stance negotiator

The other negotiator makes an extreme claim and you get the impression that any concessions will be small and a long time coming.

The essence of the strategy is to wear the other negotiator down and rely on the fact that the clear-cut concession strategy is the most common way of settling differences. By always making smaller concessions the outcome will be in their favour. The signal of this strategy is an extreme opening offer.

It is a single sided strategy; it takes no account of the other party, other than to presume that time pressure, a poor walk away alternative (BATNA) and generally high motivation to settle, will all lead the other negotiator to make the necessary compromises.

Firstly, check other party's context. If they have a good BATNA and are not under time pressure then we should expect them to follow a strong contending strategy. Secondly, check whether you need to negotiate at all.

Assuming you do, then the best response to an extreme offer is a two-pronged approach. On the issue, make a matching high (but not extreme) offer, and be resolute about it. On the process, outline a scenario of trying to package together some creative options.

Realistically this is not going to make a lot of difference at the start but it will lay a foundation for later in the negotiation. The other party is only going to change strategy when their context changes. Trying to convince them that they have a poor BATNA will only cause them to become more rigid. They need to realise that you are not going to make concessions. In strategy terms, their expectation of your strategy has to change. Be prepared to walk away.

If the other negotiator continues to negotiate (showing that an agreement is better for them than walking away) they will press for concessions (but not make any themselves). Remember the tit for tat strategy.

In response to an invitation to make a concession, put a linked and conditional 'if... then... ' concession on the table. 'If you are prepared to make a concession on delivery dates then I can look at the payment schedule.' Note that the 'you' comes before the 'I'.

If you feel it is necessary to make a unilateral concession then it must be a single concession, preferably backed up by attempts to open up the negotiation into something more creative. 'I'm prepared to look at the payment schedule and extend the period to 30 days. I will not be able to go beyond that so please don't ask for more. Delivery dates can be improved. What suggestions do you have about how this might be done?'

If at all possible avoid making two concessions in a row. It only encourages the other negotiator to become even more resolute ('raise the level of their aspiration' is the technical term). However, if your strategy analysis indicates that you are going to have to concede, then do so and get it over with.

The cooperative inviting negotiator

Often negotiators will be friendly, considerate and open and then in amongst the discussion invite you to make an opening offer. This looks cooperative, 'tell me what you think it's worth' but the intent is to have you put your price on the table so that they can spend time explaining why it won't be acceptable, and so when they state their offer it looks more acceptable.

Through your prior preparation you should have an opening position ready. When invited to make an opening offer, if you are not ready to do so, ask a question more for clarification or reopen discussion on one of the issues or perhaps summarise the differences between the parties. Don't respond by asking the other party to make their offer.

Once you have made your offer the other party will try to undermine it – don't respond to the criticisms. Remember reciprocity and the need for differentiation, both of which require the other party to put their offer on the table too. Talk through the process but if this does not work, press for their offer. 'You asked me for my offer and I've given it to you; what's your offer?' If they are evasive then press them on this equitable negotiation point. When they finally give it, perhaps a response would be, 'No wonder you did not want to tell me your offer! It is so low/high that you knew I would never accept it' though remember that there is no advantage in trying to score debating points. Keep your eye on the need for agreement.

The 'take it or leave it' offer

Check your BATNA. If you possibly can, leave it; be gracious about it but put your offer on the table and say that you will wait to hear from them if they want to agree to it. Check their BATNA too. If they cannot walk away from the negotiation either, put a 'yes-able proposition' on the table. It will be important to give the other party an excuse to back away from their take it or leave it position – 'in the light of this new information' (which does not actually have to be new, but just put in a new way) 'you might like to see if this proposal is a better one.'

If you can't leave it but they can then although it might feel good to put your own position on the table and have an argument, it is best to just agree and be done with it.

Competitiveness in the process

Negotiators can be competitive in how they approach the task of negotiating. (We should also remember Deutsch's crude law of social relations – if we see competitive behaviour across the table it may be because we are being competitive too.)

Bluffing and lying

Don't reciprocate!! Stand firm on the issue and keep asking questions in the area you suspect is not accurate. However, don't expect an open confession. The aim is to make sure the other party knows that you know they have lied. Allow the correct information to be provided at a later point – when it comes, a moment of direct eye contact will probably be sufficient rather than 'Oh that's not what you said last time.' Remember to double-check everything.

One of the advantages in taking notes is that the other party knows you will have a record of what they say and that you can always go back and check.

Remember that not being explicit about one's bottom line is not regarded as being deceitful. Also remember that if we give only partial information we might not call this lying but the other side might not see it as being honest.

Ingratiation

Through trying to impress you, the intent of the other party is to make you feel obligated towards them. Take what comes and be properly respectful in return but remember that you are not obligated to make concessions just because people say nice things about you. It is hard to know when trying to be friendly and building a working relationship becomes deliberate ingratiation so be careful about making judgements. If the other party organises a company car to meet you at your hotel to take you to the negotiation, they may be trying to make you feel obligated or they may be just trying to show respect. (Remember to do the same for them when they visit you.)

Gamesmanship

This includes things like being late or unexpectedly bringing a large negotiating team. Always remember your BATNA and theirs. Politeness and straightforwardness is disarming, as is giving an anecdote of a related situation in another negotiation where the gamesmanship tactic did not work (a high context way of calling the trick).

However also remember that – to an extent – business practices are different in different contexts. Meetings never start on time in Jakarta. This is partly because of the traffic but also because in Indonesia there is no sense of punctuality, so to arrive late is not deliberate gamesmanship.

The guilt ploy

If they emphasise how cooperative and reasonable they've been and yet we still don't have an agreement, this invites the conclusion that the deadlock is all your fault. If you can be made to feel guilty for the situation then you will feel motivated to alleviate the difficulty by making a concession. Always remember that it takes two to reach a deadlock; restate your main points and concerns.

The good cop/bad cop routine

There is some evidence that this works (Brodt and Tuchinsky, 2000) but it only works because it is allowed to. The defence, as in all these competitive ploys, lies in good preparation and having a clear statement of one's main points and concerns.

Don't retaliate by bringing in your own 'heavy hitter'. Contend on the issue. When you've had enough of their role play either call the play or, if feeling particularly confident, wind up the bad cop – he'll lose the plot eventually and have to be rescued by his own team. Best though to just let them do what ever they want and each time they finish restate your main points and concerns.

Tactics to unsettle the opponent

Beware the negotiator who likes to quickly drill down into the detail. Some people just think that way and are not being deliberately competitive – they just need to be pulled back to consider the big picture, the underlying concerns and motivations, not the detail of the history or of the technical arrangements. The detail becomes important later.

However, one way to put another negotiator off guard is to get them to focus on detail. The intent is that once flustered, the negotiator will give more information or make a concession. Other ploys directed towards putting the other negotiator off include bringing a far larger team (especially some lawyers) than you had indicated, always changing the topic, getting deliberately angry or making personal attacks.

The response, as always, is first check your BATNA, and then theirs, and then restate your main points.

Dealing with threats

The usual threat is to walk away though a variant is time-related – 'if you don't agree now, next week the price will be higher/lower.' Threats such as these work and this is because they have the effect of altering the other negotiator's perceptions of their available alternatives. Other threats can be more punitive or personal, 'if you walk away from this deal I'll make sure you never do business in this town again!'

A threat early in the negotiation does not show much respect for the other negotiator. Stating that you have an alternative and so don't really need to negotiate, or that the other party does not have any alternatives and so *has* to negotiate with you, will encourage a competitive response. It may well be true that you do have a good alternative and that the other party does not but there is no advantage to be gained by bringing that to the negotiation table early. Let the context speak for itself in the early stages.

Threats are more effective in the end-game at which point they should be more explicit (Sinaceur and Neale, 2005). The negotiators face a real choice of agreeing or not, so a threat has more impact. There will be more on managing the end-game in Chapter 8.

There is one thing to remember about all threats, even the punitive ones which are intended to unsettle you. Each threat has an implementation cost for the person making it. If the threat would indeed get you to change your mind and it cost nothing to the other party to implement their threat, they would not be talking to you but would have already done what they are threatening to do. So when the other party threatens to take you to court, you may well already know that you would lose the court case but the cost in fees and the inevitable time delay stops the other party from relying 100% on court action to achieve their desired outcome. So when a threat is made, first time ignore it but think hard about the costs to the other party of them implementing their threat. When the threat is raised again, refer to those costs and then carry on making your main points.

Of course, if you are going to lose the court case, it probably means that your case at the negotiation table is not going to be very strong either.

Handling interruptions

An easy way to unsettle another negotiator and control the discussion is through interruption and so it is a common competitive tactic.

Prevention is better than cure, so keep what you have to say short as this will deter interruptions. Secondly, don't go into too much detail, particularly early in the discussion.

Some interruptions are inevitable: one person is speaking, the other starts to say something, and then one or the other backs off, and no harm is done. This is what might be regarded as the first level of response to an interruption.

The next response is to acknowledge that the other person wants to make a point, but then carry on. Other ways of responding are shown below. It will be seen that they increase in severity. You should try to use the range of responses rather than stoically forebear the other person interrupting you until it all gets too much and you point the finger, 'if you keep interrupting me like that . . . .!!', and probably in your frustration you have interrupted the other person to tell them not to interrupt.

Don't respond to the interruption, continue to make your point.
Acknowledge but then continue with '. . . that's something we could deal with later but my main point is . . . '
Follow their interruption by going back to your main point (instead of responding to the interruption) with 'the point I have been making all along, and want to repeat now is . . . '
Refer to the ground rules of debate with 'it is only fair that each person has the opportunity to put their point of view across' or 'if there are too many interruptions, then we are not going to have much of a discussion on issues which we need to sort out.'
Maintain direct eye contact (prior to continuing with your point).
Refer directly to the other negotiator's behaviour with 'if you keep interrupting me, then you can't expect me to sit quietly while you are talking, can you?'

Handling tension

There is no doubt that humour is a great tension release but we have also probably been in situations where, in an attempt to cope with tension, someone has launched into a long story which usually turns out to be not very funny, and the tension is still there (and the embarrassment makes it worse). There is another potential difficulty with humour – some people's idea of a funny quip can be taken as a put-down of someone else; it is a comment or observation at someone else's expense. So being able to use humour – a funny interpretation or a quirky comment – is a great asset, but it is also risky (hence the question mark on the list below). So what else can be done?

Tension can be resolved by:

humour?
talking about the facts
talking about the common ground
summarising
signalling an adjournment.

Often it is just sufficient to say that an adjournment is going to be necessary, 'If we keep all this arguing up, we are going to need 'time out' for some fresh air', and that draws everyone's attention to what has been going on. The tension subsides by:

putting the issue 'on hold' and moving onto another issue
an informal 'reconciliation' – an 'impromptu' phone call or meeting
a change in personnel.

As a last resort, bringing new people into the meeting changes the dynamics.

Tension is a creative force and will be inevitable whenever people are discussing an issue of substance. Tension is an indication of the seriousness of the issue and strength of feeling, and should be distinguished from the tension which arises when the process is being managed poorly, or where some participants are not seriously searching for a resolution of the issues.

Appendix 7: Managing workplace negotiations

Workplace negotiations are one of the more obvious forms of constituency negotiations. They have all the ingredients of complexity and it is not surprising that sometimes the negotiations go very wrong, resulting in a poor outcome for all concerned. However although strikes and lockouts make the headlines, by far the greater majority of management–union negotiations result in agreements the parties can comfortably live with.

As with other constituency negotiations there will be a range of priorities within each side – that is, the management and the employees, some of whom may not be union members. In workplace negotiations, there is a lack of symmetry between the parties not evident in negotiations between two businesses. Even if one business is a conglomerate and the other small, they are still both businesses whereas a company and an employee group (whether in a union or not) are completely different entities with different negotiation resources and options. The fact that workers are the employees of the company they are negotiating with – or perhaps, against – adds to the asymmetry (Fells, 1998b). With the demise of compulsory arbitration, the union has to reach agreement with the employer but the company has options that do not involve reaching agreement with the union. Further, when management and union (or indeed any group of workers) commit to reach some form of enterprise agreement they are negotiating more than the terms of the document. They are renegotiating the terms of their interdependence (Walton and McKersie 1965), not only deciding the workplace rules but also establishing the power balance between them (Flanders, 1968). As with any other relationship, workplace relations carry their own history and the legacy of past disputes is hard to dislodge.

The negotiations are normally public in the sense that other employers, the industry association and other unions are all interested in the outcome. Negotiations in larger companies are reported in the newspapers; some become political. The legislative framework, although designed to resolve disputation, creates a framework that encourages an adversarial negotiation dynamic (Fells, 1999b) and so some employers and governments have encouraged direct negotiation between employer and employee. To the extent that these are genuine negotiations as opposed to 'take it or leave it' offers (though not usually put in such blunt terms), they are still not free from many of the complexities of the workplace.

This appendix provides some audit tools to help negotiators analyse and manage their workplace negotiations.

Treat enterprise negotiations as normal

Although different, management–union negotiations are not so very different that it is necessary to throw out all the principles of good negotiation found elsewhere in this book. There is no need for a changed approach; rather the application of the basic principles of negotiation in a different context.

Many management–union negotiations follow a traditional script. A union log of claims is submitted and rejected. Management's counter proposal is also rejected. The negotiators then sort out a number of issues but one or two 'big ticket' items remain as an opportunity for power-based brinkmanship. However, that the parties choose to use only contend or concede issue strategies does not mean that the other two strategies are not available to them. Although from the outset the parties may use actions more appropriate to the end-game, there is still a need to exchange information and test for flexibility. The script everyone has been comfortable with is not the only one.

Negotiating an enterprise agreement takes a lot of effort and can become the focus of attention for both the management and workforce for many months. It is right that such an important event – which is going to govern the working lives of employees for perhaps the next two or three years – should be regarded as important. However, it is often seen as an isolated event.

Having spent months getting to a point of agreement, negotiators often say something like 'It's a good job that this is a two year agreement and we don't have to go through all this again next year!!' Many HR managers and union officials work back from the agreement's expiry date and put a note in their diary for a month or two prior to remind them to start thinking about the next round of negotiations. Furthermore, once the agreement is signed it is left to the managers and supervisors to renegotiate the agreement terms with the employees to ensure that the changes actually occur. (This is why employees can trade away a work practice in return for a productivity payment and often can trade it away again in the next agreement.)

Rather than be treated as an isolated event – a one-off opportunity to deal with a backlog of workplace issues – the enterprise negotiations and agreement should be the culmination of work that has been done over the previous two or three years. The time to start thinking about the next enterprise agreement is the first day the current one starts to be implemented. Both parties should constantly review the operation of the agreement throughout its life and so the next enterprise agreement becomes an opportunity to consolidate all that they have been trying to achieve.

The parties should also consider how their enterprise negotiations compare with negotiations that occur at other times. There is little point trying to set up a cooperative negotiation process two to three months ahead of the agreement's expiry date if during the previous year the management has been taking an authoritative line on employee grievances and the employees have been 'working the system' as best as they can. Organisations are a form of 'negotiated order' with constant negotiation between its members as they seek to get the work done. Managers of departments negotiate with each other over production schedules; supervisors negotiate with their team when they have a 'rush job' on; employees negotiate with their manager when they can see a better way of doing their job; everyone negotiates with the IT department to jump the queue and get their computer fixed quickly!

Usually it is the management who set the tone within an organisation. If day-to-day production and other issues are routinely dealt with on an interest-based perspective then when employee grievances emerge they too will be approached and resolved in the same way. Then, when the enterprise agreement is due to be negotiated those involved will be comfortable with an interest-based script. If the day-to-day issues are 'resolved' on the basis of rights or power (to use the terminology of Ury, Brett and Goldberg, 1989) then the enterprise agreement will almost inevitably be negotiated on the same basis. Fundamental shifts in management–union relations can be achieved but this requires a combination of changing circumstances and comprehensive strategy (Fells and Skeffington, 1998; Fells, 2003; Walton, Cutcher-Gershenfeld and McKersie, 1994).

The practical implication is that the senior management of a company should establish behavioural and outcome criteria to deal with issues inside and outside the organisation. Employees at all levels need to be given the opportunity to develop the necessary skills to resolve issues constructively as they arise. The way potentially conflictive issues are dealt with should feature in any performance reviews at both the individual and organisational levels. A degree of pragmatism is necessary as it is unwise to expect any model of negotiation, no matter how rationally based and behaviourally perfect, to transition intact from the training room to the boardroom, office or shop floor. The organisation must learn from the past to build a realistic future.

Conduct a negotiation audit

As the philosopher George Santayana wrote, 'Those who cannot remember the past are condemned to repeat it.' It perhaps did not matter that you got a bit strident while negotiating with the real estate agent when selling your house as it was a one-off transaction but in the workplace the implementation of the agreement is a day-by-day affair. While the lead negotiators themselves may not have to deal with the consequences, the constituents do.

It is important to review each negotiation. The best time to do this is soon after the negotiations have concluded. Realistically this is difficult and so the review of the previous enterprise negotiation should be the first step in getting ready for the forthcoming one. The four elements to this audit – structure, process, individual action and outcome – are outlined below.

There is considerable benefit in the audit being conducted by negotiators and other key figures from both sides at a meeting specially convened for this purpose – a 'lessons learned' workshop. A critical 'ground rule' for this meeting is that nothing is to be decided. It is not a 'negotiation about a negotiation' but simply an open review providing both parties with opportunity to reflect on the past and what might be done better next time. If the parties are unwilling to work through the process jointly, there is still benefit in doing it separately.

Step one: the structure of the negotiation

Figure A7.1 presents the main elements of most workplace negotiations indicating some of the subgroups that can be within either side. It is also important to consider the alternatives open to both parties; these can be significantly impacted by workplace relations legislation.

The audit process involves simply taking a blank piece of paper and drawing the structure of the negotiations to reflect the negotiation under review. For example on the union side there may have been two unions involved so both would need to be included. On the company side, the diagram might need to show that there was input from the corporate HR

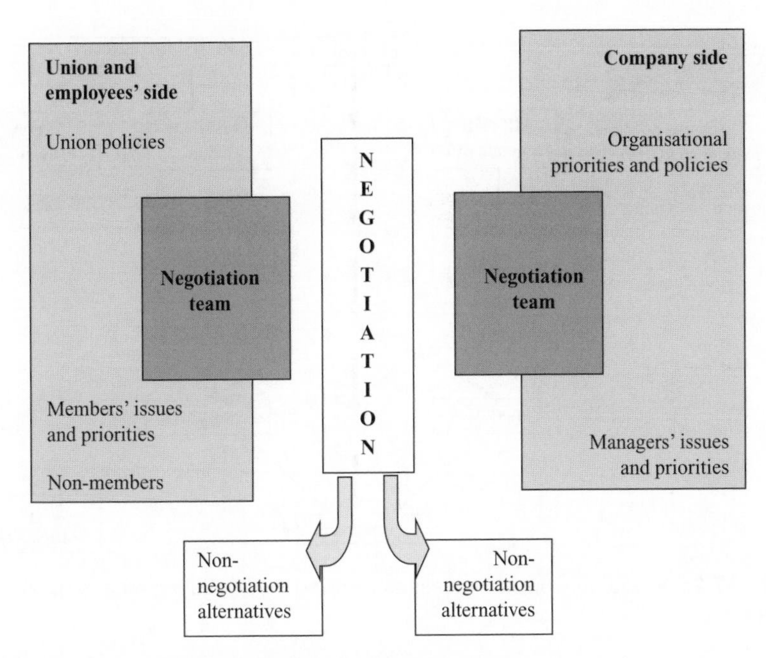

Figure A7.1: A simplified workplace negotiation structure

office as well as from the plant's HR manager. Clarifying the structure of the negotiation provides a foundation for the next step.

Step two: the process of negotiation

Figure A7.2 presents many of the complex interacting steps that have to be followed to achieve an enterprise agreement. These steps are centred on the initial claim and offer but include the dynamics within each side before and during the negotiations.

Again the audit process involves taking a blank piece of paper and drawing the actual sequence of events from start to finish in negotiation under review. It is useful to put a timeline against the sequence of events, if possible estimating the amount of time invested (and by whom) at each step. This process of recollecting what happened last time will then enable the parties to discuss what occurred and consider how the forthcoming negotiations might be improved. Some discussion questions are provided below. The review process will be enhanced if the parties can discuss these questions jointly and openly, but reviewing them in a private session is better than not reviewing the negotiations at all.

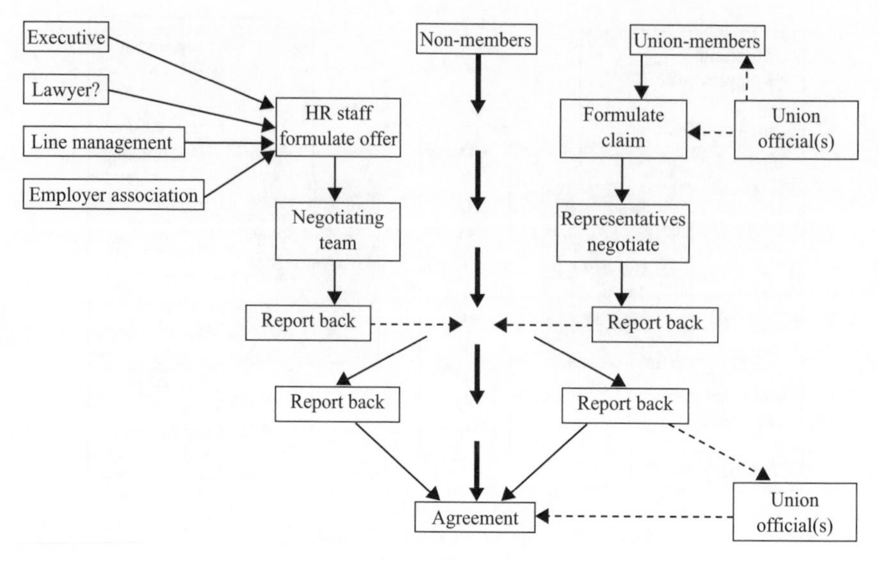

Figure A7.2: An example of the processes involved in negotiating an enterprise agreement

Negotiation review questions

What were the 'hot spots' in the process when difficulties occurred?
What was causing the problem (the focus is on difficulties in the process, not differences in the issues)?
Was there anyone who or any organisation that was not involved and should have been (even if only to have been in the communication loop)?
How might this be achieved for the coming negotiations?
Was there anyone who or any organisation that was involved and did not make a constructive contribution?
How might this (or any other outsider's) intervention be prevented/minimised/or made constructive in the coming negotiation?
What points in the other party's process caused us difficulty?
What can we do about the elements in our process that seem to cause difficulty to the other party?
What investments of time, information and other resources do we need to improve the process?
How can we improve the communication between the main negotiations and the constituencies?

Developing a new negotiation script

Discussion of the process can easily lead into discussion of the dynamics of interaction between the parties. As shown in Chapter 9, interactions in constituency negotiations are inherently competitive and require a great deal of 'balancing' by the negotiators, particularly on the union side.

Though the process will have started much earlier, the formal start of a management–union negotiation is usually the union presenting a log of claims. Union negotiators are then obliged to defend these claims – the easiest way being to attack the management's past performance and impending offer. Similarly when the management then places its own offer it is there to be defended, not 'unpacked'. Another feature which impacts on the negotiation is that both parties will be working to a document – the enterprise agreement. Normally both parties will seek to rewrite the current agreement to reflect their own positions. Working to a document invites a clause-by-clause approach (no different to when lawyers work their way through a legal contract) that in turn invites a win-lose dynamic on each point, irrespective of its importance.

The audit presents an opportunity for the participants to review their negotiation script though the extent to which the whole idea of scripts can be explored depends greatly on the willingness of the participants. Two similar scripts of cooperative workplace negotiation are Mutual Gains Bargaining and Interest Based Bargaining (Cutcher-Gershenfeld, 2003, Friedman, 1993), both derived from the Principled Negotiation Model of Fisher, Ury and Patton (1991). The Nullarbor Model of Chapter 5 or some other script might resonate with the participants. It is worth repeating the point made earlier that a new approach to enterprise negotiation will only be sustained if it is consistent with the conflict resolution climate within the organisation as a whole.

Similarly the script should recognise the fundamentally competitive dynamic of workplace relations even when the issue under discussion is an 'integrative' one. The process has to 'deliver' for the constituents on both sides and this might not be achieved if there is too much emphasis on cooperation. One extensive study of different forms of workplace bargaining across a single organisation found that competitive rather than cooperative bargaining resulted in better outcomes, at least as far as the employees were concerned (Bacon and Blyton, 2007). (This was in part because the managers seeking employee cooperation were themselves being competitive.) Rather than rely on a standard consultancy package it would be preferable if the participants preparing for a forthcoming negotiation gave some thought to developing an imagery or a broad script of their own, one that seeks to improve on past practice but which is not too divorced from it.

Managing the negotiations

The practical implication of the notion of phases (Chapter 4) is that negotiations need to be managed. Working broadly to a preferred script is one way of doing this. At the individual level, and particularly if the negotiation audit does not progress to the participants discussing the idea of a new negotiation script, it would be useful for participants to be aware of the three questions which help any negotiator to make an 'on-the-spot' action review in the midst of the negotiation (Figure A7.3).

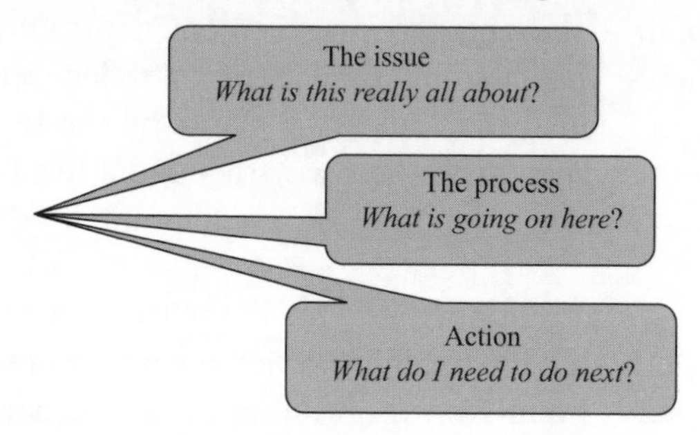

Figure A7.3: On-the-spot action review questions for negotiators

Step three: the actions of individual negotiators

The individuals taking part in the negotiation must take responsibility for what occurs and this involves taking responsibility for their own actions and contributions. Appendix 3 provides some self-reflection tools. In the context of a 'lessons-learned' workshop these may be too 'deep' and a more collaborative process might be more appropriate. The audit of behaviour could focus on the notion of a 'good negotiator'. Some discussion and reflection questions are suggested below.

Negotiator review questions

For joint discussion

What does it mean to be a good negotiator?

What do good negotiators do?

(This discussion could be started by participants thinking of someone they regard as a good negotiator and someone else – no names! – who they regard as being an unhelpful/poor negotiator.)

For individual reflection

How would you rate your contribution to the previous negotiations on a scale of 0–10? Why?

What is the particular contribution you will bring to the forthcoming negotiation? (This is a way of asking, what are your strengths as a negotiator?)
What area of your negotiating do you think you should improve?

It is sometimes suggested that parties agree ground rules for a forthcoming negotiation. As a result of conducting an audit it is probable that those involved get to see, for example, that interrupting each other is not helpful. At some point in the process they might draw all these action points together on a flip chart (a useful contribution by the facilitator if there is one) but a personal commitment to the process is probably going to have more impact on behaviour than drawing up a 'code of negotiation conduct'. A personal commitment might take the form of each participant writing down one thing each is going to do differently in the forthcoming negotiation.

Step four: the outcomes of the negotiation

The parties to a forthcoming negotiation may feel uncomfortable about reviewing the outcome of the previous negotiations in a joint session. They should be left to use the questions presented below as part of their own preparation on the issues they intend to put forward for negotiation. The questions direct the reviewers to consider their answers from the perspective of the other party.

Outcome review questions

How would the other party evaluate the substantive outcomes?
Pay and other conditions of employment?
Work effort, innovation and other task related requirements?

How would the other party evaluate the relational outcomes?
Manager–employee?
Employee–employee?
Management–union?

What would the other party say were the key reasons for these outcomes?

Appendix 8: Managing a business negotiation

Many business negotiations are also complex with elements of constituency dynamics and 'balancing' on the part of the negotiation team. They can take many forms ranging from relatively simple product sales through procurement contracts to a complex sale of an entire business operation. Except in the most straightforward of cases, the negotiators – whether company sales representatives, procurement managers or corporate lawyers – are acting on behalf of the company. They will be working to a set of expectations and priorities much the same as union negotiators work to a set of expectations and priorities set for them by their members.

As with workplace negotiations, business negotiations are different but not so very different that the basic elements of good negotiation no longer apply. The parties always use the four issue strategy and the option of walking away. The tasks of information exchange, flexibility testing and concession making are still all necessary to reach a good agreement.

This appendix reviews some important practical aspects to consider when preparing for and conducting major formal business negotiations, though the points raised apply in less formal business negotiation settings as well. It presumes an understanding of the negotiation strategy and process issues discussed in earlier chapters.

Deal prospecting: when does a negotiation start?

A small geology company had researched a major mining house, making an assessment of its internal capabilities and also of the broader geology of areas where the mining company was already operating. By their assessment the geologists believed they could contribute to the mining company's exploration and development through their own particular skill set. They asked for a meeting with a senior executive from the mining company and outlined their proposed joint arrangement. The senior executive brought the hour-long meeting to an end by saying he did not know why he was even spending time listening to their proposal.

A similar presentation was made to another mining company whose representatives quickly saw the long-term potential of what was being proposed. The two sides soon reached an understanding that they could enter into a partnership and so spent couple of hours sorting out the main parameters of an agreement covering their respective financial and expertise contributions, the broad process for evaluating mining prospects and the way any subsequent revenue would be shared. It took a further four months to finalise the details of the contract (mainly through email exchanges). Though points were contested and positions traded, the negotiations were cooperative and there were no potential deal breakers.

These examples show an important aspect of many business negotiations, that the two parties have to decide whether they even want to negotiate with each other. There has to be a process of 'deal prospecting' that precedes any formal 'deal making'. Deal prospecting involves preliminary investigation and an initial 'shadow' negotiation to reach a point where the parties commit to negotiating an agreement.

In the case of a supply contract, the initial prospecting might be through industry networks and internet searches to identify a short list of potential suppliers which might then be approached with a general proposition. The critical point is when both parties come to the view that an agreement is possible. If the issue is straightforward, such as when the supplier is being asked to supply a standard product, the parties might quickly realise that an agreement is possible provided that they can reach mutually beneficial terms. From this point on, the discussion focuses on the detailed terms in the expectation that agreement will be reached, though either party might change their view, conclude that a satisfactory agreement will not be possible and bring the negotiations to a close.

Major transactions, such as an acquisition, divestment or joint venture, are rarely opportunistic but typically occur after one of the companies has spent a lot of time (and money) thoroughly auditing suitable potential target companies and establishing a sound business case for the proposal. An internal document or information memorandum will be prepared for the company's board and if they agree to proceed then a senior level approach would be made to the preferred target. As with establishing a supply contract, the parties have to reach the critical point of deciding whether a deal is in fact possible. Although much more might be at stake, the principle is the same. The first step may be for the CEO to put the broad scope of the deal to his counterpart in the target company. If she is receptive, they may commit to more formal discussions. The 'shape', or to use Watkins' (2006) imagery 'architecture', of the proposed deal would be explained and discussed and only when both parties are reasonably confident that an agreement is possible (again provided they can reach mutually beneficial terms) will they proceed. Deal prospecting would have led into deal making (Figure A8.1). The stages portrayed in Figure A8.1 are common to most complex negotiations, though the terminology may differ

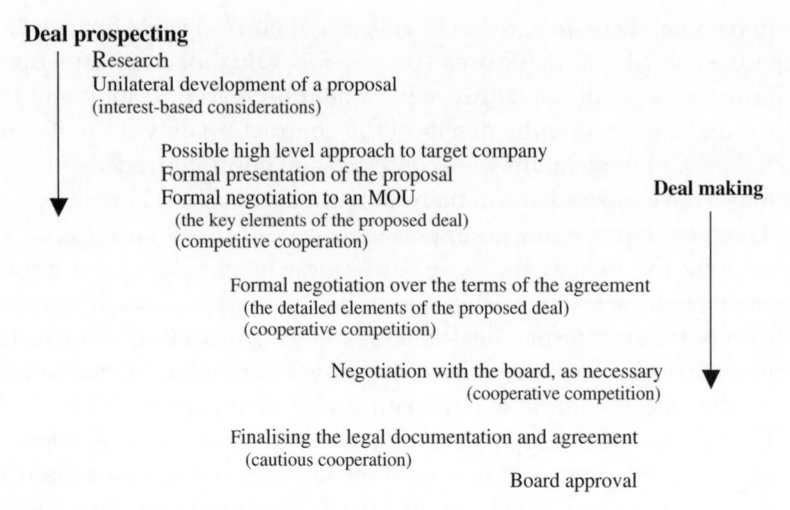

Figure A8.1: Deal prospecting and deal making

such as diagnostic, framework and detail phases (Zartman and Berman, 1982).

Aspects of preparation

Preparing the negotiating team

Major business negotiations may take many months and require a team of negotiators committed to securing an outcome that meets the company's expectations. The initiating party is at an advantage in being able to draw its team from those working on the development of the proposal.

The negotiating team has to be 'on top of the facts' so that they understand the integrative potential of the proposed deal and can evaluate the worth of trade-offs being proposed by the other party. Each person appointed to the team will be expected to contribute in their particular area of expertise, such as finance, operations, marketing or legal, but each must also understand the perspectives of others in the team and the issues their colleagues will want addressed as part of the overall settlement. For example, in a negotiation to acquire a new mine, the geologist would provide insights into the nature of the ore body but she would be expected to contribute to discussions of environmental, logistics to market and other issues. Team members must communicate fully with each other to ensure an integrated approach. This means the geologist must be prepared to work her way through complex legal documents – not just the parts dealing with the mineral aspects; while the lawyer must have an understanding of extraction processes. The lead negotiator has to understand the different perspectives each team member will bring, the issues they raise and, crucially, see how these specialist issues might impact on other areas of the proposal.

While it is important to have operational people involved to ensure that what is being agreed can be implemented, it is equally important to ensure that nobody on the negotiating team has subsidiary personal interests (such as managers who also have control of other parts of the organisation which might be adversely affected by the merger or acquisition).

Another aspect of the lead negotiator's role is to take control of the conduct of the joint sessions and to generally coach the team in how the sessions will be conducted. If others are to participate on the basis of their expertise then they must understand that their contribution is in information exchange and that the discussion reverts back to the leader when it looks like it is shifting from information exchange to debate over the validity of positions. Similarly any solutions reached in joint working parties must be reported back and are only tentative until formally proposed and accepted in the main negotiation forum.

The lead negotiator needs clear authority from the 'constituency', the senior management group. The negotiating team will inevitably have to make some unanticipated decisions and trade-offs so they need to understand how they might trade one aspect of the deal for another to achieve a final agreement. Is a combination of upfront and conditional payments acceptable? How much could be paid to gain additional control? The scope and limits of their authority must be clear for the negotiators to be properly empowered and motivated to deal effectively with these uncertainties. The lead negotiator should maintain communication with the senior management group, exercising judgement about when to update them on progress or seek further instructions – that difficult balancing act faced by all constituency negotiators. A competent lead negotiator operating with clear instructions should all but eliminate the risk of 'separation' that is a feature of many constituency negotiations.

Be clear on the strategic intent

The initiating party is again at a distinct advantage having done much research to establish the inherent worth of the proposed deal. The target company is in a reactive position (though of course their business development team may well have been alert to the prospect of an approach).

The negotiators must be clear on the strategic intent that underpins the negotiation. What's the big picture? Where is the value coming from? In what way does one party add to the other's value proposition? This should all be clear from the in-house documentation based on the prior research. This research should make clear the inherent value and risks in the target company and its modus operandi so that the negotiators can understand the proposal from both parties' perspectives. The underlying rationale for the proposal drives the exploration for ways around problems and again during periods of exchange when the negotiators are trying to 'close off' on issues. It is often at this point that the subsidiary objectives tend to come to the fore but the negotiators should not become focused on the detail at the expense of the big picture.

The proposal has to be put into negotiable terms. The key purpose would be to acquire or merge with a particular company or create a joint venture, but this will typically embrace some subsidiary objectives such as to minimise the cost of the acquisition or to maximise operational control over the new organisation. Securing a smooth implementation would involve ensuring the cooperation of key management and other employees (or alternatively minimising the impact of their departure). There may be specific legal or financial aspects that are critical in defining a successful outcome. These subsidiary objectives tend to become limits or constraints on the negotiation – 'unless we obtain the company for less than x amount of dollars we will not proceed', or 'if we can't carry their key management team, we will not proceed'. They can easily become the deal breaker. There may also be important process objectives such as to minimise the actual cost of the negotiation (such as consultant fees) and a timeframe (though being alert to the implications of being under time pressure).

Developing an opening position

Once the team has become familiar with the proposal, the next step is for the lead negotiator to make a first draft of an agreement document. The negotiating team then meets to raise any particular issues they want addressed. Experience in the industry will normally provide the core list of issues but all likely issues should be raised for discussion at this stage.

The team should then develop an issues list: for each issue, the company's preferred position, the other company's likely position in their response to the offer, the priority of the issue and a final column left for the outcome. The priority of each issue will be determined to a large extent by the strategic intent. (Any differences of view as to priorities that can't be resolved within the team should be referred to the senior management group.) There will be 'die in the trenches' issues without which any agreement will have failed to achieve its objective; key issues where negotiation and compromise is possible (a key issue might be control but the actual number of seats on the board, the precise extent of control, might be negotiable) and other 'nice to have' issues if they can be achieved. All are real issues. It is not a case of making up issues which can be 'thrown away' to create a cooperative response. All the issues will be negotiated until the closing stages, but in those closing stages it is the 'nice to have' issues which may be traded to achieve the deal. Through further discussion a proposal document is prepared and once the team is comfortable that this document reflects the company's preferred position on each of the issues, it is sent to the other company and formal negotiations can then start.

Aspects of the negotiations

Competitiveness is inevitable

Some might suggest that negotiations should be 'interest based' (see Chapter 6) and will not be helped by this issue-based preparation of an opening positional document. However, a great deal of what normally needs to be achieved through the differentiation phase – including the uncovering of underlying interests which might be beneficially matched – will have already been done through the prior research and perhaps even canvassed and confirmed through any preliminary 'deal prospecting' discussions which led to the formal negotiations. At this stage, the parties have reached the point of recognising that they have mutually beneficial interests but also that these mutual interests now need to be examined more closely.

Even though both parties have recognised their mutual interests from an early stage in the negotiation they can still uncover new insights and opportunities as the negotiations progress. However – and this is also the case in an ongoing management–union relationship – when the parties sit down to negotiate they should not anticipate being able to completely reframe the negotiations out of an inherently competitive orientation through the uncovering of unrealised underlying interests. The negotiations will be cooperative because the parties are looking to create joint value but they will be competitive as each seeks to achieve its particular interests – hence the descriptor 'competitive cooperation' in Figure A8.1. Even when emphasising cooperation in business negotiations, some recommended processes and tactics have a competitive edge such as Acuff's (2008) 'resistance' and 'hard bargaining' phases and Requejo and Graham's (2008) advice to 'make no concessions until the end'.

The importance of commitment

The primary task for the parties is to establish whether the proposal can be made to work. Clearly no company, not even one being approached in a friendly merger or acquisition, is going to reveal critical information about its operation, yet without that critical information it is impossible to make sound financial decisions. Therefore, as the parties begin their negotiations they are also evaluating the prospect of whether the negotiators themselves can build a relationship that will enable them to actually put the deal together. This informal relationship building (which does not mean the negotiators actually have to like each other) will be reinforced through an understanding that the first task is to negotiate a formal memorandum of understanding (MOU) that will list the key issues and the broad outcomes on each of these issues. The MOU will set the limits within which an agreement would be reached and so reduces the risk to each party in proceeding. It would be a firm indication of what the final agreement will look like (see Box A8.1).

Box A8.1: Examples of issues that might appear in an MOU

The parties' expectations in terms of contributions and benefits from the joint venture.
Market issues confirming the value creating (or market exploiting) product or service.
Technical issues (technical and managerial capability; legal & standards compliance; quality assurance; performance measurement systems etc.) to show how each party will will actually deliver its contribution.
Financial issues (financial systems; taxation issues; valuations) which underpin the parties' contributions/benefits.
Ownership; governance.
Exclusivity.
Intellectual property issues.
Risk management issues.

The signing of this MOU would be indication that both parties are committed to reaching agreement. It indicates that they will exchange full information, including any due diligence, and so the negotiations can move into their second stage of working through the detail. For example the MOU might have specified a range for the valuation of a particular major asset. On closer examination of the financial and other technical information, the two teams of negotiators will reach their own views on the precise value of that asset. If these differ they have to reach an agreed valuation either through a compromise valuation or through offsetting this against some other issue as part of the total package. The negotiations at this stage have been characterised as 'cooperative competition' in Figure A8.1. They will be competitive because the parties may be pushed to their negotiating limits and the issues themselves may be financially significant. They will be cooperative because the parties are fully aware of the strategic intent of the negotiation and are operating within the commitment of the MOU. Clear-cut compromises would be frequent as the negotiations draw to a close.

There are two further elements to the process. The first is the negotiations between the lead negotiator and the board if the parameters of the board's remit are being tested. Because the future of the proposal is at stake, these intra-party negotiations may be tense and competitive between those who believe the negotiations should continue and those who do not. The second element is that the draft documents the negotiators will have been working on have to be finalised into comprehensive legal documentation. This is a task for the lawyers from both sides. While they must protect the interests of their company and be alert to risk, it is not their role to seek any further gains out of the deal. Negotiations over the form of words to fully reflect the intent of what has been agreed should be cautious, but cooperative.

Appendix 9: A culture checklist

It is important for a negotiator to envisage the negotiation from the *other* party's perspective, which means taking account of how their cultural perspective might influence how they approach the task of negotiation. Tables 10.1, p. 151 and 10.2, p. 154 in Chapter 10 are useful starting points. This Appendix provides some further steps to help prepare for a cross-cultural negotiation; the example relates to negotiating with Australians.

Step 1: what do we know about their culture?

Review the cultural dimensions (Table 10.1) and approaches to communication (Table 10.2). Are negotiators from the other party more likely to do those things associated with individualism or with collectivism? Check against each dimension in turn. It is unlikely that you will have specific knowledge of each attitude or behaviour listed – rely first on what you know from your own experience, from the advice of others with experience of the culture and then from written sources, either of general culture or negotiation checklists. Be aware of the need to test one's conclusions as the negotiations develop.

Step 2: how might this affect how they might negotiate?

The issue dimension

What would a good agreement look like from their perspective?
To answer this, use the Strategy Framework – see Chapter 3 specifically Box 3.1, p. 52 and Appendix 4, p. 178.

The process dimension

Can we envisage the negotiation script they might be working to?

The behavioural dimension

How will they approach the tasks of negotiation?
To answer this, use Tables 10.6, 10.7 and 10.8 on pp. 166, 167 and 168 respectively to consider how they might exchange information, indicate flexibility and exchange concessions. Choose the more likely of the two

lists in each case but remember that these are just 'tendency statements', not a firm prediction of precise behaviour.

Step 3: what should I be aware of and try to do?

This needs to be a short list, probably noting just one thing that the other party might regard as normal negotiating which you would find difficult, and similarly one characteristic of your own behaviour you think they might have difficulty with.

When they . . . then I will try to . . .
When I normally would . . . I will try to . . .

An example: negotiating with Australians

Step 1: what do we know about Australian culture?

Bearing in mind that an Australian can be of British, Italian, South African, or Vietnamese extraction for example (and that a cultural profile of Indigenous Australians would be different again) you might anticipate that Australian negotiators:

- are expressive of attitudes and opinions
- acknowledge the presence of conflict and will actively seek to resolve the difference and move on
- are individualistic rather than collective
- have a sense of empowerment and are able to contribute to decisions
- recognise authority but may be challenged by it
- are more egalitarian than hierarchical
- are willing to take risks
- encourage change
- are innovative
- are generally low in uncertainty avoidance
- are assertive
- are results oriented and competitive with a 'win' orientation
- understand that precise outcomes should be kept
- are 'masculine'
- value early returns more highly
- are conscious of emerging difficulties or 'downsides' and will want to address them

have a linear perception of processes or approaches to a task
are focused on the immediate task and are action oriented
are conscious of time
will tend towards a short rather than long temporal perspective
deliver precise and relevant statements
deliver statements that will reflect opinions, feelings and reactions
seek information that will be sought through questioning
favour low rather than high context forms of communication.

Step 2: how might this affect how Australians might negotiate?

The issue dimension

Question: What would a good agreement look like from their perspective?

Answer: A firm agreement, suggesting wanting to get the detail sorted out, so inclined to be direct and focused; a sense of fairness and equity.

Using the Strategy Framework, they might be concerned about time and susceptible to the pressure of poor alternatives.

The process dimension

Question: Can we envisage the negotiation script they might be working to?

Answer: 'Rock and roll' – linear, wanting to get on and sort out the issues.

The behavioural dimension

Question: How will they approach the tasks of negotiation?
Answer:
Using Table 10.6, when exchanging information, Australians:
are direct and to the point, efficient
deal with the present
will outline the history and context; only to explain the present situation
will use PowerPoint for impact
will encourage structured, open discussion
will, ideally, outline interests, priorities and seek reciprocal information
will use rational arguments to explain linkages, goals, priorities
will ask open, priority questions
equally possible, will take positional approach and be hesitant in information exchange.

Using Table 10.7, when indicating flexibility Australians:
will want to 'unpack' any suggestion

will produce ideally creative solutions from an interest-based discussion
more likely: unilateral problem solving leading to a new proposal.

Using Table 10.8, when exchanging concessions Australians:
will want an outcome
will make detailed proposals
will spell out expectations of the other party
will clearly state limits ('we can't do that') with justification
will reject unacceptable offers outright
will outline alternatives (BATNA)
will be comfortable with differences, any disagreements will be expressed at the negotiating table until addressed.

Step 3: what in particular should I be aware of and try to do?

When Australians try to push on to sort out some of the issues then I will try to summarise and put what they are trying to do into a broader context, but at the same time make sure I'm not looking to be evasive.

When I normally would simply restate our position and anticipate thinking about their new proposals once the meeting was over, I will try to at least make some observation about what they have proposed.

References

Acuff, F. L. (2008) *How to Negotiate Anything with Anyone Anywhere Around the World*, Amacom, New York.

Adair, W. L. (2003) 'Integrative Sequences and Negotiation Outcome in Same- and Mixed-Culture Negotiations', *International Journal of Conflict Management*, 14, (3/4), pp. 273–96.

Adair, W. L. and Brett, J. M. (2004) 'Culture and Negotiation Processes' in M. J. Gelfand. and J. M. Brett (eds) *The Handbook of Negotiation and Culture*, Stanford Business Books, Stanford, CA, pp. 158–76.

Adair, W. L. and Brett, J. M. (2005) 'The Negotiation Dance: Time, Culture, and Behavioral Sequences in Negotiation', *Organization Science*, 16, (1), pp. 33–51.

Adair, W., Brett, J., Lempereur, A., Okumura, T., Shikhirev, P., Tinsley, C. and Lytle, A. (2004) 'Culture and Negotiation Strategy', *Negotiation Journal*, 20, (1), pp. 87–111.

Adair, W. L., Weingart, L. and Brett, J. M. (2007) 'The Timing and Function of Offers in U.S. and Japanese Negotiations', *Journal of Applied Psychology*, 92, (4), pp. 1056–68.

Amabile, T. M., Hadley, C. N. and Kramer, S. J. (2002) 'Creativity Under the Gun', *Harvard Business Review*, August, pp. 52–61.

Anton, R. J. (1990) 'Drawing the Line: An Exploratory Test of Ethical Behavior in Negotiations', *International Journal of Conflict Management*, 1, (3), pp. 265–80.

Axlerod, R. (1990) *The Evolution of Co-Operation*, Penguin Books, London.

Bacharach, S. B. and Lawler, R. J. (1981) *Bargaining*, Jossey-Bass, San Francisco.

Bacon, N. and Blyton, P. (2007) 'Conflict for Mutual Gains', *Journal of Management Studies*, 44, (5), pp. 814–34.

Barker, J. R. (1993) 'Tightening The Iron Cage: Concertive Control in Self-Managing Teams', *Administrative Science Quarterly*, 38, pp. 408–37.

Barry, B. and Friedman, R. A. (1998) 'Bargainer Characteristics in Distributive and Integrative Negotiation', *Journal of Personality and Social Psychology*, 74, (2), pp. 345–59.

Barry, B., Fulmer, I. S. and Van Kleef, G. A. (2004) 'I Laughed, I Cried, I Settled. The Role of Emotion in Negotiation' in M. J. Gefland and J. M.

Brett (eds) *The Handbook of Negotiation and Culture*, Stanford University Press, Stanford, CA., pp. 71–94.

Bazerman, M. N. and Neale, M. A. (1983) 'Heuristics in Negotiation: Limitations to Effective Dispute Resolution' in M. H. Bazerman and R. J. Lewicki (eds), *Negotiating in Organizations*, Sage, Beverley Hills, CA, pp. 51–67.

Bazerman, M. H. and Neale, M. A. (1992) *Negotiating Rationally*, Free Press, New York.

Bazerman, M. N., Curhan, J. R., Moore, D. A. and Valley, K. L. (2000) 'Negotiation', *Annual Review of Psychology*, 51, pp. 279–314.

Bazerman, M. H., Tenbrunsel, A. E. and Wade-Benzoni, K. (1998) 'Negotiating With Yourself and Losing: Making Decisions With Competing Internal Preferences', *Academy of Management Review*, 23, (2), pp. 225–41.

Beersma, B. and De Dreu, C. K. W. (1999) 'Negotiation Processes and Outcomes in Prosocially and Egoistically Motivated Groups', *International Journal of Conflict Management*, 10, (4), pp. 385–402.

Ben-Yoav, O. and Pruitt, D. G. (1984a) 'Resistance to Yielding and the Expectation of Cooperative Future Interaction in Negotiation', *Journal of Experimental Social Psychology*, 20, pp. 323–35.

Ben-Yoav, O. and Pruitt, D. G. (1984b) 'Accountability to Constituents: A Two-Edged Sword', *Organizational Behavior and Human Performance*, 34, pp. 283–95.

Boulle, L. (1996) *Mediation Principles, Process, Practice*, Butterworths, Sydney.

Breaugh, J. A. and Klimoski, R. J. (1977) 'The Choice of a Group Spokesman in Bargaining: Member or Outsider?', *Organizational Behavior and Human Performance*, 19, pp. 325–36.

Brett, J. M. (2000) 'Culture and Negotiation', *International Journal of Psychology*, 35, (2), pp. 97–104.

Brett, J. M. (2007) *Negotiating Globally*, (2nd edn), John Wiley and Sons, San Francisco.

Brett, J. M. and Gelfand, M. J. (2006) 'A Cultural Analysis of the Underlying Assumptions of Negotiation Theory' in L. L. Thompson (ed.) *Negotiation Theory and Research*, New Psychology Press, York, pp. 173–201.

Brett, J. M. and Okumura, T. (1998) 'Inter-and Intracultural Negotiations: U.S. and Japanese Negotiators', *Academy of Management Journal*, 41, (5), pp. 495–510.

Brett, J. M., Pinkley, R. L. and Jackofsky, E. F. (1996) 'Alternatives to Having a BATNA in Dyadic Negotiation: The Influence of Goals, Self-Efficacy and Alternatives on Negotiated Outcomes', *International Journal of Conflict Management*, 7, (2), pp. 121–38.

Brett, J. M., Shapiro, D. L. and Lytle, A. L. (1998) 'Breaking the Bonds of Reciprocity in Negotiations', *Academy of Management Journal*, 14, pp. 410–24.

Brislin, R. W. and Kim, E. S. (2003) 'Cultural Diversity in People's Understanding and Uses of Time', *Applied Psychology: An International Review*, 53, (3), pp. 363–82.

Brodt, S. E. and Tuchinsky, M. (2000) 'Working Together But in Opposition: An Examination of the "Good Cop/Bad Cop" Negotiating Team Tactic', *Organizational Behavior and Human Decision Processes*, 81, (2), pp. 155–77.

Buelens, M. and Van Poucke, D. (2004) 'Determinants of a Negotiator's Initial Opening Offer', *Journal of Business and Psychology*, 19, (1), pp. 23–35.

Butler, J. (1999) 'Trust, Expectations, Information Sharing, Climate of Trust and Negotiation Effectiveness and Efficiency', *Group and Organization Management*, 24, (2), pp. 217–38.

Calhoun, P. S. and Smith, W. P. (1999) 'Integrative Bargaining: Does Gender Make a Difference?,' *International Journal of Conflict Management*, 10, (3), pp. 203–24.

Carlisle, J. and Leary, M. (1981) 'Negotiating in Groups' in R. Payne. and C. Cooper (eds) *Groups at Work*, John Wiley and Sons, Chichester, Hants, 165–88.

Carnevale, P. J. (2008) 'Positive Affect and Decision Frame in Negotiation', *Group Decision and Negotiation*, 17, pp. 51–63.

Carnevale, P. J. D. and Lawler, E. J. (1986) 'Time Pressure and the Development of Integrative Agreements in Bilateral Negotiation', *Journal of Conflict Resolution*, 30, pp. 636–59.

Chamberlain, N. W. and Kuhn, J. W. (1965) *Collective Bargaining*, McGraw Hill, New York.

Citera, M., Beauregard, R. and Mitsuya, T. (2005) 'An Experimental Study of Credibility in E-negotiations', *Psychology and Marketing*, 22, (2), pp. 163–79.

Crott, H., Kayser, E. and Lamm, H. (1980) 'The Effects of Information Exchange and Communication in an Asymmetrical Negotiation Situation', *European Journal of Social Psychology*, 10, pp. 149–63.

Cummings, C. and Wilson, D. (eds) (2003) *Images of Strategy*, Blackwell, Malden, Mass.

Curhan, J. R., Neale, M. A., Ross, L. and Rosencranz-Englemann, J. (2008) 'Relational Accommodation in Negotiation: Effects of Egalitarianism and Gender on Economic Efficiency and Relational Capital', *Organizational Behavior and Human Decision Processes*, 107, pp. 192–205.

Cutcher-Gershenfeld, J. E. (2003) 'How Process Matters. A Five Phase Model for Examining Interest-Based Bargaining' in T. A. Kochan. and D. B.

Lipsky (eds) *Negotiations and Change*, Cornell University Press Ithaca, New York, pp. 141–59.

Dahl, R. (1957) 'The Concept of Power', *Behavioral Science*, 2, pp. 201–15.

Dawson, R. (1999) *Secrets of Power Negotiating for Salespeople*, Career Press, Franklin Lakes, NJ.

De Dreu, C. K. W. (2003) 'Time Pressure and Closing of the Mind in Negotiation', *Organizational Behavior and Human Decision Processes*, 91, pp. 280–95.

De Dreu, C. K. W., Weingart, L. R. and Kwon, S. (2000) 'Influence of Social Motives on Integrative Negotiation: A Meta-Analytic Review and Test of Two Theories,' *Journal of Personality and Social Psychology*, 78, (5), pp. 889–905.

Deutsch, M. (1990) 'Sixty Years of Conflict', *International Journal of Conflict Management*, 1, (3), pp. 237–63.

Donohue, W. A. (2004) 'Critical Moments as "Flow" in Negotiation', *Negotiation Journal*, 20, (2), pp. 147–51.

Douglas, A. (1957) 'The Peaceful Settlement of Industrial and Intergroup Disputes', *Journal of Conflict Resolution*, 1, pp. 69–81.

Douglas, A. (1962) *Industrial Peacemaking*, Columbia University Press, New York.

Drake, L. E. (1995) 'Negotiation Styles in Intercultural Communication', *International Journal of Conflict Management*, 6, (1), pp. 72–90.

Druckman, D. (1978) 'Boundary Role Conflict' in I. W. Zartman (ed.) *The Negotiation Process*, Sage Publications, Beverley Hills, CA, pp. 87–110.

Druckman, D. (2001) 'Turning Points in International Negotiation', *Journal of Conflict Resolution*, 45, pp. 519–44.

Druckman, D., Husbands, J. L. and Johnston, K. (1991) 'Turning Points in the INF Negotiations', *Negotiation Journal*, 7, (1), pp. 55–67.

Drummond, H. (1998) 'Go and Say, "We're Shutting": Ju Justu as a Metaphor for Analysing Resistance', *Human Relations*, 51, (6), pp. 741–59.

Eyuboglu, N. and Buja, A. (1993) 'Dynamics of Channel Negotiations: Contention and Reciprocity', *Psychology and Marketing*, 10, (1), pp. 47–65.

Fang, T. (1999) *Chinese Business Negotiating Style*, Sage Publications, Thousand Parks, CA.

Fells, R. E. (1986) *Movement, Phases and Deadlocks. A Study in the Process of Industrial Relations Negotiation*, Monograph no.12, Industrial Relations Research Centre, University of New South Wales, Sydney.

Fells, R. E. (1993) 'Developing Trust in Negotiation', *Employee Relations*, 15, (1), pp. 33–45.

Fells, R. E. (1996) 'Preparation for Negotiation: Issue and Process', *Personnel Review*, 25, (2), pp. 50–60.

Fells, R. E. (1998a) 'Overcoming the Dilemmas in Walton and McKersie's Mixed Bargaining Strategy' *Relations Industrielles, Industrial Relations*, 53, (2), pp. 300–22.

Fells, R. E. (1998b) 'A Critical Examination of the Process of Workplace Negotiation', *Labour and Industry*, 9, (1), pp. 37–52.

Fells, R. E. (1999a) 'Settlement Process or Tactical Opportunity? Mediation in Industrial Relations', *Journal of Industrial Relations*, 41, (4), pp. 594–611.

Fells, R. E. (1999b) 'Competitive Negotiation and the Question of Union Negotiating Rights', *Labour and Industry*, 9, (3), pp. 99–12.

Fells, R. E. (2000a) 'Of Models and Journeys: Keeping Negotiation and Mediation on Track', *Australasian Dispute Resolution Journal*, 11, (4), pp. 209–19.

Fells, R. E. (2000b) 'Labour–Management Negotiation: Some Insights into Strategy and Language', *Relations Industrielles Industrial Relations*, 55, (4), pp. 583–603.

Fells, R. E. (2000c) 'Negotiating 'Strategically' in A. Travaglione. and V. Marshall (eds.) *Human Resource Strategies: An Applied Approach*, McGraw-Hill, Sydney, pp. 81–116.

Fells, R. E. (2001) 'Wages Policy and Enterprise Bargaining in the Western Australian Public Sector', *Labour and Industry*, 12, (1), pp. 43–64.

Fells, R. E. (2003) 'Human Resource Management and the Collective Employment Relationship – A Negotiation Perspective' in R. Weisner. and B. Millett (eds.) *Human Resource Management: Challenges and Future Directions*, John Wiley and Sons, Milton, Qld, pp. 104–16.

Fells, R. E. and Savery, L. K. (1984) 'Leadership as a Productive Strategy in Negotiation', *Leadership and Organisational Development Journal*, 5, (1), pp. 21–4.

Fells, R. E. and Skeffington, R. (1998) 'Moving Beyond Adversarialism: Industrial Relations and Change in the Australian Shearing Industry', *Industrial Relations Journal*, 29, (3), pp. 234–46.

Fisher, R. (1971) *Basic Negotiation Strategy*, The Penguin Press, London.

Fisher, R. (1983) 'Negotiating Power', *American Behavioral Scientist*, 27, (2), pp. 149–66.

Fisher, R. (1989) 'Negotiating Inside Out: What Are the Best Ways to Relate Internal Negotiations with External Ones?', *Negotiation Journal*, 5, (1), pp. 33–41.

Fisher, R. and Davis, W. (1999) 'Authority of an Agent. When is Less Better?' in R. H. Mnookin. and L. E. Susskind (eds) *Negotiating on Behalf of Others*, Sage Publications, Thousand Oaks, CA, pp. 59–80.

Fisher, R., Kopelman, E. and Schneider, A. K. (1994) *Beyond Machiavelli. Tools for Coping with Conflict*, Harvard University Press, Cambridge, Mass.

Fisher, R., Ury, W. and Patton, B. (1991) *Getting To Yes*, Penguin, New York.

Flanders, A. (1968) 'Collective Bargaining: A Theoretical Analysis, *British Journal of Industrial Relations*, 6, pp. 1–26.

Foo, M. D., Elfenbein, H. A., Tan, H. H. and Aik, V. C. (2004) 'Emotional Intelligence and Negotiation: The Tension Between Creating and Claiming Value', *International Journal of Conflict Management*, 15, (4), pp. 411–29.

Friedland, N. (1983) 'Weakness as Strength: The Use and Misuse of a "My Hands are Tied" Ploy in Bargaining', *Journal of Applied Social Psychology*, 13, (5), pp. 422–26.

Friedman, R. A. (1993) 'Bringing Mutual Gains Bargaining to Labor Negotiations: The Role of Trust, Understanding, and Control', *Human Resource Management*, 32, (4), pp. 435–59.

Friedman, R. A. (1994) *Front Stage Backstage*, The MIT Press, Cambridge, Mass.

French, J. R. P. and Raven, B. (1959) 'The Bases of Social Power' in D. Cartwright (ed.) *Studies in Social Power*, Institute for Social Research, Ann Arbor, Mich., pp. 150–67.

Fulmer, I. S. and Barry, B. (2004) 'The Smart Negotiator: Cognitive Ability and Emotional Intelligence in Negotiation', *International Journal of Conflict Management*, 15, (3), pp. 245–72.

Galinsky, A. D. and Mussweiler, T. (2001) 'First Offers as Anchors: The Role of Perspective-Taking and Negotiator Focus', *Journal of Personality and Social Psychology*, 81, (4), pp. 657–69.

Gelfand, M. J. and Christakopoulou, S. (1999) 'Culture and Negotiator Cognition: Judgement Accuracy and Negotiation Processes in Individualistic and Collectivistic Cultures', *Organizational Behavior and Human Decision Processes*, 79, (3), pp. 248–69.

Gelfand, M. J. and McCusker, C. (2002) 'Metaphor and the Cultural Construction of Negotiation: A Paradigm for Research and Practice' in M. J. Gannon, and K. L. Newman (eds) *The Blackwell Handbook of Cross-Cultural Management*, Blackwell, Oxford, pp. 292–314.

Gentner, D., Loewenstein, J. and Thompson, L. (2003) 'Learning and Transfer: A General Role for Analogical Encoding', *Journal of Educational Psychology*, 95, (2), pp. 524–75.

Gesteland, R. R. (2005) *Cross Cultural Business Behavior*, Copenhagen Business School Press, Copenhagen.

Ghauri, P. and Usunier, J. (1996) *International Business Negotiations*, Pergamon, Oxford.

Green, G. M. and Wheeler, M. (2004) 'Awareness and Action in Critical Moments', *Negotiation Journal*, 20, (2), 349–64.

Greenhalgh, L. (1987) 'The Case Against Winning in Negotiations', *Negotiation Journal*, 3, (2), pp. 167–73.

Greenhalgh, L. and Gilkey, R. W. (1999) 'Our Game, Your Rules: Developing Effective Negotiating Approaches' in R. J. Lewicki, D. M. Saunders and J. W. Minton (eds) *Negotiation. Readings, Exercises and Cases*, (3rd edn), Irwin McGraw Hill, Boston, pp. 360–69.

Gudykunst, W. B. (1998) 'Individualistic and Collective Perspectives on Communication: An Introduction', *International Journal of Intercultural Relations*, 22, (2), pp. 107–34.

Hall, E. T. (1959) *The Silent Language*, Doubleday, New York.

Hall, E. T. (1960) 'The Silent Language of Overseas Business', *Harvard Business Review*, 38, pp. 87–96.

Hall, E. T. (1976) *Beyond Culture*, Doubleday, New York.

Hall, E. T. (1983) *The Dance of Life*, Doubleday, New York.

Halpern, J. (1994) 'The Effect of Friendship on Personal Business Transactions', *Journal of Conflict Resolution*, 38, (4), pp. 647–64.

Halpern, J. (1997) 'Elements in a Script for Friendship in Transactions', *Journal of Conflict Resolution*, 41, (6), pp. 835–68.

Halpern, J. J. and Parks, J. M. (1996) 'Vive La Difference: Differences Between Males and Females in Process and Outcomes in a Low-Conflict Negotiation', *International Journal of Conflict Management*, 7, (1), pp. 45–70.

Hendon, D. W., Hendon, R. A. and Herbig, P. (1996) *Cross-Cultural Business Negotiations*, Praeger, Westport, CT.

Hendon, D. W., Roy, M. H. and Ahmed, Z. U. (2003) 'Negotiation Concession Patterns: A Multicountry, Multiperiod Study', *American Business Review*, 21, pp. 75–83.

Heron, J. (1989) *The Facilitator's Handbook*, Kogan Page, London.

Hofstede, G. (1980) *Culture's Consequences*, Sage Publications, Beverly Hills, CA.

Hofstede, G. (1991) *Culture in Organisations*, McGraw Hill, London.

Hofstede, G. (1994) 'The Business of International Business is Culture', *International Business Review*, 3, (1), pp. 1–14.

Holmes, M. E. (1992) 'Phase Structures in Negotiation' in L. L. Putnam and M. E. Roloff (eds) *Communication and Negotiation*, Sage, Newbury Park, CA., pp. 83–105.

Honey, P. (1976) *Face to Face*, Institute of Personnel Management, London.

Huber, V. L. and Neale, M. A. (1986) 'Effects of Cognitive Heuristics and Goals on Negotiation Performance and Subsequent Goal Setting', *Organizational Behavior and Human Decision Processes*, 38, pp. 342–65.

Johnson, J. L. and Cullen, J. B. (2002) 'Trust in Cross-Cultural Relationships' in M. J. Gannon and K. L. Newman (eds) *The Blackwell Handbook of Cross-Cultural Management*, Blackwell, Oxford, pp. 335–60.

Kemp, K. E. and Smith, W. P. (1994) 'Information Exchange, Toughness and Integrative Bargaining: The Role of Explicit Cues and Perspective Taking', *International Journal of Conflict Management*, 5, (1), pp. 5–21.

Kern, M. C., Brett, J. M. and Weingart, L. R. (2005) 'Getting the Floor: Motive-Consistent Strategy and Individual Outcomes in Multi-Party Negotiations', *Group Decision and Negotiation*, 14, pp. 21–41.

Klimoski, R. J. (1972) 'The Effects of Intragroup Forces on Intergroup Conflict Resolution', *Organizational Behavior and Human Performance*, 8, pp. 365–83.

Klimoski, R. J. and Ash, R. A. (1974) 'Accountability and Negotiator Behavior', *Organizational Behavior and Human Performance*, 11, pp. 409–25.

Klimoski, R. J. and Breaugh, J. A. (1977) 'When Performance Doesn't Count: A Constituency Looks at Its Spokesman', *Organizational Behavior and Human Performance*, 20, pp. 301–11.

Kolb, D. (1983) *The Mediators*, MIT Press, Cambridge, Mass.

Kolb, D. and Coolidge, G. G. (1991) 'Her Place at the Table. A Consideration of Gender Issues in Negotiation' in J. W. Breslin and J. Z. Rubin (eds), *Negotiation Theory and Practice*, Harvard Program on Negotiation, Cambridge, Mass., pp. 261–77.

Kray, L. and Babcock, L. (2006) 'Gender in Negotiations: A Motivated Social Cognitive Analysis' in L. L. Thompson (ed.) *Negotiation Theory and Research*, New Psychology Press, York, pp. 203–24.

Kumar, R. and Worm, V. (2004) 'Institutional Dynamics and the Negotiation Process: Comparing India and China', *International Journal of Conflict Management*, 15, (3), pp. 304–34.

Kurtzberg, T. R. (1998) 'Creative Thinking, Cognitive Aptitude and Integrative Joint Gain: A Study of Negotiator Creativity', *Creativity Research Journal*, 11, (4), pp. 283–93.

Lang, M. D. and Taylor, A. (2000) *The Making of a Mediator*, Jossey-Bass, San Francisco.

Latham, G. P. and Yukl, G. A. (1975) 'A Review of Research on the Application of Goal Setting in Organisations', *Academy of Management Journal*, 18, (4), pp. 824–45.

Lax, D. A. and Sebenius, J. K. (1986) *The Manager as a Negotiator*, Free Press, New York.

Lax, D. A. and Sebenius, J. K. (2002) 'Dealcrafting: The Substance of Three-Dimensional Negotiations', *Negotiation Journal*, 18, (1), pp. 5–28.

Leung, K. and Tjosvold, D. (eds) (1998) *Conflict Management in the Asia Pacific*, John Wiley and Sons, Singapore.

Levitt, S. D. and Dubner, S. J. (2005) *Freakonomics*, William Morris, New York.

Lewicki, R. J. and Hiam, A. (2006) *Mastering Business Negotiation*, Jossey-Bass, San Francisco, CA.

Lewicki, R. J. and Litterer, J. A. (1985) *Negotiation*, Richard D. Irwin, Homewood, Ill.

Lewicki, R. J., McAllister, D. J. and Bies, R. J. (1998) 'Trust and Distrust: New Relationships and Realities', *Academy of Management Review*, 23, (3), pp. 438–58.

Lewicki, R. J., Minton, J. W. and Saunders, D. M. (2006) *Negotiation* (5th edn), Irwin McGraw Hill, Boston, Mass.

Lewicki, R. J. and Stevenson, M. A. (1997) 'Trust Development in Negotiation: Proposed Actions and a Research Agenda', *Business and Professional Ethics Journal*, 16, pp. 99–133.

Lewicki, R. J. and Wiethoff, C. (2000) 'Trust, Trust Development and Trust Repair' in M. Deutsch and P. T. Coleman (eds) *The Handbook of Conflict Resolution*, Jossey-Bass, San Francisco, pp. 86–107.

Lituchy, T. R. (1997) 'Negotiations Between Japanese and Americans: The Effects of Collectivism on Integrative Outcomes', *Canadian Journal of Administrative Sciences*, 14, (4), pp. 386–95.

Locke, E. A. (1968) 'Towards a Theory of Task Motivation and Incentives', *Organizational Behavior and Human Performance*, 39, (2), pp. 157–89.

Lytle, A. L., Brett, J. M. and Shapiro, D. L. (1999) 'The Strategic Use of Interests, Rights, and Power to Resolve Disputes', *Negotiation Journal*, 15, (1), 31–51.

Ma, Z., Wang, X., Jaeger, A., Anderson, T., Wang, Y. and Saunders, D. (2002) 'Individual Perception, Bargaining Behavior, and Negotiation Outcomes: A Comparison Across Two Countries,' *International Journal of Cross Cultural Management*, 2, (2), pp. 171–84.

Magee, J. C., Galinsky, A. D. and Gruenfeld, D. H. (2007) 'Power, Propensity to Negotiate, and Moving First in Competitive Interactions', *Personality and Social Psychological Bulletin*, 33, (2), pp. 200–12.

Magenau, J. M. and Pruitt, D. G. (1979) 'The Social Psychology of Bargaining: A Theoretical Synthesis' in G. M. Stephenson and C. J. Brotherton (eds) *Industrial Relations: A Social Psychological Approach*, John Wiley and Sons, Chichester, pp. 181–210.

Mayfield, M., Mayfield, J., Martin D. and Herbig, P. (1997) 'Time Perspectives of the Cross-Cultural Negotiations Process', *American Business Review*, 15, pp. 78–85.

Mnoonkin, R. H., Peppet, S. R. and Tulumello. A. S. (2000) *Beyond Winning*, Harvard University Press, Cambridge, Mass.

Moore, D. A. (2004) 'The Unexpected Benefits of Final Deadlines in Negotiation', *Journal of Experimental Social Psychology*, 40, (1), pp. 122–7.

Morgan, G. (1986) *Images of Organisation*, Sage, Newbury Park, CA.

Morgan, J. N. (1949) 'Bilateral Monopoly and the Competitive Output', *Quarterly Journal of Economics*, 63, p. 376.

Morely, I. E. (1992) 'Intra-Organisational Bargaining' in J. F. Hartley and G. M. Stephenson (eds) *Employment Relations*, Oxford, Blackwell, pp. 203–24.

Morley, I. E. and Stephenson, G. M. (1977) *The Social Psychology of Bargaining*, Allen and Unwin, London.

Morris, M., Nadler, J., Kurtzberg, T. and Thompson, L. (2002) 'Schmooze or Lose: Social Friction and Lubrication in E-mail Negotiations', *Group Dynamics: Theory Research and Practice*, 6, (1), pp. 89–100.

Mosterd, I. and Rutte, C. G. (2000) 'Effects of Time Pressure and Accountability to Constituents on Negotiation', *International Journal of Conflict Management*, 11, (3), pp. 227–47.

Murninghan, J. K., Babcock, L., Thompson, L. and Pillutla, M. (1999) 'The Information Dilemma in Negotiations: Effects of Experience, Incentives and Integrative Potential', *International Journal of Conflict Management*, 10, (4), pp. 313–39.

Nadler, J. (2004) 'Rapport in Legal Negotiation: How Small Talk Can Facilitate E-mail Dealmaking 9, *Harvard Negotiation Law Review*, pp. 223–51.

Naquin, C. E. and Paulson, G. D. (2003) 'Online Bargaining and Interpersonal Trust', *Journal of Applied Psychology*, 88, (1,) pp. 113–20.

Natlandsmyr, J. H. and Rognes, J. (1995) 'Culture, Behavior, and Negotiation Outcomes: A Comparative and Cross-Cultural Study of Mexican and Norwegian Negotiators', *International Journal of Conflict Management*, 6, (1), pp. 5–29.

Neale, M. A. and Bazerman, M. H. (1985a) 'The Effects of Framing and Negotiator Overconfidence on Bargaining Behaviors and Outcomes', *Academy of Management Journal*, 28, pp. 34–49.

Neale, M. A. and Bazerman, M. H. (1985b) 'The Effect of Externally Set Goals on Reaching Integrative Agreements in Competitive Markets', *Journal of Occupational Behaviour*, 6, pp. 19–32.

Newhouse, J. (2000) *Boeing versus Airbus*, Vintage Books, Random House, New York.

O'Connor, K. M. and Adams, A. A. (1999) 'What Novices Think About Negotiation: A Content Analysis of Scripts', *Negotiation Journal*, 15, (2), pp. 135–47.

Olekalns, M., Brett, J. M. and Weingart, L. R. (2003) 'Phases, Transitions and Interruptions: Modelling Processes in Multi-Party Negotiations', *International Journal of Conflict Management*, 14, (3/4), pp. 191–211.

Olekalns, M., Lau, F. and Smith, P. L. (2007) 'Resolving the Empty Core: Trust as a Determinant of Outcomes in Three-Party Negotiations', *Group Decision and Negotiation*, 16, (6), pp. 527–38.

Olekalns, M. and Smith, P. L. (2000) 'Understanding Optimal Outcomes. The Role of Strategy Sequences in Competitive Negotiations', *Human Communications Research*, 26, (4), pp. 527–57.

Olekalns, M. and Smith, P. L. (2003) 'Testing the Relationships Among Negotiators' Motivational Orientations, Strategy Choices and Outcomes', *Journal of Experimental Social Psychology*, 39, pp. 101–17.

Olekalns, M., Smith, P. L. and Walsh, T. (1996) 'The Process of Negotiating: Strategy and Timing as Predictors of Outcome', *Organizational Behavior and Human Decision Processes*, 68, (1), pp. 68–77.

Osgood, C. E. (1962) *An Alternative to War or Surrender*, University of Illinois Press, Urbana, Ill.

Paese, P. W., Schreiber, M. and Taylor, A. W. (2003) 'Caught Telling the Truth: Effects of Honest and Communication Media in Distributive Negotiations', *Group Decision and Negotiation*, 12, pp. 537–66.

Patton, B. (2005) 'Negotiation' in M. L. Moffitt and R. C. Bordone (eds) *The Handbook of Dispute Resolution*, Jossey-Bass, San Francisco, pp. 279–303.

Pinkley, R. L., Griffith, T. L. and Northcraft, G. B. (1995) '"Fixed Pie" a la Mode: Information Availability, Information Processing and the Negotiation of Suboptimal Agreements,' *Organizational Behavior and Human Decision Processes*, 62, pp. 101–12.

Pinkley, R. L., Neale, M. A. and Bennett, R. J. (1994) 'The Impact of Alternatives to Settlement in Dyadic Negotiation', *Organizational Behavior and Human Decision Processes*, 57, pp. 97–116.

Pruitt, D. G. (1981) *Negotiation Behavior*, Academic Press, New York.

Pruitt, D. G. (1983a) 'Strategic Choice in Negotiation', *American Behavioral Scientist*, 27, (2), pp. 167–94.

Pruitt, D. G. (1983b) 'Achieving Integrative Agreements' in M. H. Bazerman and R. J. Lewicki (eds) *Negotiating in Organisations*, Beverly Hills, Sage Publications, pp. 35–50.

Pruitt, D. G. and Carnevale, P. J. (1993) *Negotiation in Social Conflict*, Open University Press, Buckingham.

Pruitt, D. G. and Syna, H. (1985) 'Mismatching the Opponent's Offers in Negotiation', *Journal of Experimental Social Psychology*, 21, pp. 103–13.

Putnam, L. L. (1990) 'Reframing Integrative and Distributive Bargaining: A Process Perspective' in B. L. Sheppard, M. H. Bazerman and R. J. Lewicki (eds) *Research on Negotiations in Organizations*, JAI Press, Greenwich, Conn., pp. 3–30.

Putnam, L. (1994) 'Productive Conflict: Negotiation as Implicit Coordination', *International Journal of Conflict Management*, 5, (3), pp. 284–98.

Putnam, L. L. and Jones, T. S. (1982) 'Reciprocity in Negotiations: An Analysis of Bargaining Interaction', *Communication Monographs*, 49, pp. 171–91.

Rackman, N. and Carlisle, J. (1978) 'The Effective Negotiator Parts 1 and 2', *Journal of European Industrial Training*, Part 1: 2, (6), pp. 6–11; Part 2: 2, (7), pp. 2–5.

Raiffa, H. (1982) *The Art and Science of Negotiation*, Harvard University Press, Cambridge, Mass.

Requejo, W. H. and Graham, J. L. (2008) *Global Negotiation. The New Rules*, Palgrave Macmillan, New York.

Rhoades, J. A. and Carnevale, P. J. (1999) 'The Behavioral Context of Strategic Choice in Negotiation: A Test of the Dual Concerns Model', *Journal of Applied Social Psychology*, 29, (9), pp. 1777–802.

Robinson, R. J., Keltner, D., Ward, A. and Ross, L. (1995) 'Actual Versus Assumed Differences in Construal: "Naïve Realism" in Intergroup Perception and Conflict', *Journal of Personality and Social Psychology*, 68, (3), pp. 404–17.

Robinson, R. J., Lewicki, R. J. and Donahue, E. M. (2000) 'Extending and Testing a Five Factor Model of Ethical and Unethical Bargaining Tactics: Introducing the SINS Scale', *Journal of Organizational Behavior*, 21, pp. 649–64.

Roloff, M. J. and Jordan, J. M. (1991) 'The Influence of Effort, Experience and Persistence on the Elements of Bargaining Plans', *Communication Research*, 18, pp. 306–12.

Rubin, J. Z. and Brown, B. R. (1975) *The Social Psychology of Bargaining and Negotiation*, Academic Press, New York.

Rubin, J. Z. and Zartman, I. W. (1995) Asymmetrical Negotiations: Some Survey Results that May Surprise,' *Negotiation Journal*, 11, (4), pp. 349–64.

Salacuse, J. W. (1998) 'Ten Ways that Culture Affects Negotiating Style: Some Survey Results', *Negotiation Journal*, 14, (3), 221–40.

Salacuse, J. W. (2004) 'Negotiating: The Top Ten Ways that Culture Can Effect Your Negotiation,' *Ivey Business Journal*, 69, (1), pp. 1–6.

Sandy, S. V., Boardman, S. K. and Deutsch, M. (2000) 'Personality and Conflict' in M. Deutsch. and P. T. Coleman (eds) *The Handbook of Conflict Resolution*, Jossey-Bass, San Francisco, pp. 289–315.

Savage, G. T., Blair, J. D. and Sorenson, R. L. (1989) 'Consider Both Relationship and Substance When Negotiating Strategically', *Academy of Management Executive*, 3, (1), pp. 37–48.

Schelling, T. (1960) *The Strategy of Conflict,* Harvard University Press, Cambridge, Mass.

Schneider, A. K. (2002) 'Shattering Negotiation Myths: Empirical Evidence on the Effectiveness of Negotiation Style', *Harvard Negotiation Law Review,* 7, pp. 143–233.

Schroth, H. A., Bain-Chekal, J. and Caldwell, D. F. (2005) 'Sticks and Stones May Break Bones and Words Can Hurt Me: Words and Phrases that Trigger Emotions in Negotiations and their Effects', *International Journal of Conflict Management,* 16, (2), pp. 102–27.

Schuster, C. and Copeland, M. (1996a) *Global Business,* Dryden Press, Fort Worth, Texas.

Schuster, C. and Copeland, M. (1996b) 'Cross-Cultural Communication: Issues and Implications' in P. Ghauri and J. Usunier, *International Business Negotiations,* Pergamon, Oxford, pp. 131–152.

Schweitzer, M. E. and Croson, R. (1999) 'Curtaining Deception: The Impact of Direct Questions on Lies and Omissions', *International Journal of Conflict Management,* 10, (3,) pp. 225–48.

Sebenius, J. K. (2001) 'Six Habits of Merely Effective Negotiators', *Harvard Business Review,* April, pp. 87–95.

Sebenius, J. K. (2002a) 'Caveats for Cross-Boarder Negotiators', *Negotiation Journal,* 18, (2), pp. 121–33.

Sebenius, J. K. (2002b) 'The Hidden Challenges of Cross-Boarder Negotiations', *Harvard Business Review,* 80, (3), pp. 4–12.

Shell, G. R. (2001) 'Bargaining Styles and Negotiation: The Thomas-Kilmann Conflict Mode Instrument in Negotiation Training', *Negotiation Journal,* 17, (2), pp. 155–74.

Sinaceur, M. and Neale, M. A. (2005) 'Not All Threats are Created Equal: How Implicitness and Timing Affect the Effectiveness of Threats in Negotiations', *Group Decision and Negotiation,* 14, pp. 63–85.

Sivanathan, N., Pillutla, M. M. and Murnighan, J. K. (2008) 'Power Gained, Power Lost', *Organizational Behavior and Human Decision Processes,* 105, pp. 135–46.

Song, F., Cadsby, C. B. and Morris, T. (2004) 'Other-Regarding Behavior and Behavioral Forecasts: Females Versus Males as Individuals and as Group Representatives', *International Journal of Conflict Management,* 15, (4), pp. 340–63.

Sorenson, R. L., Morse, E. A. and Savage, G. T. (1999) 'A Test of the Motivations Underlying Choice of Conflict Strategies in the Dual-Concerns Model,' *International Journal of Conflict Management,* 10, (1), pp. 25–44.

Stevens, C. (1963) *Strategy and Collective Bargaining,* McGraw Hill, New York.

Stuhlmacher, A. F. and Champagne, M. V. (2000) 'The Impact of Time Pressure and Information on Negotiation Process and Decisions', *Group Decision and Negotiation*, 9, pp. 471–91.

Thompson, L. (1991) 'Information Exchange in Negotiation', *Journal of Experimental and Social Psychology*, 27, pp. 161–79.

Thompson, L. and Hastie. R. (1990) 'Social Perception in Negotiation', *Organizational Behavior and Human Decision Processes*, 4, pp. 98–123.

Thompson, L. and Hrebec, D. (1996) 'Lose-Lose Agreements in Interdependent Decision Making', *Psychological Bulletin*, 120, pp. 396–409.

Thompson, L. and Leonardelli, G. (2004) 'The Big Bang: The Evolution of Negotiation Research', *Academy of Management Executive*, 18, (3), pp. 113–17.

Thompson, L., Neale, M. and Sinaceur, M. (2004) 'The Evolution of Cognition and Biases in Negotiation Research' in M. G. Gefland and J. M. Brett (eds) *The Handbook of Negotiation and Culture*, Stanford Business Books, Stanford CA, pp. 7–44.

Thompson, L., Peterson, E. and Brodt, S. E. (1996) 'Team Negotiation: An Examination of Integrative and Distributive Bargaining', *Journal of Personality and Social Psychology*, 70, (1), pp. 66–78.

Tinsley, C. H. (2001) 'How Negotiators Get to Yes: Predicting the Constellation of Strategies Used Across Cultures to Negotiate Conflict', *Journal of Applied Psychology*, 86, (4) pp. 583–93.

Tinsley, C. H., Curhan, J. J. and Kwak, R. S. (1999) 'Adopting a Dual Lens Approach for Examining the Dilemma of Differences in International Business Negotiations', *International Negotiation*, 4, pp. 5–22.

Tinsley, C. H., O'Connor, K. M. and Sullivan, B. A. (2002) 'Tough Guys Finish Last: The Perils of a Distributive Reputation', *Organizational Behavior and Human Decision Processes*, 88, pp. 621–42.

Triandis, H. C. (1995) *Individualism and Collectivism*, Westview Press, Boulder, Col.

Tung, R., Worm, V. and Fang, T. (2008) 'Sino-Western Business Negotiations Revisited – 30 Years after China's Open Door Policy', *Organizational Dynamics*, 31, (1), pp. 60–74.

Ury, W. (1991) *Getting Past No: Negotiating with Difficult People*, Bantam Books, New York.

Ury, W. L., Brett, J. M. and Goldberg, S. B. (1989) *Getting Disputes Resolved*, Jossey-Bass, San Francisco, CA.

Usunier, J. and Lee, J. A. (2005) *Marketing Across Cultures*, Prentice Hall, Harlow, Essex.

Valley, K. L., Neale, M. A. and Mannix, E. A. (1995) 'Friends, Lovers Colleagues and Strangers: The Effects of Relationships on the Process and Outcome of Dyadic Negotiations' in R. J. Bies, R. J. Lewicki. and B. H. Sheppard (eds) *Research on Negotiation in Organisations Handbook of Negotiation Research,* vol 5, JAI Press, Greenwich, CT, pp. 65–93.

Van Boven, L. and Thompson, L. (2003) 'A Look into the Mind of the Negotiator: Mental Models in Negotiation', *Group Processes and Intergroup Relations,* 6, (4), pp. 387–404.

Walters, A. E., Stuhlmacher, A. F. and Meyer, L. L. (1998) 'Gender and Negotiator Competitiveness: A Meta-Analysis', *Organizational Behavior and Human Decision Processes,* 76, pp. 1–29.

Walton, R. E., Cutcher-Gershenfeld, J. E. and McKersie, R. B. (1994) *Strategic Negotiations,* Harvard Business School Press, Boston, Mass.

Walton, R. E. and McKersie, R. B. (1965) *A Behavioral Theory of Labor Negotiations,* McGraw-Hill, New York.

Warr, P. (1973) *Psychology and Collective Bargaining,* Hutchinson, London.

Watkins, M. (1998) 'Building Momentum in Negotiations: Time-Related costs and Action-Forcing Events', *Negotiation Journal,* 14, (3), pp. 241–56.

Watkins, M. (1999) 'Negotiating in a Complex World', *Negotiation Journal,* 15, (3), pp. 245–70.

Watkins, M. (2004) 'Anxious Moments: Openings in Negotiation', *Negotiation Journal,* 20, (2), pp. 153–69.

Watkins, M. (2006) *Shaping the Game,* Harvard Business School Press, Boston, Mass.

Weiss, S. E. (1994). 'Negotiating with "Romans"', *Sloan Management Review,* Part 1: 35, (2), pp. 51–61; Part 2: 35, (3), pp. 85–99.

Wiengart, L. R. and Olekalns, M. (2004) 'Communication Processes in Negotiation' in M. J. Gelfand and J. M. Brett (eds) *The Handbook of Negotiation and Culture,* Stanford Business Books, Stanford, CA, pp. 143–57.

Weingart, L. R., Thompson, L. L., Bazerman M. H. and Carroll, J. S. (1990) 'Tactical Behaviour and Negotiation Outcomes', *International Journal of Conflict Management,* 1, (1), pp. 7–33.

Winkler, J. (1981) *Bargaining for Results,* Pan Business Management, London.

Wolfe, R. J. and McGinn, K. L. (2005) 'Perceived Relative Power and its Influence on Negotiations', *Group Decision and Negotiation,* 14, pp. 3–20.

Zartman, I. W. and Berman, M. R. (1982) *The Practical Negotiator,* Yale University Press, New Haven, Conn.

Index